PRAISE FOR
HIRED! FIRED! RETIRED!

"*Hired! Fired! Retired!* by John Henry Weiss is one of those books that just clicks if you're trying to figure out your career—whether you're starting out, picking yourself up after a fall, or eyeing the finish line. It's packed with real talk about nailing your dream job, handling the curveballs like getting let go, and even making retirement something you actually look forward to. What hit me hardest was how Weiss totally gets today's work world, from AI flipping everything upside down to the impact of globalization or the constant need to adapt. But he doesn't just point out the problems; he hands you practical solutions, like how to negotiate your pay without breaking a sweat or rebuild your confidence after a rough patch. It truly feels like sitting down with the best career coach you can have. If you're ready to do more than just scrape by in today's job scene, grab this book!"

—Dr. Patrick Behar-Courtois, author of *Maximizing Organizational Performance: A Guide to Effective Performance Coaching*

"*Hired! Fired! Retired!* reminds me of numerous changes that define the employment journey. A reliable nondidactic road map in a day when GPS and AI define destination, alternative routes, and expected time of arrival, this book delivers reasoned guidance and a compelling endgame.

"Many chapters echoed my career path on one-lane roads and multilane highways. The culminating pages speak to a purposeful retirement. While this book offers solid advice for different stages, I believe it will find a special niche with retirees who want to establish an encore career. My journey led me to publish several works, manage a column in a regional newspaper, serve as a regional representative for a writers' organization, and preside over a statewide political party auxiliary.

"John's optimism informs every passage in the book. Perhaps it might be more appropriate to title it *Hired! Fired! Reinvented!* Alternatively, *Reinvested or Redeemed!* Worth the read at any age."

> —Vincent James Vezza, author, champion for writers, public speaker, storyteller, and Representative for the North Carolina Writers Network

"John Henry Weiss correctly identifies that the real challenge of AI for today's professional isn't technical—it's strategic. This book is the indispensable resource for understanding that strategic impact and integrating it into your career planning. For anyone looking to future-proof their career, I can't recommend this modern approach highly enough."

> —Joe Sipher, author of *Outsmart the Learning Curve*, founder of HealthScout AI

Hired! Fired! Retired!
Navigating Your Career in the Worldwide Workplace

by John Henry Weiss

© Copyright 2025 John Henry Weiss

ISBN 979-8-88824-833-1

All rights reserved. No part of this publication may be reproduced, stored in a retrieval system, or transmitted in any form or by any means—electronic, mechanical, photocopy, recording, or any other—except for brief quotations in printed reviews, without the prior written permission of the author.

Published by

3705 Shore Drive
Virginia Beach, VA 23455
800-435-4811
www.koehlerbooks.com

HIRED! FIRED! RETIRED!

Navigating Your Career in the Worldwide Workplace

JOHN HENRY WEISS

VIRGINIA BEACH
CAPE CHARLES

ALSO BY JOHN HENRY WEISS

Welcome to the Real World: A Complete Guide to Job-Hunting for the Recent College Grad

Operation Job Search: A Guide for Military Veterans Transitioning to Civilian Careers

Moving Forward in Mid-Career: A Guide to Rebuilding Your Career After Being Fired or Laid Off

The Big Book of Job-Hunting Hacks: How to Build a Résumé, Conquer the Interview, and Land Your Dream Job (in conjunction with the American Library Association and Brenda Bernstein)

For Roger Rogalin, 1949–2024,
principal of Packanack Elementary School,
adjunct instructor at Seton Hall University,
and former president of MacMillan/McGraw-Hill.
Rest in peace, dear friend.

CONTENTS

Introduction 1
PART 1: HIRED! 11
   1: Understanding Today's Worldwide Workplace 13
   2: How The Workplace Is Structured 20
   3: Employment Is A Legal Contract Between
      Employer And Employee 29
   4: Matching The Real You With A Real Career
      Using The NEXTERCISE 37
   5: Gender, Race, And Ethnicity In The Workplace 41
   6: Crafting A Résumé And Digital Profile
      While Employed 46
   7: Conquering The Interview For A New Job
      While Employed 53
   8: Learning About Your Potential Employer Before, During,
      And After An Interview 75
   9: Negotiating Salary, Benefits, And Remote
      Working Conditions 80
   10: How To Quit Your Job Gracefully 87
   11: Starting Your Own Business Or
       Purchasing A Franchise 94
   12: Government Jobs 105
   13: Career Objectives And AI 111
   14: Discovering Your Aptitude, Identity, Persona,
       And Character 118
   15: Twelve Tips For Understanding The
       Worldwide Workplace 124

PART 2: FIRED! 129
   16: Terminated! Why Me? 131
   17: Overcoming Grief And Depression 137
   18: Severance And Your Rights Under
        Employment Law 145
   19: Protecting Your Financial Security 150
   20: Insurance Protection 159
   21: Family Matters Do Matter 168
   22: Résumés, Interviews, And AI 175
   23: Overcoming Opposition To Your Candidacy 177
   24: Finding Employment At Job Fairs, Conventions,
        Trade Shows, Office Parks, And Online 185
   25: Rebuilding Your Career By Starting
        Your Own Business 207
   26: Connecting With Career Coaches And Counselors,
        Outplacement Services, And Recruiters 210
   27: Building And Maintaining Your Identity 220
   28: Twelve Tips For Rebuilding Your Career After Being
        Fired Or Laid Off 226

PART 3: RETIRED! 229
   29: Retirement Planning 231
   30: When, Why, And How Workers Retire 238
   31: Financial Planning And Will Preparation 245
   32: Maintaining Insurance Coverage 256
   33: Overcoming Loss Of Identity 267
   34: Pursuing An Encore Career 271
   35: Peace, Happiness, And Pickleball In Retirement .. 276
   36: Ten Tips For Making Retirement Work 279

Acknowledgments 282
Appendix 284
The Author 301
Index 303

INTRODUCTION

Work is nothing less than a juggernaut—an inexorable force, a movement, a behemoth that defines and dictates everything we do. It tells us what kind of clothes to wear. What time to wake up. What time to go to bed. What to do with our spare time. What to eat. Where to live. How to define ourselves. Workers are struggling every day to put this juggernaut to rest, to take control of their workplace and find meaning, understanding, purpose, and identity in their careers. But there is more to consider.

Media like *The New York Times*, *The Wall Street Journal*, *The Washington Post*, the *Chicago Tribune*, and the *Los Angeles Times* fill their pages with talk about artificial intelligence (AI) as though it is a newly revealed phenomenon, but it is already inextricably tied into the world around us. We are still uncertain exactly how it will affect the job market; we know it will replace many jobs and create others, but we cannot say what jobs will be lost or added. This is something that readers of this book will need to track on a daily basis.

We do know one thing for certain: Employers will require job candidates to know about AI in detail because going forward, it will affect the way workers perform their required tasks.

TERMS USED TO DESCRIBE WORK

There are a number of terms we hear when navigating the workplace: career, job, profession, occupation, vocation. Let's look at a broad definition of each.

- **Career.** In this book we use this term to mean the occupation you hold to make a living. It includes your training, education, and skills. Examples of careers are doctor, nurse, administrative assistant, carpenter, truck driver, technology director, sales manager, teacher.
- **Job.** This refers to the tasks you perform in your career.
- **Occupation.** This term refers to a field of career interest over time. An example of an occupation is that of a carpenter who has worked alone or for general contractors for several years. It could also refer to a sales representative who has worked selling products or services for several companies.
- **Profession.** This term refers to very specialized interest and training. Examples of those who hold a profession are doctors, dentists, nurses, lawyers, university professors.
- **Vocation.** This term derives from the Latin *vocare*, which means a "calling" and has religious implications, as though a worker were called to a specific job by God. As an example, a person might be called by God to be a doctor or a priest or a minister.

THE PURPOSE OF THIS BOOK

Hired! Fired! Retired! Navigating Your Career in the Worldwide Workplace is a book for all workers trying to survive one day to the next by making money to pay for the "big three" items necessary for survival: food, clothing, and shelter. The purpose of this book is to help workers search for careers and job satisfaction and answer questions regarding their true personal, social, and work identities.

THE TRANSFORMATION OF THE WORKPLACE

The workplace was changed forever by the COVID-19 pandemic, which began in China in Q4 of 2019, leaving millions dead and seriously ill throughout the world. While the pandemic affected the health of millions, regardless of race, ethnicity, gender, and religion, it also caused widespread unemployment, nearly bringing the economy to a screeching halt. It touched the lives of all workers: entry-level workers, recent college grads, chief executive officers (CEOs), lawyers, entrepreneurs, and trade workers.

No one escaped its reach. In the United States, a booming economy in 2019 with an unprecedented 3.6 percent unemployment rate quickly fell into disarray. By April 2020 the unemployment rate had increased to an astounding 15.8 percent.[1] While workers deemed "essential" worked harder than ever, millions of others were laid off, millions took on part-time jobs, and millions more continued in their jobs by working remotely from their homes. The daily routine for remote workers included never-ending Zoom meetings, disrupting normal homelife. Parents working from home suddenly had to care for children who were attending school remotely. This dual role caused extreme burnout, resulting in mass resignations by those who could no longer manage. Meanwhile, many became caregivers for elderly family members.

Some of those who were fortunate to survive being laid off and find another job worked for lower wages and reduced benefits. It was only after the release of COVID vaccines that a portion of the workplace began returning to "normal." The development of these vaccines was completed in record time because of the American government's initiative, Operation Warp Speed. However, COVID variants soon spread throughout the world, necessitating the development of booster shots. The result? More disruption.

Many economists agree that the most severe effect of the pandemic was this workplace transformation. Workers suffered

---

[1] "Unemployment rises in 2020, as the country battles the COVID-19 pandemic," Bureau of Labor Statistics, June 2021, https://www.bls.gov/opub/mlr/2021/article/unemployment-rises-in-2020-as-the-country-battles-the-covid-19-pandemic.htm.

bouts of stress as they struggled to find work that provided the means to purchase food, shelter, and clothing for themselves and their dependents. For example, outbound sales representatives, whose daily routine had included calling on potential customers personally, had to revert to video calls, which were much less effective at generating sales. Why? Because potential customers are often hesitant to place orders without establishing a trusting relationship.

Enter AI. As workers struggled to make ends meet, something else was transpiring that brought untold benefits and simultaneously cast doubt on the future of work. This doubt about career longevity led to a surge of introspection across the workforce. Previously, workers concentrated on only two parts of the career-hunting process:

- Crafting a dynamite résumé and sending it off to as many job boards as possible.
- Conquering the interview, if they were fortunate to land one.

The COVID pandemic and AI changed the paradigm. Desperate workers began thinking about this juggernaut called work, what it meant in the short and long term. The result was a renewed emphasis on understanding meaning and identity in the workplace—an emphasis that continues to this very day. Importantly, it has changed the paradigm for career hunting as well. Now workers are asking career-centered questions like these:

- What are my captivating interests?
- What are my greatest abilities?
- If I combine my abilities and interests, what kinds of jobs suit my career goals?
- Who am I, a leader or a follower?
- What will I take away from work in addition to the paycheck and benefits?

- Is there any meaning in the work that I've done up to this point?
- Where do I want my career to be twenty years from now?
- How will AI alter my career path and the jobs therein?
- Is my identity defined only by the job I have?
- Have I ever experienced work–life balance?
- What will I do when I retire?

Organizations like the Pew Research Center tell us that workers will quit their jobs if they can't find answers to these vital questions. Introspection leads to the realization that a person needs more than a paycheck. Workers want to take control of their workplace rather than having someone else tell them what to do every working day.

OBJECTIVES OF THIS BOOK

We have limited our objectives to five categories that affect all workers currently employed and those seeking new careers:

1. To provide students and workers with information to understand how the worldwide workplace is structured.
2. To help students and workers discover the meaning of work in their individual careers.
3. To help students and workers learn how their identity is critical to finding a job that provides not only money but also fulfillment and satisfaction.
4. To prepare students and workers for changes in the workplace caused by technology and unforeseen events like the recent pandemic and the increased use of AI.
5. To inform students and workers that employment is a legal contract between employer and employee.

HOW THIS BOOK IS ORGANIZED

Hired! Fired! Retired! is divided into three interrelated parts and thirty-six chapters, which may be read sequentially (recommended) or in the order the reader desires. To this end, much advice and many resources may be repeated as necessary.

Part 1. "HIRED!" This part focuses on the lives of workers who are currently employed. Key topics include career selection; the challenges of working remotely from home; persona, character, and identity; the hiring process; employment law; starting your own business; leadership and followership; government careers; negotiating salary and benefits; the role technology and AI will play in employment; and practical tips for career searching. In addition, we explore how the workplace has changed and how these changes will alter the way workers conduct career hunting going forward. Succinct tips are included for dealing with the possibility of being terminated and what to do now to prepare for your retirement.

There is more to being employed than a paycheck and job satisfaction. When you are employed, you enter into a legal contract that gives you and your employer distinct legal rights. For example, in most states, employers can terminate at will, which means that you could be fired at any time for no reason and have no legal recourse. Also, many employment contracts state that employees who leave a company must agree not to work for a competitor for a specific period within a specific geographical area. This is commonly called a "noncompete agreement." Thankfully, Congress is now considering changes to the noncompete and termination-at-will clauses found in many job offers.

Part 2. "FIRED!" Being let go may seem like a lonely proposition, but rest assured that you will have plenty of company if you get the axe. According to the Bureau of Labor Statistics, 55,000 workers in America are let go every day in "normal" times and even more during recessions, depressions, pandemics, and government downsizings.

This part focuses on how and why employers fire and lay off workers when they are least expecting it. Considerable time is devoted to the process workers can use to move forward from grieving to rebuilding their careers. A portion of "FIRED!" deals with financial matters. As an added bonus, we will explore your legal rights and what you and your lawyer can do to ensure fair treatment from your former employer.

Nomenclature enters the picture, too. You can be let go, fired, laid off, downsized, reorganized out, replaced, or whatever the term might be tomorrow.

Part 3. "RETIRED!" Yes, retirement is an important and distinct part of the work cycle. It's no longer sixty-five and out, left to play in the sand with your grandchildren, read books, or travel to foreign lands until RIP appears behind your name. "RETIRED!" analyzes what happens when workers retire, whether they are thirty-five or sixty-five, and how the concept of retirement is a dynamic that continues to evolve as workers determine what they want to do and when they want to do it. Here you will find practical tips for dealing with four major issues of retirement:

➤ Finding an encore career to remain active and productive.
➤ Crafting a budget to pay for continuing expenses.
➤ Redefining your identity.
➤ When to retire. Many said an early goodbye to the active workplace during the pandemic only to regret that decision when faced with a challenge like how to pay for all current expenses and have money left over for enjoyment.

DATA SOURCES

There is much data in this book taken from what we consider to be reliable nonpolitical resources. These sources will keep

you apprised of the employment picture during a recession or pandemic and during "normal" times:
- ➤ The Bureau of Labor Statistics (BLS) (BLS.gov). Two locations are most helpful: the Employment Situation Summary; and the Job Openings and Labor Turnover Survey (JOLTS), frequently called the JOLTS report.
- ➤ The US Census Bureau (Census.gov)
- ➤ The World Atlas (WorldAtlas.com)
- ➤ The Pew Research Center (PewResearch.org)
- ➤ *The Occupational Outlook Handbook.* This information-packed print book and online resource produced by the US Department of Labor is a treasure for job seekers at every level. It is updated every two years. The *Handbook* lists hundreds of jobs in multiple industries, along with job descriptions, job functions, job environments, educational requirements, required experience and expertise, salaries, the number of jobs available in the US, and the projected job outlook for the next ten years. Make this book an integral part of your career library. It is a resource for every worker.
- ➤ OpenAI (OpenAI.com) and other AI sources appearing almost daily

HOW AI IS CHANGING THE WORKPLACE

We witness it every day. The workplace is changing due to the increasing use of AI. Many of today's jobs will not be here tomorrow, or next month or next year. AI is a quick and cost-effective way to accomplish job objectives that were previously performed by workers. Keep this in mind when seeking new employment opportunities. Always ask, "Will this job opportunity that I'm applying for today be here next year?"

The use of AI in everyday business transactions is moving rapidly. And, at present, companies like McDonald's,

Johnson&Johnson, Moody's, and eBay have incorporated AI into their products and operations. For detailed information about AI, visit Investopedia.com and other current sources.

Fortunately, the job market has rebounded from the pandemic, albeit with significant changes that workers need to understand. However, we still find that most print and digital career books focus narrowly on two items: résumés and interviews. There is much more involved. Making a career change is a process involving numerous initiatives, all described in this book.

All workers will experience each part of the career cycle: being hired or employed; being terminated or fired; and being retired. In addition, all workers must learn to delve into their psyche to have peace and happiness during their time in the workplace and in retirement. To help you through this process, we focus on finding understanding, meaning, purpose, and identity in this juggernaut called work.

PART 1
HIRED!

SEARCHING FOR UNDERSTANDING, MEANING, PURPOSE, AND IDENTITY WHEN EMPLOYED

CHAPTER 1

UNDERSTANDING TODAY'S WORLDWIDE WORKPLACE

INCLUDING AI

It's here! It took centuries to develop, and with the help of technology, it has arrived. We're talking about the worldwide workplace, where we spend at least ten hours a day providing services in return for money to buy the "big three" (food, shelter, clothing) and become self-sufficient. Yesterday, workers limited their career searches to their local neighborhoods, where they could be at the workplace in thirty minutes. Today it's a far different story. The place we work now encompasses the entire globe.

Today's human beings are a mobile group and leave their place of birth regularly to pursue job opportunities in other domestic locations and foreign countries. For example, over one million legal immigrants come to the United States each year from all over the world. Add a vast number of undocumented immigrants, and we ask, "What's the attraction?" The primary reason is to take advantage of America's job basket, the largest in the world.

Americans, too, leave their native land voluntarily to pursue career opportunities or because their employer transferred them to workplaces in a foreign country. It happens every day, and some real-life examples will add to our understanding.

WORKERS ON THE MOVE

Elon Musk, CEO of Tesla, was born in 1971 in Pretoria, South Africa. When he was seventeen, he immigrated to Canada and then to the United States to pursue education opportunities that were not available in South Africa or Canada. After receiving his BS in physics from the University of Pennsylvania, he developed many major companies, including PayPal, SpaceX, and Tesla. Musk is worth billions of dollars, making him the richest person on earth.

And then we have Marshall from Maryland, who graduated from the University of Wisconsin with degrees in psychology and entrepreneurship. He was already bilingual in English and Spanish, resulting from his attending a Spanish-immersion K–6 school in Montgomery County, Maryland. His college semester abroad was spent in Madrid, Spain, where he familiarized himself with the culture and discovered there were many teaching jobs available. Education being one of his career choices, he found work in Madrid as a private school teacher. In addition, he graduated with an MA in philosophy from Universidad Complutense de Madrid. Now Marshall is employed full-time with a Spanish digital newspaper, planning for dual citizenship, and firmly entrenched in Spanish culture. To supplement income early in his teaching career, Marshall taught English to Chinese students in Beijing—online, of course—and now creates websites.

Now consider Gus from Silver Spring, Maryland. He recently graduated from James Madison University in Virginia with a BS in business. Caving in to his spirit of adventure, Gus moved to Denver, Colorado, and found work after only six weeks. He was hired by a company based in Bellevue, Washington, to service customers throughout the US while working remotely from his home in Denver. Now Gus works from home as national sales manager for a company based in Nebraska. Here we have a man from Maryland who moved to Denver to work remotely for companies based elsewhere, servicing customers in all fifty states. A few years ago, that would have been an exception, but today it is commonplace.

And consider Nick Johnson, born and raised in Pennsylvania and who graduated from the University of Pennsylvania with a degree in finance. After working several jobs on the East Coast, Nick moved to Seattle, where he became part of a transportation company serving all fifty states. Now he is head of finance for a prominent AI company based in San Francisco. He lives in the Los Angeles area, working in the worldwide market. His physical location appears meaningless as he has worked for a number of months in South America and recently in Fiji and Paris. He can fulfill his job requirements from anywhere on the planet with approval of his employer.

The experiences of Elon, Marshall, Gus, and Nick are repeated everyday throughout the world. The workplace is not limited to where you were born. It's everywhere, and opportunities for workers vary greatly. Add remote working practices for many workers, and we have a workplace that is truly global. A few of my personal experiences will add meaning to our thesis.

Recently I visited three large cities in India: Delhi, Agra, and Jaipur. The contrast between the rich and poor was striking. I had heard so much about the great tech job opportunities that existed there, and I focused on finding them. Yes, technology jobs were available, but they existed behind gated buildings and in high-rise "work cities." By chance I had a lengthy conversation with a man in his early twenties who was working in a menial job at a New Delhi restaurant. He held a degree from an Indian technology college but had not found related work beyond that of a customer services representative ensconced in a cubicle in a high-rise office building, taking calls from customers in America. Wanting more than that, he applied for immigration to America and was in his second year waiting for clearance.

"Please take me with you when you return to America," he joked.

I had another moving experience in Warsaw, Poland. While touring the city, I stayed at an upscale hotel that provided a lavish buffet breakfast each morning. It included all the standard breakfast fare in addition to Polish specialties like homemade kielbasa and fresh-baked ham that was sliced to order by a young woman dressed in a white apron and wearing a white chef's hat. Her name tag read Marta. I said hello and asked for some of that mouthwatering baked ham.

"Yes sir. How many slices do you want?" Marta's crystal-clear English surprised me, and I asked where she learned to speak the language fluently. She responded, "Here in Poland, English is a required second language in our elementary schools and high schools. I am so thankful for that because my dream is to immigrate to New York City to pursue job opportunities in technology. I can hardly wait to get there!" Her enthusiasm was so genuine I wanted to smuggle her back to America.

Going forward, your workplace could be a traditional office setting where you work every day for eight hours or a remote location like your home where you accomplish a set of objectives on your own time schedule, or it could be a combination.

THE ORIGIN AND EVOLUTION OF WORK

So how did this thing called work begin? Some anthropologists and paleontologists posit that we became self-sufficient human beings when we began to stand on two feet and walk upright. There is good reason for this premise. Recent discoveries in Ethiopia include fossil remains of upright walkers from 4.4

million years ago. The first was a female called Ardi, a shortened name for the hominid *Ardipithecus ramidus*. What Ardi was able to do in addition to climbing trees was walk on two feet. This ability enabled her to hunt rabbits and other wild beasts and pick her own food from both trees and the ground. Ardi had no idea that walking to find food would become the most important thing human beings do to survive.

One could argue that this was the beginning of entrepreneurial work in its most rudimentary form. Of course, concepts like careers, jobs, benefits, job hunting, unemployment, and recruiting did not exist 4.4 million years ago, but the search for the "big three" was similar to our present-day workplace in many ways.

However, today we've become more sophisticated. We've invented assistants to help us find the big three. These assistants are computers, Instagram, AI, Amazon, email, trucks, airplanes, tractors, cars, Costco, and Walmart, just to name a few.

At some time in our not-too-distant past, about 700 BC, the Lydians invented metal coins, which workers received for their labor in place of tangible survival items. The Chinese invented paper money in 800 BC. Workers began to use money, both coin and paper, to buy food, shelter, and clothing—though there were some interesting exceptions. The Romans paid their soldiers with salt instead of money. Hence the word "salary." Salt was highly valued for its ability to preserve food, a handy forerunner to modern-day refrigerators.

Our survival model has been refined over the years. Maybe cryptocurrencies will be the next step in this evolution.

If you work, chances are excellent that you will be fired or laid off, maybe tomorrow at 5 p.m., just before leaving your place of employment. This is a serious concern because when you are terminated, your paycheck and your benefits disappear, and for some, so does your identity.

After you have survived being hired and fired and rehired and refired for fifty years, you will most likely elect to retire. Once more your paycheck and benefits and identity will disappear. This work cycle can be satisfying or unpleasant—very unpleasant. It depends on how you prepare for it. It's your career. Finding your personal understanding, meaning, and identity will determine your level of peace and happiness.

Human beings are complicated. Philosophers, psychologists, academics, and clerics have penned millions of print and digital pages disclosing what they have discovered in their search for understanding, meaning, and identity. An internet search for "the meaning of life" will verify the premise. We are especially prone to search for answers in that universal activity that occupies most of our time: work. Work does not quit. Work does not take a rest. Work is an overpowering force that continues moving forward in time and place.

To put it all in perspective: We are born, we die, and in between, we work.

KEY TAKEAWAYS

- The primary purpose of work is to make money to purchase food, shelter, and clothing, the big three items that are necessary for survival, regardless of age, gender, race, ethnicity, beliefs, and values.
- The workplace is not limited to where you were born. It's everywhere, and people are constantly on the move to find jobs in this expanding global environment.
- Workers can therefore increase their chances of being hired by learning another language, or maybe two. Try online companies like Babble, Berlitz, or eTour.
- To be hired in the worldwide workplace, workers must prepare by acquiring technology proficiency, including not only the basics but also expertise in coding, robotics, and AI.

- The work cycle consists of three distinct parts: employment, termination, and retirement.

PRINT AND DIGITAL RESOURCES
- *The Occupational Outlook Handbook* by the US Department of Labor. This book is available in print and online.

CHAPTER 2

HOW THE WORKPLACE IS STRUCTURED

Finding the "right" career requires knowledge of the workplace structure. Just plunging into an opportunity posted on a job board, a career page, or an ad by an online recruiter is a plan for continued career unhappiness.

Using the information in this chapter will enable you to move ahead by selecting an industry you like, finding companies in that industry that are appealing, and then looking for specific career opportunities in those companies.

The workplace is not just a random collection of careers. It comprises industries, companies within those industries, careers within those companies, and jobs within careers. Jobs with the same title, such as "marketing director," may have different functions depending on the industry. For example, the functions of a marketing job in the transportation industry can be different from a marketing job in the healthcare industry.

Before crafting a résumé or even looking online at multiple job boards, learn how the real workplace works. This is critically important because if you don't understand how the workplace is structured, you will experience nothing but frustration.

LARGE AND IMPORTANT INDUSTRIES

The largest and most important industries are, of course, food, shelter, and clothing. Without them human beings could not survive. Each industry has multiple companies, both large and small, and employs millions of workers. Let's explore a company in each industry for an eye-opening introduction to how our workplace is structured.

Food Companies

Human beings cannot survive more than four days without water and three weeks without food. These statistics highlight the critical nature of the food-production and distribution industry.

The availability of food and drink is often taken for granted. Most Americans never have to search for it. It's always there. If you do not have money to pay for it, the government will provide it for you through the food-stamp program known as the Supplemental Nutrition Assistance Program, or SNAP. However, in many countries, food and drink are scarce commodities, and people spend most of their time striving for them.

One of the largest international food companies is Kroger. It is based in Cincinnati, Ohio, and has twenty-one companies in its corporate family, which are scattered throughout thirty-five states. In addition, Kroger sells its products through stores in China. Kroger data reveals that the average person makes 221 food-related decisions every day.[2] This company's mantra is that everyone deserves access to fresh, affordable, and delicious food, no matter who you are, how you shop, or what you like to eat.

Kroger employs over 430,000 workers and is always in hiring mode. Their workforce includes more than the workers you see on store floors. Most jobs are behind the scenes in sales, marketing, accounting/finance, technology, supply chain

---

2   "Brand Guide," the Kroger Company, April 2025, https://www.thekrogerco.com/brand-guidelines/.

management, human resources, and more. In addition, Kroger has formed partnerships with fifty colleges and universities to help train future employees through internships and education. Check out Kroger at TheKrogerCo.com for company and career information.

Other food producers and distributors to explore are Nestlé, PepsiCo, Tyson Foods, Kraft Heinz, Mondelez International, General Mills, Conagra, Hormel Meats, and Campbell Soup Company. If your interests lie in helping people survive and live healthy lives, the food industry may be your answer.

Shelter Companies

You will find hundreds of companies in the shelter industry. Shelter includes both residential and commercial buildings. One such nationwide company is the Lennar Corporation (Lennar.com). Since 1954 Lennar has built over one million homes for people across America. Workers in this industry include hands-on workers in the various trades, like carpenters, bricklayers, electricians, and plumbers, and executive workers like president, CEO, and various vice presidents. Without this critical industry, people would die from exposure or violence.

Clothing Companies

The clothing industry includes companies that manufacture apparel for women, men, and children for all seasons. One such company is L.L. Bean, based in Freeport, Maine, with fifty-six retail stores across twenty states. It was founded in 1912. International stores are located in Costa Rica, Japan, Hong Kong, and Taiwan. Explore their job opportunities at LLBean.com.

Jobs in the clothing industry include fashion designers, technical designers, sales representatives, stylists, public relations managers, graphic designers, marketing directors, textile designers, and more.

BEYOND FOOD, SHELTER, AND CLOTHING

There are many other important industries worldwide where you can find viable job opportunities attuned to your interests and skill sets. Below are listed some of the most important.

Healthcare

The healthcare industry is massive and accounts for 20 percent of the US gross domestic product (GDP). Expenditures are being driven upward by an increasing population and technology that includes remote diagnostics, AI, and robotics. The industry includes hospitals like Johns Hopkins in Baltimore, pharmaceutical manufacturers like Johnson&Johnson, outpatient clinics like your local urgent care center, pharmacies like CVS, medical device manufacturers like Medtronic, health insurers like United Healthcare, and many others.

Some careers in this industry include physician, dentist, nurse, midwife, physical therapist, sonographer, physician assistant, nurse practitioner, genetic counselor, healthcare administrator, radiologist, and nursing assistant. This is an industry that rarely experiences mass terminations and is always seeking new workers for a variety of jobs.

Insurance

Insurance is one of the oldest industries in America. The first fire insurance company in America was founded in Charleston, South Carolina, in 1735. In 1752, Benjamin Franklin founded a homeowners insurance company that still exists today: the Philadelphia Contributionship, which offers a variety of insurance products. Other companies such as MassMutual, MetLife, and State Farm were founded over a hundred years ago.

Some say that insurance is boring, but when it comes to

stability, longevity, and hefty profits, boring is good. Are you looking for a long-term career? Consider the insurance industry.

Finance

Another critical American industry that employs millions of workers across all fifty states and abroad is the banking and finance industry. Some big names include Goldman Sachs, Bank of America, Wells Fargo, Vanguard, and Fidelity. These venerable institutions hire workers not only with a math or finance background but also in sales, marketing, human resources, and law. The largest bank in America is JP Morgan Chase & Co. (JPMorganChase.com). Review their website for job opportunities if you find finance interesting.

Technology

The ever-growing technology industry includes more than icons like Apple, Adobe, and Microsoft. New and exciting companies focusing on AI and robotics are everywhere. Consider RG Group, a sixty-year-old company focused on motion-control products and solutions and robotics. RG is located in York, Pennsylvania, and provides services to companies in America and abroad. Another tech company is AssemblyAI, which provides services to companies such as *The Wall Street Journal*, BBC, Dow Jones, and Spotify. This company is headquartered in San Francisco, and its staff works remotely from across the world. Learn more about them at AssemblyAI.com.

Transportation

The broad-based transportation industry includes companies that manufacture devices from bicycles to spacecraft and provide services like moving you from one place to another. This industry is constantly evolving. For example, automobiles are changing from gas-fired to battery-operated. And not just

Tesla. Companies in China, Japan, India, and other countries are active in the transition to electric vehicles as well. Soon gas-fired cars will be in the same category as the horse and buggy. In the near future, middle-class citizens might be able to book a flight to outer space from SpaceX, an Elon Musk–owned company.

The transportation industry is often overlooked by workers seeking long-term careers, but the world would grind to a screeching halt without companies like American Airlines, Union Pacific Railroad, FedEx, UPS, XPO Logistics, and Deutsche Bahn.

Government

Yes, the government is an industry offering millions of jobs to workers of all stripes at the local, state, and federal levels. The number of jobs in American government, local, state and federal, approaches twenty million. This industry is often overlooked because many workers believe, mistakenly, that all government jobs are political. While this might be true for some of the highest-level jobs, such as federal cabinet positions, most government jobs are similar to what one would find in the corporate world. Government jobs pay well, offer generous benefits, and are meaningful. Look for open positions by googling your state and entering "job opportunities." Do the same for jobs at the local level. To learn how jobs at the federal level work, your best source is FederalJobs.net.

The Self-Employment and Franchise Industry

The global workplace has another important facet: the self-employment industry. This industry includes all businesses that are owned and operated by individuals, not corporate entities like Apple or Disney. The self-employment and franchise industry offers opportunities to those workers who choose to open and fund their own businesses. It could be a storefront business like a small restaurant or a technology consulting service operated by an individual working from home.

In chapter 11, "Starting Your Own Business or Purchasing a Franchise," we'll go into detail about how entrepreneurship works.

MAJOR FUNCTIONAL DEPARTMENTS WITHIN A COMPANY

As a general rule, companies are divided into various departments like marketing, sales, accounting/finance, legal, technology, human resources, research and development, production, and product development. Overseeing the various departments is the executive branch, which includes the C-level workers whose department designation is preceded by the word "chief," like the chief executive officer and chief financial officer (CFO); the president; and various vice presidents, such as VP of marketing. Usually, each department is headed by a vice president or a director. Under the director is a manager. And finally, there are hands-on workers who report to the manager.

Overseeing the entire company is often a board of directors that includes the executive staff and usually one or two executive-level members from outside the company.

However, there could be a different departmental organization depending on the company's number of employees, its revenue, and its products and services. For example, in a company with under 500 employees, sales and marketing might be combined into one department.

When evaluating a company for potential employment, a job candidate should know the organizational structure and the names and background of the various department heads, both C-level and below.

GENERATIONS THAT FORM OUR WORKFORCE

Frequently we hear the media discuss the various social generations. Here is a list of those peer groups who have already become fully entrenched in the workforce, their birth years, and the personality characteristics they carry into the workplace.

- The Silent Generation, born between 1925 and 1945. This generation is noted for its silence about matters pertaining to government and figures in authority. Most workers in this class are now retired.
- Baby boomers, born between 1946 and 1964. Workers in this class were born in the "baby boom" following WWII and are noted for their ambivalent attitudes and actions relating to diversity, gender, sexuality, race relations, and what has been called pop culture.
- Generation X, born between 1965 and 1980. This class demonstrates political and cultural awareness and burgeoning familiarity with technology.
- Generation Y (or millennials), born between 1981 and 1996. This group includes workers who have been referred to as "digital natives," people who were born into a world that was learning to use the latest technologies to its advantage.
- Generation Z, born between 1997 and 2012. This group has demonstrated acute cultural and political awareness because of their familiarity with all forms of technology, especially social media.

Understanding how each generation functions in a company is especially important for corporate managers. For more information on this topic, review the work of Dr. Jean Twenge (JeanTwenge.com).

THE SURVIVAL OF OUR SPECIES

What does all this talk about work really mean? Does it matter? We get up in the morning. We go to work. We come home. We go to bed and repeat the same day in and day out.

All work is done for the same reason: to survive as a species. The prime industry is food because it enables us to survive. For example, an ear of corn comes to our table because it is supported by workers who plant the seeds. It is harvested by workers in the field. It is transported to wholesale and retail food companies by trucks driven by workers. Trucks move on tires that were manufactured by workers. Without the workers who make tires, our ear of corn would never get to our table. All workers and work itself are interrelated.

KEY TAKEAWAYS

- The workplace consists of industries, companies within those industries, and careers and jobs within those companies.
- Food, shelter, and clothing are industries required for our survival.
- The insurance industry is noted for its steady and significant profits and its longevity.
- AI will continue to change the workplace. A working knowledge of AI will enhance your prospects for employment in every industry.
- There are over twenty million government jobs at the local, state, and federal levels.

PRINT AND DIGITAL RESOURCES

- *The Occupational Outlook Handbook* by the US Department of Labor
- FederalJobs.net, run by Dennis Damp
- "Organizational Structure for Companies with Examples" on Investopedia.com

CHAPTER 3

EMPLOYMENT IS A LEGAL CONTRACT BETWEEN EMPLOYER AND EMPLOYEE

One of the most flagrant errors a worker can make is to assume that a career can be built around nothing more than a handshake with the HR director and the new boss. Unfortunately, this assumption can result in multimillion-dollar lawsuits by employers against their workers or by workers against their employers.

OFFER LETTERS AND EMPLOYMENT

Employment offers are written by company human resources directors and reviewed and approved by the company legal department. Frequently they are called offer letters, a confusing term that gives a false sense of security to the prospective worker. Adding to the confusion are the many internet sites providing information about offer letters. Offer letters are just proposals that contain information about the job. An offer letter is not legally binding even if you sign it and return it to the prospective employer unless it contains a provision stating that it is a legally binding contract.

The Offer Letter

The usual written offer letter includes the starting date, salary, benefits, job title and responsibilities, work location, remote working provisions, and the name and title of your boss. In addition, it often contains two nasty provisions:

1. An at-will provision that gives the employer the right to terminate you at any time for any reason

2. A noncompete provision that restricts you from working for a competitor for a specified number of years in a specified geographical area

Employers usually want you to sign the offer letter before moving on to the next step, the employment contract. Do not sign the offer letter.

The Employment Contract

The employment contract is a written document, reviewed and approved by the company legal department, stating the legally binding provisions of your employment. They will contain all the provisions in the offer letter plus the rights and responsibilities of both you and the employer. The contract must be signed by both you and the employer to be legally binding.

Before signing any employment contract, consult an employment attorney to ensure that your rights are not being violated and that the provisions are reasonable for the length of time you are employed. Yes, the attorney will charge a fee, which could be between $300 and $500, a small price to pay for sound legal advice about your career. Many job candidates refuse to hire an employment lawyer because of the cost but come to regret that mistake when they are terminated six months after starting work.

SERIOUS ISSUES IN OFFER LETTERS AND EMPLOYMENT CONTRACTS

At-will and noncompete provisions in employment offers and contracts vary between states and companies, and some companies do not include these onerous provisions in their employment offers and contracts. There are no national laws dealing with these two offensive provisions. Many states are now in the process of rescinding these laws, and there are legislators at the national level working to prohibit these provisions as well.

Never, under any circumstances, sign or orally agree to at-will and noncompete provisions in employment contracts or offer letters. If the employer insists, walk away from the job opportunity.

The Noncompete Provision

The noncompete provision could cause extreme hardship for a terminated worker. Here is a real-life example:

Joe was a sales rep working in the state of New Jersey for a publishing company producing instructional materials for the K–12 education market. After two years on the job, he was terminated. His employer gave no reason for the termination *and* told him he could not take a new job with a competing company in New Jersey for two years. That's when Joe came to me for recruiting assistance. I reviewed his employment contract, which included termination-at-will and noncompete provisions.

I learned from Joe that he had been offered a new job with a competing company in New Jersey, but before he could start, he received a call from an attorney employed by his previous employer, who told him he could not accept that job because of the two-year noncompete provision. If he did take the new job, the company would file a lawsuit because he had violated the noncompete agreement.

Joe was shocked! He was married with two elementary school children, owned a home with a hefty mortgage, and needed the money. My first step was to contact the president of his previous employer to explain Joe's financial situation and ask for an exception to the noncompete, which was legally binding in New Jersey. The president refused, citing that Joe was a highly respected sales rep with a good following among New Jersey educators and that he would take away business.

Joe could not wait two years. His only recourse was to accept a sales job outside of the publishing industry at a much lower salary.

The noncompete provision is confusing. It is legal in some states but not in others. The best way to deal with this issue is to take advice from your employment attorney.

The Termination-at-Will Provision

The termination-at-will provision gives the employer the right to terminate a worker at any time for no reason whatsoever. At-will applies for the duration of the agreement.

It works like this. On a Friday at 4 p.m. the HR director could call you into her office and say you are being terminated and to turn in your company documents and leave the office. When you ask why, she could just respond that the company believes it is the appropriate thing to do at this particular time. She need not give any reason, specific or general, for your termination.

Her action reflects the legally binding provision in your employment contract. However, this provision can work in favor of the employee. Make sure that the contract states that the employee can likewise terminate their job at any time without stating a reason and without liability.

FEDERAL LEGALLY BINDING EMPLOYMENT PROVISIONS

There are legally binding workplace provisions enacted by Congress to protect workers from unscrupulous employers. Here are five important federal acts covering workplace rights, duties, obligations, and enforcement.

The Family and Medical Leave Act (FMLA)

Enacted in 1993 and under jurisdiction of the Department of Labor, FMLA is a federal law that provides eligible employees with paid and unpaid leave. Also, it includes job-protected leave for specified events for a specific period. As a hypothetical example, Mary has a baby and elects to stay home nurturing the newborn for the maximum amount of leave offered by FMLA, which is twelve workweeks. The company must hold Mary's job open for the amount of time she is off work. When she returns, the company must place her back in the same job at the same salary. To be eligible, Mary must have been employed for twelve months for a specified number of hours per week. The same applies to workers taking time off to care for sick family members.

Rules and regulations covering FMLA leave can change and have different interpretations. Many lawsuits have been filed regarding FMLA provisions. For current information go to DoL.gov/FMLA. Also, contact your HR director. You may consider contacting an employment lawyer if the picture is still not clear. Most employers with fifty employees or more are covered by FMLA.

The Fair Labor Standards Act (FLSA)

Established by Congress in 1938 and directed by the Department of Labor, FLSA establishes a federal minimum wage, overtime pay, recordkeeping, and youth employment standards affecting employees in the private sector and in federal, state, and local governments. Covered nonexempt workers are entitled to a minimum wage of not less than $7.25 per hour, effective July 24, 2009. Overtime pay at a rate not less than one and one-half times the regular rate of pay is required after forty hours of work in a workweek.

In 2019 the minimum salary from FLSA increased to $684 per week and $35,568 per year. Each year, check the adjusted amount by viewing the FLSA website.

Once again, there have been many lawsuits filed by workers over the interpretation of the provisions in this act, which can change suddenly. In addition, there are many state laws regarding labor matters. For current information, go to DoL.gov. Also, check your state website.

The Occupational Health and Safety Act (OSHA)

Safety and health conditions in most private industries are regulated by OSHA or OSHA-approved state programs. These safety and health conditions cover public-sector employers as well. Employers covered by OSHA must comply with OSHA's regulations and safety and health standards. Laws are enforced through OSHA inspections and investigations.

If you observe hazardous working conditions, report them to your boss and HR director and request compliance with OSHA requirements. If they do not comply and correct the situation, contact your state OSHA department to report the unsafe conditions.

Equal Employment Opportunity Commission (EEOC)

The EEOC is responsible for enforcing federal laws that make it illegal to discriminate against a job applicant or an employee because of the person's race, color, religion, sex, national origin, age, disability, or genetics. Employment laws apply to all types of work situations, including hiring, firing, promotions, harassment, training, wages, and benefits. Thousands of lawsuits have been filed by workers against employers who have violated employment laws protecting human rights.

The Pregnant Workers Fairness Act

This federal law, which went into effect in June 2023, requires employers with fifteen or more employees to reasonably accommodate pregnant workers who have temporary work restrictions.

Other Provisions

There are many additional federal acts covering a variety of issues in the workplace, such as veterans' rights, migrants' rights, unemployment compensation, construction regulations, transportation regulations, company closings, layoffs, and many others.

Employers hire HR specialists and lawyers to interpret and administer federal and state employment laws. For example, many employers belong to a nationwide organization called HR Specialist (TheHRSpecialist.com) to keep updated on employment law and practices through comprehensive monthly newsletters and live conferences.

In addition, most companies belong to the Society for HR Management (SHRM), the world's largest human resources organization. This organization provides frequent newsletters, online advice, and annual or quarterly personal conferences. You do not have to be a company HR director to belong to SHRM. Go to their website (SHRM.org) for important employment information and join SHRM for a modest fee.

Workers have nobody working on their side unless they belong to a union. However, there is a growing trend to establish local labor unions to look after worker rights. For example, workers in a number of Starbucks stores have formed local unions to voice their concerns to the Starbucks corporation.

Workplace laws can be complicated, confusing, and subject to change. Keep up to date by checking both federal and state laws, online, at least once a month to make sure your rights are not being compromised by your employer.

KEY TAKEAWAYS

- Always hire an employment lawyer to review offer letters, employment contracts, and termination documents.
- Human resources departments are constantly updated on employment law. To even the playing field, workers should subscribe to the HR Specialist newsletter, even if represented by a union. Special price offers are frequently available. Cost for this newsletter can be as low as $97 per year.
- Become a member of SHRM.
- Do not sign an employment contract that contains a noncompete provision or a termination-at-will provision.

PRINT AND DIGITAL RESOURCES

- Chelle Law (ChelleLaw.com) is a nationwide employment law firm based in Scottsdale, Arizona, that provides online and print advice and videos about employment and termination matters.

CHAPTER 4

MATCHING THE REAL YOU WITH A REAL CAREER USING THE NEXTERCISE

"Plan your work. Work your plan." This was the response I received from an entrepreneur in Minneapolis who owned three auto dealerships when I asked him, "How did you become so successful?" These six words are among the most important in this book.

How do you begin a meaningful career search? We have created an exercise to help you navigate what can be a confusing worldwide network of careers. We call it the NEXTERCISE.

The NEXTERCISE will guide you through the process leading to career opportunities that align with your interests and skills. This is a career exploration exercise for all workers: entry level, experienced, and middle-aged, terminated workers looking for a new career, military veterans entering the civilian workforce, and retired workers seeking an encore career. Race, gender, ethnicity, and your location play no part. The NEXTERCISE applies worldwide. Follow the script, step by step:

FIRST: List, in writing, your twelve major interests.
Here is an example:

My Interests

1. Healthcare
2. Sports
3. Architecture
4. Finance
5. World affairs
6. Government
7. Transportation
8. Travel
9. Cooking
10. Legal matters
11. Politics
12. Environment

NEXT: List in writing your twelve major skills.
Here is an example:

My Skills

1. Par-level golfing
2. Preparing gourmet meals
3. Writing articles on current affairs
4. Gardening
5. Managing my personal finances, including my IRA
6. Auto maintenance
7. Communication with peers
8. Interior and exterior house painting
9. Selling high-dollar products
10. Reading with comprehension
11. Parenting
12. Leadership

NEXT: Match your top interests with your top-level skills. We'll use three from each list as an example:

Matching My Interests and Skills

- 3. Architecture *and* 8. Interior and exterior house painting
- 2. Sports *and* 1. Par-level golfing
- 9. Cooking *and* 2. Preparing gourmet meals

NEXT: Now that you've matched your top-level interests and skills, let's match them with industries.

Matching My Interests and Skills with Industries

- Architecture/interior and exterior house painting *with* the shelter industry
- Sports/par-level golfing *with* the professional sports industry
- Cooking/preparing gourmet meals *with* the food industry

NEXT: Match your industry with companies therein.

Matching My Industries with Companies

Companies in the Shelter Industry:
- Lennar
- Home Depot
- Sherwin Williams
- Bechtel
- D.R. Horton

Companies in the Professional Sports Industry:
- Philadelphia Eagles football team
- National Basketball Association (NBA)
- Pickleball Central
- Chicago Cubs baseball team

Companies in the Food Industry:
- Costco
- PepsiCo
- Mondelez International
- McDonald's
- Kroger

NEXT: Visit the company websites to learn about the company products, services, and career opportunities. When you find the right job opportunity, learn the name of the HR director or the hiring manager and send your résumé and cover letter to that person. Do not send your letter and résumé to a job number or job title. They must be sent to a named person to have any meaning.

KEY TAKEAWAYS
- Plan your work. Work your plan.
- Follow the NEXTERCISE to discover your personal interests and skills. Then, match them with corresponding industries and companies therein. Do this periodically to make sure you are on the right career path.
- Explore each company on your list and decide which ones are not only appealing but also have job opportunities that are in sync with your interests, background, and experience.
- You will find peace and happiness if your work embraces the real you.

CHAPTER 5

GENDER, RACE, AND ETHNICITY IN THE WORKPLACE

Diversity, equity, and inclusion: "DEI" is what we frequently hear from workers who see a workplace riddled with discrimination. Some of this rhetoric is valid, but much of it is hype to entice the American workforce to hire job candidates based on identity rather than qualifications. This has caused much angst in the workforce, which has resulted in lawsuits—some justified, some contrived. As a result of both this and political pressure, many companies, large and small, are eliminating their DEI practices.

Having been in the recruiting business for twenty-five years, I have witnessed a sincere effort on the part of corporate presidents, CEOs, and HR directors to make the workplace flat. When a company executive comes to me with a job description for a new employee, entry to executive level, my mandate is to present qualified candidates of all stripes.

The employer has an obligation to make money in order to grow the business for the sake of customers, workers, and shareholders. The employer fulfills this mission by hiring workers who are qualified to produce quality products and services regardless of race, gender, or ethnicity. "But why," some cry, "are more than half of all workers on the floor of a big retailer like Costco or Walmart White?" Population statistics will give us the answer. Our population of 340 million breaks down like this: 70 percent White, 12 percent African American, 16 percent Hispanic and Latino, and 2 percent mixed Asian and Indian.

ORGANIZATIONS PROMOTING WOMEN IN THE WORKFORCE

According to the United States Census Bureau, women make up close to 47 percent of the US workforce, 32 percent of them in executive-level roles.[3] However, the picture changes when we talk about specific industries. For example, 75 percent of K–12 teachers in America are women.[4] In the healthcare industry, women make up about 50 percent of "entry-level, managerial, and executive roles."[5] Some of the largest highly visible companies have had female CEOs, like Mary Barra, CEO of General Motors; Carol Tomé, CEO of United Parcel Service; Vicki Hollub, CEO and president of Occidental Petroleum; and Jane Fraser, CEO of Citigroup.

There are many helpful online organizations whose mission is to protect women's rights and provide initiatives for moving forward:

- Ms. Career Girl, a popular site offering workplace guidance and advice for young women (MsCareerGirl.com).
- The National Organization for Women, founded in 1966, is the largest organization of feminist activists,

---

3   Chris Gilligan, "States With the Highest Percentage of Female Top Executives," US News, March 6, 2023, https://www.usnews.com/news/best-states/articles/2023-03-06/states-with-the-highest-percentage-of-women-in-business-leadership-roles
4   Katherine Schaeffer, "Key facts about public school teachers in the U.S.," Pew Research Center, September 24, 2024, https://www.pewresearch.org/short-reads/2024/09/24/key-facts-about-public-school-teachers-in-the-u-s.
5   "Elevating Women in Health Care—All the Way to CEO," Boston Consulting Group, January 6, 2025, https://www.bcg.com/publications/2025/elevating-women-in-health-care.

boasting over 500,000 members in America alone. It offers guidance to women of all ages about identity, work, persona, and character (NOW.org).
- Women's Media Center conducts research and advocates for the visibility of women and girls in the media (WomensMediaCenter.com).
- Women Who Code, an international organization whose mission is to inspire women to select technology careers in the workplace (WomenWhoCode.com).
- Girls Who Code, an international organization whose mission is to close the gender gap in technology (GirlsWhoCode.com).

ORGANIZATIONS PROMOTING MINORITY EMPLOYMENT

The career opportunities for minorities have never been better, and there are many examples to substantiate this thesis. For example, Charles Payne, an Air Force veteran, is the host on the popular *Fox Business News* that airs daily. Charles has authored several books on the world of finance. Then we have Paul Goodloe, the key featured meteorologist on the Weather Channel since 1999. And Rosalind Brewer, an African American woman, is considered one of the most brilliant female business leaders in the worldwide workforce. She was Starbucks' first Black chief operating officer (COO), Walgreens' first Black CEO, and the first woman CEO of Sam's Club before that.

Prompted by racial discrimination in hiring, a number of organizations have been founded to promote a level field for minority workers:
- The National Association for the Advancement of Colored People was founded in 1908 to promote justice and equal rights in society generally, and the workplace in particular, for people of African lineage (NAACP.org).

- The National Urban League, founded in 1910, promotes the educational, social, and economic inclusion of African Americans across 300 communities and thirty-seven US states. They achieve this by implementing a range of social programs and by public advocacy (NUL.org).
- More in Common aims to combat narratives that divide communities and societies. They partner with organizations to advance community inclusion and encourage open dialogue on issues that polarize people (MoreinCommon.com).
- OneTen aims to close the opportunity gap for Black talent in America. Working with job candidates, it creates programs to earn success and ignite potential for Black workers. OneTen connects Black talent to well-paying job opportunities through its Career Marketplace and has partnerships with many leading companies across America, such as IBM, Lowe's, Cisco, Delta, Walmart, Target, AT&T, PepsiCo, JP Morgan Chase & Co., Allstate, and Bank of America. Review their website for more information (OneTen.org).
- The Black Data Processing Associates is an international organization founded in 1975 as a network for underrepresented minorities working in the IT and computer science fields (BDPA.org).
- The Black Professionals in Tech Network aims to connect Black tech professionals and help corporations strengthen their diversity initiatives. This organization helps corporate partners understand how to attract, hire, retain, and promote Black tech talent by changing not only the way they hire but also how they structure their internal culture (BPTN.org).

KEY TAKEAWAYS

- While there are still cases of discrimination in the worldwide workplace related to gender, race, and ethnicity, workers can confidently move forward in their search for meaningful careers. Companies will always hire qualified workers who add to the bottom line and display intelligence, energy, and passion for a specific job opening. All workers are protected by numerous federal and state employment laws that prevent discrimination.
- Women and minority job candidates should frequently check the websites listed for the organizations above to remain updated on recent legislation and changes in the workplace.

PRINT AND DIGITAL RESOURCES

- *Career Forward: Strategies from Women Who've Made It* by Grace Puma and Christiana Smith Shi

CHAPTER 6

CRAFTING A RÉSUMÉ AND DIGITAL PROFILE WHILE EMPLOYED

One grave mistake that employed workers make is to assume their present job will last forever. This can lead to a false sense of security because the company culture could change with the hiring of a new CEO, prompting you to leave the company and find an alternative job. One of your initiatives while still employed should be to craft an up-to-date résumé. Why? Because your old résumé, that five-year-old piece of dynamite, is probably outdated in both content and style.

Be ready to move on because tomorrow you might have good reason to quit and look elsewhere, regardless of your present rank and salary. It makes no difference if you are the president, a mid-level manager, or a field sales representative. Don't be caught off guard. Frequently, a company will be planning behind closed doors to terminate thousands of jobs before it becomes public knowledge. Note changes in the new company culture or the behavior of its executives. For verification, watch daily financial TV programs and read financial publications like *The Wall Street Journal*.

If you quit your job for any reason, you will have good company. Millions of workers quit their jobs each day to find something better aligned with their interests, skills, and aspirations. And remember that you may be terminated in person or by email on a sunny Friday afternoon for no reason whatsoever—one of those 55,000 workers terminated each day in America.

Crafting a résumé is just one initiative in the process of finding alternative employment. The purpose of the résumé is to motivate the reader (maybe the HR director or the hiring manager) to invite you for an in-person or Zoom interview. Remember that the résumé alone will not land you a new job. Take these important steps while you are still employed:

- Read prospective companies' quarterly financial reports.
- Read daily financial newspapers like *The Wall Street Journal* and watch the daily financial programs on CNBC or Bloomberg. Pay particular attention to AI.
- Do not use AI to write your résumé. Hiring managers and HR directors know the difference between a personally crafted résumé and one created by AI.

BEFORE CRAFTING YOUR RÉSUMÉ

Many workers plunge forward in the career hunting process by reading online job openings, but first crafting a viable résumé and digital profile in keeping with today's style and format is necessary to move your candidacy forward to the interview.

A résumé is a picture of you in words. It tells the reader who you are and what you have accomplished, your education, and the skills that will take you forward. It's critically important to keep the future in mind when writing your résumé. While hiring managers may find your past interesting and important, they are always thinking, even subconsciously, about what you can do for the company going forward.

Workers often wonder whether they should write a general résumé to submit to potential employers they find on job boards or career pages or craft the résumé for a specific job with a specific company. The latter is the proper way to go. Always write the résumé in response to a specific job opening and send it to a named person with a specific job title. Sending your résumé to a general job posting will yield the same result as sending it addressed to the third ring of the planet Saturn: Nothing.

Here are action items to implement before putting pen to paper or finger to key:

- Decide what industry and companies in that industry you would like to pursue using the NEXTERCISE in chapter 4.
- View online sources to determine the best current résumé styles. There are plenty of free résumé styles to view from reliable sources. You will find that most are similar if not identical.
- Decide what you would like to delete from your old résumé.
- Decide what you would like to add to your new résumé.

THE MAIN PARTS OF YOUR RÉSUMÉ

All résumés should follow a time-tested order for placement of major headings. Use these major headings for your résumé in this order and remember to include your AI experience.

- Contact. Begin with your name and contact information at the top of the first page. Be sure to include your home city and state, phone number, and email address. Resist the temptation to play big-time techie and assume that all you need is your name and email address. Do that and your résumé will be trashed.
- Summary. State your present job title, company affiliation, and a concise description of your present job responsibilities. Include AI experience.
- Work Experience. List your work experience

chronologically, starting with the most recent and working backward, in bullet-point format. State the name of the employer, job title, and a description of your job responsibilities, including AI experience.
- Technology Skills. List your technology expertise and capabilities in bullet-point format. Remember to include any AI experience.
- Awards and Special Recognition. In bullet-point format, list all recognitions going back to your high school years. Frequently a hiring manager will look at this part of your résumé first.
- Community Service. In bullet-point format, list any charitable community work you have performed. Employers frequently form nonprofit partnerships with community organizations and welcome employees who do the same.
- Education. List all education chronologically line by line. State the name of the college, university, or trade organization, followed by the type of degree received. You do not need to include dates.
- Certifications and Continuing Education. In today's technology-focused workplace, potential employers like to see that you are continuing your education. Include AI education.

To summarize, here is your résumé outline by major heading:
- Contact
- Summary
- Work Experience
- Technology Skills
- Awards and Special Recognition
- Community Service
- Education
- Certifications and Continuing Education

At this point in the process there is no need to list things like hobbies, special interests, or references.

While the résumé, a summary of you in writing, is important, you want to show how your experience will enable you to perform in the new job and beyond. To meet this criterion, under your summary and technology skills, include something like this: "My AI and robotic skills will enable me to fulfill the increasingly important tasks required by this job and beyond."

AI AND YOUR RÉSUMÉ

Some workers believe that using AI to write a résumé is acceptable. They match the job description with their personal information and let AI do the rest. This is not acceptable to hiring managers. They can easily detect your AI-written résumé and will reject your candidacy.

But AI does have a place in your résumé. Throughout the résumé, be sure to articulate your AI experience and expertise, no matter how slight it may be. Going forward, AI will change the workplace generally and your job or occupation in particular.

COMMON RÉSUMÉ MISTAKES

You want the reader to see "you" on paper without mistakes. You want hiring managers and HR directors to be impressed with your candidacy and not be distracted by common errors, which will cause your résumé to be dismissed. Also, resist the temptation to inject humor into your résumé, unless you are applying for a job as a comedian. Here are the most frequent reasons for résumé dismissal:

- ➤ Typos. In addition to using your spellchecker, read your résumé aloud and have a trusted colleague do the same. Why? One typo and you are out of the running.

The hiring manager will never tell you that your résumé contained a spelling error. They will just trash it, and your candidacy will be history.
- Grammar mistakes. Again, one mistake and you are history. Run your résumé through the grammar checker. Read it aloud and have a trusted colleague do the same.
- Inconsistent formatting and style. Throughout the résumé, use only one typeface and size, like twelve-point Times New Roman. Do not use anything fancy like a script typeface.
- Missing metrics. Quantify as much as possible. Generalities will get you nowhere. If you managed a sales team, state how many sales reps reported to you and the dollars they generated.
- Gaps in employment history. Gaps in your employment history will raise serious concerns. If you were out of the workforce between jobs, state the reason. It could be personal or family illness or FMLA leave. Whatever it is, state the reasons for the employment gap to erase speculation.
- Photos and fancy design. The reader could be distracted by photos, which could be out of style. Avoid design features like colors, shading, or boxing. Keep it clean. Keep it simple.

YOUR DIGITAL PROFILE

In today's world, your profile could be on various Meta Platforms (formerly Facebook) apps, LinkedIn, or other social media. When hiring managers are evaluating your candidacy, they will not only read your résumé but also check your social media profiles. Your profile should be in sync with your résumé for consistency. If they do not jibe, the hiring manager could ask silently, "Will the real Mary Jones please come forward?"

KEY TAKEAWAYS

- Always keep your résumé updated. You never know when you will be terminated or find reasons to leave your job.
- Include AI experience and expertise in your résumé.
- Make sure that your résumé and digital profile are in sync.
- Hiring managers are forward-looking. Tailor your résumé and profile to reflect that your skills will serve you well in the future.
- Never use AI to write your résumé.

PRINT AND DIGITAL RESOURCES

- *How to Write a Stellar Executive Resume: 50 Tips to Reaching Your Job Target* by Brenda Bernstein, JD
- *How to Write a Killer LinkedIn Profile* by Brenda Bernstein

CHAPTER 7

CONQUERING THE INTERVIEW FOR A NEW JOB WHILE EMPLOYED

Interviewing for a new job while you are still employed can be a daunting task. There is the possibility that your seeking new employment could get back to your boss and others in your company, resulting in an uncomfortable relationship going forward. Your employer could consider this a lack of loyalty and wonder if you are disclosing confidential information to a competitor. Discretion is advised. Take every precaution possible to ensure the interview will be conducted with strict confidence. Let the interviewers know your thoughts about this and ask them to maintain confidence and to avoid contacting references for the time being.

Millions of words have been written about interviews. Google "job interviews," and you will get thousands of hits. Go to the business and career section on Amazon or at a Barnes & Noble bookstore, and you will find dozens of books on the topic. All of us have read internet articles titled "Ten Tips for Killer Interviews," "Ace the Interview in Three Easy Steps," or "Interviews for Dummies." All of this tells us that the interview is an important part of the career-hunting process and that we should prepare for it carefully.

THE PURPOSE OF THE INTERVIEW

Before we get into the heart of the interview, let's reconstruct the bigger picture. The interview is part of the process that enables both you and the company to determine whether the relationship will work to the advantage of both the company and the candidate. When that happens, everyone wins. The company makes money from your productive work in order to pay your salary and benefits, expenses, and taxes, perhaps contribute to charitable causes, and still have enough left over to be a profitable business. You win because you make money to become self-sufficient, take care of your family, and contribute money and time to the community.

WHO'S HOLDING THE ACES?

Even though the interviewer appears to hold all the cards, this is not so. The hiring manager needs someone like you to fill an important position and is under pressure to find the right candidate as soon as possible. While the hiring manager is evaluating the person sitting across the desk, smart candidates are sizing up the hiring manager as well. It is important that the hiring manager is someone you respect, someone who shows courtesy and honesty. If you find that the interviewer lacks these qualities, erase that company from your list. You may need a job, but you do not want it at the expense of working on a ship of fools. If you think this listing ship might change once the company hires you, remember this rule: You can't fix crazy!

LISTEN AND LEARN

Your instinct might be to tout your accomplishments with a recitation of what's on your résumé. The interviewer has most likely checked out who you are and what you have done and is not interested in a retelling. Remembering, the person sitting across the desk from you is forward-looking. Keep that in mind when the interviewer begins the conversation by asking questions. Listen and comprehend, because how you respond is what really counts. In his well-known book *The Seven Habits of Highly Effective People*, Stephen Covey says, "Most people do not listen with the intent to understand; they listen with the intent to reply. They are either speaking or preparing to speak."

A good example that supports Covey's theory is the TV interview. Interviewers are often more concerned with presenting their own agendas than with listening to responses to their questions. Before the response is even completed, interviewers interrupt with their own statements. Why don't they permit the person to complete the answer? Your interviewer might have the same tendency, so be sure to maintain the integrity of the interview to make your point. If the interviewer interrupts before you have responded completely, you must make an appropriate remark to keep the interview on an even keel, even though your gut reaction might be "Shut up. Let me finish my answer to your question."

Here is what you might say when this happens: "To complete my response to your first question, here is what I was going to say . . ." That should keep the interview on the right track and make for a fruitful exchange of ideas and courteous discourse. The interview is a conversation where two people listen, comprehend, and then respond.

BASIC RULES FOR INTERVIEWS

There are two basic rules for interviews: 1) Be courteous; and 2) be honest. These two rules build the foundation for all personal relationships. This holds true no matter how young, how old, or how senior the interviewer is. The person sitting across the desk from you may be older than you are and may be a director or vice president. To reach that point in the corporate hierarchy, this person has been doing something right. On the other side of the age situation, the interviewer may be ten years your junior and display arrogance that is nothing short of irritating. Suck it up, because you cannot do anything about it. Build the relationship by expressing interest in this person's rise to a position of responsibility. Regardless of the situation, the only way to deal with these variables is to be prepared to answer the questions in a mature manner and on your own terms. When you prepare for the interview, resolve to look at the hiring manager as a potential friend.

If you are still employed, be sure to tell the interviewer that you are still employed and wish to keep this confidential. State why you want to leave your present career and company. Honesty also applies if you have been laid off or fired from your last job. If the interviewer asks why you left your previous job, be honest and say that you were let go. If you were laid off, state the circumstances: a reorganization, downsizing, rightsizing, or bankruptcy. If you were fired, don't talk around it. Be forthcoming and state why you were fired: that you did not meet the job expectations or you and your boss were on different pages. Admit it and follow by saying that you have learned your lesson and that you have resolved to move forward using your newfound persona and your reconstructed character. As a matter of fact, the interviewer has likely learned that you were fired for cause after some preliminary background checking before you came for the interview.

HOW THE INTERVIEWER JUDGES YOU

Four important items on an employer's checklist appear so self-evident that many candidates overlook them. However, if you fall short on these, your chances of moving ahead in the process are diminished.

Appropriate Dress

Your appearance is the first thing a hiring manager will notice. If you come to an interview dressed inappropriately, you are history. Case closed. No second chance. With the workplace becoming more casual, there is a tendency to dress down, even for an interview. We might see mid-level and executive-level workers in casual dress when on the job, but an interview is a different occasion. I have asked human resources directors about this, and their advice is to dress a cut above casual for an interview, in business attire. In fact, several commented that many experienced candidates dress too casually for interviews, which does not help their candidacy.

Verbal Communication

After dress, the most important checklist item is verbal communication, which includes vocabulary. Avoid clichés and slang. Answer questions using business speak that you have learned throughout your working years. The hiring manager expects no less. For example, one of the questions most frequently asked is "Why do you want to work here?" Deliver your answer in business language such as this: "I want to work with your company because I'm impressed with your record of generating revenue. For example, in the last quarter your revenue was up ten percent over a comparable quarter a year ago. This tells me that you have a viable business model. I would like a chance to work for such a company and contribute my time and talents to help the company continue to grow."

Content

The content part of the interview should reflect your research on the company's finances, your interest in the job opportunity at hand, and your qualifications for helping the company move forward. Delivery should be made using business speak. Avoid clichés such as "awesome." Be sure to explore the company's AI initiatives. Also, the interviewer will ask about responsibilities in your present job. Disclose them honestly.

Body Language

Much has been written on this subject, but it still comes down to a few basics. Sit straight, make eye contact, relax, smile, and display your personality. If you are not accustomed to using your hands to make a point, do not make an awkward attempt to do this in an interview. You are having a conversation about how you can help the company going forward, not auditioning for a part in a movie. To learn more, conduct a Google search on body language.

Here is a real-life situation that I encountered recently while conducting a search for a vice president. This story demonstrates that delivery, particularly the body language part of it, is just as important as content.

Fred from California had a personal two-hour interview with the CEO of a major company located in Los Angeles. The position, vice president for international sales and marketing, required the candidate to live in the home office area, and Fred met that requirement. He did not need to relocate. This was a huge problem out of the way. On paper, he met every job requirement and more. So far, so good. However, something problematic happened during the interview process. The CEO rejected his candidacy, citing these two reasons: First, "Fred's answers seemed shallow." In other words, the CEO did not buy the content. Second, "Fred appeared insecure, lacking confidence, and appeared to be distracted."

Fred's body language created a disconnect. His eyes were wandering during the interview, his posture was strained, his arms were folded much of the time, and his legs were crossed.

Fred's body language told the CEO that he was not buying into the conversation. I counseled Fred on the basics of body language and persuaded the CEO to have a second interview with Fred. Specifically, I told Fred to sit erect, facing the interviewer, make direct eye contact throughout the interview, sit with hands resting in his lap rather than arms folded, rest legs on the floor rather than tightly crossed, and avoid fidgeting and letting eyes wander if there were interruptions from office sources, like a ringing phone. Also, I told Fred to relax and maintain a friendly smile during the interview.

The CEO obliged by granting Fred a second interview, and the results were startling. The interview proceeded as a conversation, and the CEO and Fred learned they had much in common on a personal level. Both were star performers on their college swim teams and had similar current interests. After another round of interviews with company executives, Fred was hired.

PREPARING A WRITTEN INTERVIEW AGENDA

I am always impressed when a candidate comes to an interview with a written agenda that includes questions about both the position and the company. I'm equally impressed when the candidate hands me a written agenda and requests a brief discussion of each topic if time permits. A written agenda sends a powerful message that you have carefully prepared for the interview and that you are pursuing this particular opportunity, not just any job. Here is a sample agenda that you can use as a model for crafting your own, which you can then print on your letterhead and hand to the interviewer before beginning the interview.

Sample Interview Agenda

Begin your agenda as you would a memo:

To: Mr. Fred Kowalski, Director of Marketing, XYZ Corp.
From: Lisa Hopkins, Candidate for the Marketing Manager Position
Date: April 29, 2026

I would appreciate the opportunity to discuss the following questions during my interview with Mr. Kowalski:

1. Why is this position open?
2. If someone else had this job, why did that person leave the company?
3. Why are you considering me for this position?
4. Would superior performance in this position lead to a promotion?
5. What are the three major expectations for the marketing manager?
6. To whom does this job report, and what is that person's management style?
7. What is the background of the person to whom this position reports?
8. What is the company's revenue goal for this fiscal year? How much of an increase is that over the previous year's revenue?
9. Has the use of AI made this company a leader in the industry?
10. Does the company participate in community outreach programs?
11. Does the company require ongoing professional development courses?
12. Why should I join your company?

> I thank you for discussing these issues during our interview.
>
> Sincerely,
> Lisa Hopkins

Answers to these questions are a tool for evaluating the position and company. You need this information to determine whether you want to continue the process or decline. Using the written interview agenda will separate you from the rest of the pack. Do not hesitate to use this technique for every interview.

THE INTERVIEW PROCESS

The interview process has four sections, each with its own set of procedures:

1. The beginning of the interview: This is the introductory phase, which sets the tone for the interview.
2. The body of the interview, which takes place after the greetings are completed.
3. Interviewing the interviewer.
4. The end of the interview, a critically important action item.

The Beginning of the Interview

Before each interview, write your plan detailing how you will begin the interview. After the usual observations about the weather, it's showtime. Trying to anticipate what the interviewer will ask can be futile. To level the playing field and keep this a true give-and-take rather than an interrogation, plan to incorporate some or all of these five topics into the interview:

- You are here because you have learned there is a specific employment opportunity.
- You have researched the company and would like to work there for several reasons. State what they are. Some reasons could be your interest in their product, company profitability, glowing reports from company workers, or the steady increase in the price of the company stock.
- You would like an opportunity to increase company profitability by using your talents, intelligence, energy, passion, and your facility using AI.
- Highlight your successes and awards for achievement. Verbalize the key points on your résumé under the major headings "Awards and Special Recognition" and "Community Service."
- State your career goals and do not be shy. If you really would like to be the company president someday, say so. Tell your interviewer how and why you believe you could work your way up to that position.

One never knows where an interview will go, and it is up to the candidate to set the direction and tone of the interview. Your written agenda will help accomplish this. Naturally, the interviewer has a certain number of questions, but you do not know these in advance. However, the interviewer will ask one question in almost every situation: "Would you tell me about yourself?"

It appears to be a trivial question, but you must prepare for it. If you are caught off guard, you might end up reciting your family history or rendering a chronological account of your life from birth to the present. What the hiring manager wants to hear is what you might do for the company if you are hired rather than hearing that you like a latte better than a cappuccino. How do you answer that question? It could go several ways, but here is a script that you might use; it gives direction to the interview and sets the tone for a dialogue instead of a Q and A session:

> I'm the kind of person who takes responsibility for my own life, and that includes having a position that will give me income to continue to be self-sufficient and accomplish my career goals. I do not have that in my present position. I'm here because I believe that your company can provide that opportunity. My research indicates that your last quarter generated revenue that exceeded expectations and that your past three years were profitable. I want to be part of a company with that kind of track record because it means that you are doing something right. I would like to build on that success by applying my intelligence, energy, and passion to make this company even better and more profitable. Also, my career vision includes a vice president–level position, and hopefully I can find that here.

Read this aloud several times until you make it your own. Modify it to include some hard numbers and specifics from your résumé.

The Body of the Interview and Frequently Asked Questions

Candidates, understandably, are curious about what the interviewer will ask. The kinds of questions asked in an interview follow a somewhat standard format. Here are questions the interviewer may ask regardless of the company or position:

1. Would you tell me something about yourself?
2. How did you find out about us?

3. Why do you want to work here?
4. What are your major qualifications for this position?
5. Are there any areas where you think you need to improve, like the use of AI?
6. What are your career goals?
7. Can you tell me about a work problem you encountered and how you resolved it?
8. What are your compensation requirements?
9. When could you begin work with us if we agree this is the right job for you?
10. Have you participated in community outreach programs?
11. What is your main academic interest?
12. What books have you read recently?
13. Can you give me an example of how you use social media like YouTube, Twitter, Instagram, Facebook, and LinkedIn?
14. What do you want to know about the company and the job?
15. Why did you leave your last job?

You don't know how many of these questions the interviewer will ask, but be prepared to answer all of them. Conduct a rehearsal before the interview by having a trusted friend ask these questions and then deliver your responses. Practice until you feel comfortable with your answers. Remember to quantify as much as possible.

Interviewing the Interviewer

You can begin evaluating the hiring manager by asking a question like "Could you tell me about your job experience, such as how long you have been here, what your responsibilities are, and what you did before taking this job?" Such dialogue permits the hiring manager to brag a little and share some success stories. Your expressed interest in the hiring manager's accomplishments helps build the relationship and provides valuable information. In addition, it makes the interview conversational rather than interrogative. Remember, this is your interview, and you are entitled to ask as many questions as necessary to learn about the company and its people. Do not be intimidated by the interviewer's status or title. This is your time, your career, your life.

You will likely have your own list of questions, but here are five you should always ask, according to Jeff Haden, a very successful executive recruiter and author of many articles and a book on job hunting and interviewing. This material appeared in his article "5 Questions Great Job Candidates Ask," which appeared in an issue of *INC.* online magazine.[6]

1. "What are a few things that really drive results for the company?" Every profitable company has rubrics that account for its success. Learn what these are, and you will know much about the company and what it expects from its workers. If you hear something like "Everyone here works like crazy, even coming in on Saturdays and Sundays," consider it a yellow flag. You should not have to spend seven days a week meeting job expectations, and you should not be expected to be on call via texts and email twenty-four seven, unless you are a medical

---

6 Jeff Haden, "5 Questions Great Job Candidates Ask," *Inc.*, August 6, 2012, https://www.inc.com/jeff-haden/5-questions-great-job-candidates-ask-interviewers.html.

professional or a law enforcement officer . . . or president of the United States.

2. "What do employees do in their spare time?" This might be a difficult question for the interviewer to answer, especially in a large company. However, the answer will tell you much about the kind of people the company hires and if these are your kind of people. Do they spend off-work hours at a sports bar? Do they volunteer their off-work hours for company-sponsored outreach programs? Do some of them take graduate-level courses to improve their work skills?

3. "How do you plan to deal with . . . ?" The blank part of this question could be any number of items that aroused your curiosity while doing your research on the company and the industry. The question could be "How do you plan to deal with lower margins for your technology products?" The answers to these questions will tell you whether the company recognizes its problems and how it plans to deal with them going forward.

4. "What do you expect me to accomplish in the first 60 to 90 days?" This question lets the interviewer know that you are no slouch. You want the company hiring manager to know that you are ready, willing, and able to be productive immediately. You are job ready.

5. "What are the common attributes of your top performers?" The answer to this question will tell you a lot about the corporate culture, the company expectations, and what workers are willing to do to be successful there.

The End of the Interview

There is a definite way to end the interview. Salespeople ask for the order after making their product presentation instead of just saying, "Thank you for your time" and leaving. The same holds true for the interview. Close by saying thank you, and if you are interested in the job and the company, ask, "What are the next steps in the process? I really would like to work here based on your answers to my questions and my research about the company. When can I start?"

If the interviewer gives a nebulous answer to your closing statements, counter with an action item like "Thanks for your time. I'll follow up with you by phone or email to check on the status of my candidacy. May I please have your contact information? By the way, what is your hiring deadline?" If you are not interested in the job, say so, and leave after saying, "Thank you for your time. I really do not think this is a good fit. I'm sure that you will find a candidate better suited for this position." Remember to send a follow-up message even if you are no longer interested in the job. Always maintain the relationship regardless of the results of the interview.

PANEL INTERVIEWS

Occasionally, a panel will conduct the interview instead of just one person. The panel interview may sound intimidating, but it can work to your advantage. Panels usually consist of the hiring manager, the company HR director, and a worker from the department where the job is located. For example, if you are interviewing for an editorial manager position with a publishing company, the worker may be an associate editor. The purpose of the panel interview is to save time, not to intimidate the candidate.

When you walk through the door, you might not know whether the interview will be with one person or with a panel, so be prepared mentally for both. Usually, a panel interview means that the company is seriously interested in your candidacy. It's a positive sign for you. Be reassured and confident that the interview is going to work to your advantage. After the interview begins, determine the person who appears to be most friendly and supportive and make an effort to build a relationship with them. Interviewing with a panel is advantageous for a number of reasons. In the one-on-one interview, if you do not connect with the person across from you, there is nobody else you can turn to for help. In a panel interview, you have options for building strong relationships with more than one person.

BREAKFAST, LUNCH, OR DINNER INTERVIEWS

Occasionally the hiring manager will invite you to interview over breakfast, lunch, or dinner. The reason is not hunger. Rather, this type of interview gives the manager an opportunity to observe your behavior in a real-life setting. Candidates for customer-contact jobs in sales or marketing are frequently subjected to interviews over a meal. There are several basic rules for such interviews:

- Table manners should be scrupulously observed. That means chewing with your mouth closed, not leaning on the table, and not slurping your soup or coffee.
- Never lick your fingers.
- Never drink alcoholic beverages at meal interviews, even if the interviewer does.
- Never take calls on your smartphone. In fact, turn it off and put it in your pocket or purse.
- Treat the waitstaff and cleanup crew with respect.
- Remain focused regardless of circumstances.

These may sound like adolescent suggestions, but I have included them because I have observed violations of basic manners while interviewing mid-career candidates. On one occasion, I was interviewing a candidate for the presidency of a publishing company, and she licked her fingers after finishing her entrée. In effect, she licked her way out of a job.

I have interviewed many job candidates over breakfast and lunch. Most observed our rubric, but a number did not, with devastating results—loss of a job opportunity.

VIRTUAL INTERVIEWS

Time is a standard consideration of the job-hunting process because of the large number of candidates applying for posted jobs and because of the distance between candidate and interviewer. When HR directors have a hundred applicants for one position, they make the first cut using the candidate's résumé and information from other sources like social media. After the list is narrowed to a handful of candidates, the next step is to evaluate them with a phone or virtual interview using Zoom. Company execs claim the phone and Zoom interview process is cost-effective.

The only purpose of the virtual interview is to move your candidacy to the next step, the personal interview with the hiring manager. Few candidates are hired because of a phone or Zoom interview. It simply permits the interviewer to screen out unqualified candidates.

These interviews usually are not conversations but rather interrogations that leave candidates with little time to do more than answer rapid-fire questions. The interviewer has a list of questions on the desk and wants to run through them as quickly as possible. It is a robotic procedure. The candidate is rarely given the opportunity to offer more than a perfunctory answer to questions posed by the interviewer.

Try to avoid the virtual interview by volunteering to come in for a personal interview, even if this means driving three hours each way to the company location. Face-to-face communication is what you need to move forward in the search process. If you cannot avoid the phone/Zoom interview, learn to live with it and do your best.

The Virtual Interview Preparation Checklist

Talking on the phone or on a Zoom interview comes naturally to some people, but most of us have a less-than-winning virtual personality. However, with adequate preparation, anyone can accomplish the mission successfully. Prepare for the interview using this checklist:

- Find a private location for the interview, preferably your home office where there will be absolute quiet.
- Eliminate traffic noise, barking dogs, crying babies, and music playing in the background. If there are two phones in your location, turn off the one not being used. The last thing you want is your alternate phone ringing during an interview.
- Avoid holding the interview in casual settings such as a restaurant, car, bar, or train. This is a business call, not a casual call. If there are barking dogs or clinking glasses in the background, the interviewer will surely hear the background noise, and you will be history. There are no second chances.
- Conduct the interview at a table or desk where you can spread out documents for reference. You cannot do this while driving your car.
- Have your résumé, the job description, company information, and a written interview agenda listing your questions in front of you during the interview. Also, have a tablet or notebook and a pen for note-taking. Handwrite notes instead of entering them on your desktop or laptop computer or smartphone. With today's sensitive audio technology, keyboard noise is distracting to the person on the other end of the line.
- Stay focused. On a separate sheet of paper, write the

name of the company, the name and title of the person with whom you will be speaking, the date, time, and location of the interviewer.

- If the interviewer is located in another time zone, make the adjustment. If you are in New York and the interviewer is in Denver, there will be a two-hour time difference, so plan accordingly. If the call is scheduled for 9 a.m., Mountain Time, it will be 11 a.m. in New York. If you miscalculate the time difference and the caller cannot reach you, you are history.
- Conduct the interview dressed in business attire because the way you dress sets the stage for your behavior. If you are dressed in a yoga outfit, your conversation could easily become too casual. The same applies to your body language. If you go into the interview with feet resting on top of your desk, you could slip into casual mode and begin using words like "awesome."
- Prepare to answer the question "Would you tell me something about yourself?"
- Select the three most important questions from your written agenda. Usually virtual interviews are time sensitive, so you want to make sure you have covered what is important to you. If the interviewer permits you to continue, go beyond the first three questions. Phone and Zoom interviews, like personal interviews, should be a two-way conversation, which entitles you to be a proactive part of it. Your time is just as valuable as that of the interviewer.
- Have your laptop or desktop computer running with the company website on the screen.
- Smile during the interview. A smile on your face will relax you and make the tone more conversational. Think of the smile as virtual body language.

➤ If you are using a smartphone for the interview, conduct a test run to make sure the connection works.

Virtual Interview Etiquette

Navigating the virtual interview begins with basics like how to address the interviewer. Should you address the interviewer by first or last name? Is it Mrs., Ms., Mr., Dr., or Mary? It is important to get it right. Here are some guidelines that follow the "listen first" rule. If the interviewer introduces herself as Mrs. Smith, human resources director, then you address her as Mrs. Smith throughout the interview. If she introduces herself as Barbara Smith, call her Barbara. Never, under any circumstances, address a person using a nickname like "Barb" if she introduces herself as Barbara. If the interviewer introduces himself as Dr. William Ford, call him Dr. Ford throughout the interview. If the interviewer introduces himself as Bob Ford, sales manager, call him Bob. If the interviewer introduces himself as John Cupcake, call him John, not Jack. A common error is to assume it is permissible to call a person by a shortened version of their name. I have found that the most frequently abused first name is Robert. Why does everyone revert to Bob?

After You Say Hello

The first thing to ask after you say hello and make introductory chitchat is "How much time do we have?" Knowing this will tell you how much time to spend answering questions and how much time you have for asking the questions on your interview agenda. Write the end time on a piece of paper and refer to it throughout the conversation. After learning the amount of time, tell the interviewer that you have several questions and ask when it would be appropriate to ask them. It could be the last thing on the agenda or the first.

The conclusion is the same for the phone or Zoom interview.

Learn the interviewer's phone number and email address, say thank you for the interview, and ask for the job. The script for closing all interviews is the same: "Thank you for your time and consideration. What are the next steps in the process? I really would like to work here based on your answers to my questions and my research about your company. When can I start?" After the interview, follow up by sending a thank-you message.

INTERVIEW FOLLOW-UP

Courtesy dictates that you send a follow-up message to the interviewer after every personal or virtual interview. This is a business document, so format it accordingly. Include the following items:

- A thank-you for the opportunity to interview for the position.
- A reaffirmation of your interest in the position and the company.
- A statement asking for the job.
- A postscript (PS) after your closing signature such as "I will call you on Wednesday, March 10, to continue the conversation and answer any questions you might have about my candidacy. What is the best time to call?"

All types of interviews have one purpose: to see if you and the employer are on the same page for continuing the process. If you believe you are, pursue the job until you get an offer or a definite rejection. Do not let the process hang unresolved.

KEY TAKEAWAYS

- Build a friendly relationship with the interviewer. Friends hire friends.
- Body language is crucial nonverbal communication.

- Observe basic manners during interviews at restaurants.
- Control the interview process by preparing a written agenda to share with the interviewer.
- Practice reciting answers to possible questions.
- The purpose of the phone or Zoom interview is to move your candidacy to the next step, the personal interview.

PRINT AND DIGITAL RESOURCES

- "12 Job Interview Tips for Women" on EducatetoAdvance.com
- *The 7 Habits of Highly Effective People: Powerful Lessons in Personal Courage* by Stephen Covey
- *Inc. Magazine* (Inc.com)
- Articles by Jeff Haden dealing with interviews of all types at Inc.com/author/jeff-haden
- *Building a Better Vocabulary* by Kevin Flanigan (TheGreatCourses.com)
- *Career Forward: Strategies from Women Who've Made It* by Grace Puma and Christiana Smith Shi

CHAPTER 8

LEARNING ABOUT YOUR POTENTIAL EMPLOYER BEFORE, DURING, AND AFTER AN INTERVIEW

Most workers seeking new career opportunities do very little research about a company before applying. They read a job description from a potential employer's website or an online job board and respond by sending their résumé. It's a reflex action: Look at job postings; find an interesting career or job description; send a résumé; and wait for a response.

That course of action is unlikely to lead to a satisfying conclusion. To avoid heartache, you must do your own evaluation and due diligence before applying for any position. The road to successful employment is filled with land mines, but you can avoid them by evaluation. Disregard a company that displays evidence of poor financial management, being uncaring about its employees and customers, and producing products and offering services that are inferior to the competition.

BEFORE THE INTERVIEW

Find answers to these questions before submitting your résumé or talking with anyone employed by the company:

- Is the company profitable? Has the company consistently missed its financial goals? Review the company's finances for the past five years. You can find this information online using Google and by reading the company's quarterly and annual reports.
- How long has the company been in business? Is it 100 years old or a recent start-up?
- Who are the president, the CEO, and the person who would be your boss? What are their records of achievement? Have they ever been involved in company litigation? Have they ever been indicted or accused of a civilian or work-related misdemeanor or felony? How long have they been with the company? Who were their previous employers? What is their education background?
- What is the specific job title, and what are the specific responsibilities? Why is the position open? Was the previous person in this job fired, laid off, or did they just quit? How long has the position been open?
- How many employees have been in the open position over the last five years?
- What are the company's products and services? Where does the company stand in relation to its competitors?
- Is the company using AI?
- After applying, was your candidacy evaluated promptly, or did you wait three months before hearing back from the company?

Review the background information on the company and its executives on LinkedIn and other online sources. You can also use resources like *Bloomberg Businessweek* and *The Wall Street Journal*.

DURING THE INTERVIEW

Unfortunately, most interviews deteriorate into question-and-answer sessions after the usual greetings and introductions. Do not permit that to happen. An interview should be a conversation between you and the interviewer. The main goal is to establish a friendship with the interviewers. Why? Because friends hire friends. And the interview can be your main source for learning about the company. Here is what you need to learn and observe to make an adequate evaluation of the company and the job.

- Were the interviewers courteous, complete, and prompt in their responses to your questions?
- Did company contacts break appointments at the last minute or keep you waiting for an hour before calling you in for your scheduled personal interview?
- Was the physical work environment cheerful, or was it depressing?
- Does the workspace that you would occupy appear professional, or was it just another cubicle?
- Is the interviewer your potential boss?
- Does your potential boss come from the same industry, or is she an outsider with much to learn?
- Does the company reserve the right to terminate at will—that is, without giving a reason?
- Does the company have a noncompete provision in their employment contract?
- Is the company engaged in litigation of any sort?
- Has the company ever been sued for discrimination by an employee?
- Would you be required to sign a noncompete agreement if you left the company voluntarily or if you were terminated?
- What is the salary range for the position?
- What are the company benefits?

- How much of the job is on the premises and how much is remote?
- How many internal company candidates are there for this position?
- Does the company offer a pension plan or an IRA?
- When does the company intend to make an offer to the right candidate? Obtain contact information for the interviewer, including phone number and email address.

AFTER THE INTERVIEW

- Follow up with a message of thanks to the interviewers as soon as possible. Yes, snail mail is still acceptable and sometimes preferable to an email, text, or voicemail.
- In your follow-up communication, state your reaction to the interview and ask for additional information you might need about the company.
- Contact individuals in your personal network to learn more about the company and about the interviewers.
- Review the company on Glassdoor.com and other online sources.
- If you see any yellow or red flags about the company, your potential boss, or other interviewers and you have decided not to follow up, state as much in your follow-up communication. It does not need to be elaborate. Something like this is adequate: "Dear Mr. Jones, Thank you for your time during our recent interview. After considering the position, I believe it is not the right fit for me. Sincerely, Mary Smith."

MONEY, POWER, STATUS

Some economists believe that companies and their individual employees are driven by power, status, and money.

- Money can be the main driver in any company even

to the point of taking unfair or illegal action against a competitor. While making money is a requirement for employers, it must be done properly.
- Power, another word for covert control by one's boss, can have a devastating effect on workers. It can cause depression, anxiety, physical health problems, and isolation.
- Status is one's reputation, like being viewed in a complimentary manner.

KEY TAKEAWAYS
- Make friends with the interviewer. Friends hire friends.
- Interviews should be a conversation, not a Q and A session.
- Trust but verify.
- Seek socially responsible employment.
- Learning about potential employers is critical to your success.

PRINT AND DIGITAL RESOURCES
- Glassdoor (Glassdoor.com)
- For information on employers and their workers, go to GoodHire.com.

CHAPTER 9

NEGOTIATING SALARY, BENEFITS, AND REMOTE WORKING CONDITIONS

Many workers believe that negotiating important items like salary or benefits are out of the question. They are what the company states in the interview. Case closed. In actuality, most items are negotiable and will result in your favor if handled appropriately.

NEGOTIATING SALARY

Salary is only a part of your total compensation. The base salary will vary greatly with location, experience, and education. For example, the base salary for a nurse working in Montana will be considerably less than the base salary for a nurse working in Philadelphia. Negotiating base salary is possible in most instances except positions in federal, state, or local governments.

How do you negotiate for a higher base salary? Assuming you have done your salary-comparison research for similar jobs in your location, just ask for a higher number. For example, you have learned that the going salary for customer service reps in the Chicago area is $60,000, but the hiring manager offers you $45,000. Respond by asking for $65,000, citing the going rate and figuring in additional money for your expertise. The result will be acceptance, a flat no, or a compromise.

Many workers hesitate to negotiate because of fear or ignorance of how the job market works. Remember that most things in life are negotiable. Negotiating does not need to be acrimonious. It's all a matter of knowing how business works. Negotiating will probably impress the hiring manager because it tells him that you have some business sense.

NEGOTIATING BENEFITS

To determine what you really make, you must add benefits because they are not free. Someone must pay for them. Numerous sources like the Bureau of Labor Statistics tell us that benefits paid by your employer cost approximately 30 percent of your base salary. For example, Tom has a base salary of $120,000 per year as an IT director, but that does not include company-paid benefits. Add the cost of these benefits, 30 percent or $36,000, to his base salary of $120,000, and you get $156,000, which is Tom's real total compensation. When you need to disclose your salary, like to a potential employer or a recruiter, remember to add in the benefits.

Net Worth and Wages of the American Working Classes

So, what's the average income and net worth for the lower, middle, and upper classes in America? According to sources such as Yahoo! Finance, here are recent numbers:[7]

Lower class: annual income, $30,000–58,000
Middle class: annual income, $58,000–153,000
Upper class: annual income, greater than $153,000

---

7   Douglas Warren, "The income you need to fall in America's lower, middle and upper classes—find out where you rank and how these social levels are defined," Yahoo! Finance, February 3, 2024, https://finance.yahoo.com/news/income-fall-americas-lower-middle-122100515.html

LEGALLY REQUIRED BENEFITS

There are legally required government-mandated benefits the employer must pay to you, and they are not negotiable. However, they are in a constant state of flux, so go online for the latest information. Make sure your employer is paying you what is legally owed to you.

Legally Required Federal and State Benefits
- Social Security
- Medicare: This government-provided health insurance is available only to workers sixty-five years of age or older.
- Workers' compensation insurance
- Unemployment insurance
- The Family and Medical Leave Act

The FMLA is one of the most important benefits and includes twelve workweeks of leave in a twelve-month period for 1) the birth of a child and care for the newborn child within one year of birth; 2) the placement of a child for adoption or foster care and care for the newly placed child within one year of placement; 3) care for the employee's spouse, child, or parent who has a serious health condition.

In addition, FMLA entitles eligible employees of covered employers to take unpaid, job-protected leave for specified family and medical reasons with continuation of group health insurance coverage under the same terms and conditions as if the employee had not taken leave. Eligible employees are entitled to benefits if 1) a serious health condition makes the employee unable to perform the essential functions of their job; or 2) any medical condition arises because the employee's spouse, son, daughter, or parent is a covered military member on "covered active duty." Entitlement includes twenty-six workweeks of leave during a single twelve-month period to care for a covered service member with a serious injury or illness if the eligible employee is the service member's spouse, son, daughter, parent, or next of kin.

FMLA provisions are among the most important legally required benefits, and all covered employers must abide by them. They are subject to interpretation, and many workers have filed lawsuits against their employers disputing certain provisions that are subject to change. Go online monthly to monitor FMLA provisions, or consult an employment lawyer.

Company-Paid Benefits

The following benefits are not legally required by the federal government. However, some are required by individual states or municipalities. Also, some are negotiable and some are not.

- Paid sick leave. The US does not have a required sick leave benefit. This is up to the states and municipalities. The exception is FMLA and workers' compensation.
- Paid vacations
- National, state, and local holidays
- Health insurance in addition to Medicare and Medicaid. There is no legally required federal health insurance in the US. This is up to the states and municipalities.
- Dental insurance
- Long-term disability insurance
- Short-term disability insurance
- Pension plans
- Retirement accounts like an individual retirement account (IRA) or 401(k). Employers are not legally required to provide retirement plans.
- Tuition assistance for employees' children
- Professional development education
- Profit sharing
- Stock options
- Life insurance

One of the most important benefits listed above is long-term disability insurance. Why? Life is unpredictable. For example, tomorrow morning you could wake up in extremely good health. However, at 6 p.m. when you are driving home from work, some fool could blow a red light and hit your car broadside, leaving you with a fractured femur that will keep you out of work for six months. Your company short-term disability insurance will cover only six weeks of compensation, and then your income stops. Now what? To protect from unforeseen occurrences like this, purchase long-term disability insurance from companies such as Northwestern Mutual, Unum, Breeze, Assurity, Mutual of Omaha, Guardian Life, and Principal Financial Group. Go online to review their coverage and premiums. After you purchase long-term disability, ask your employer to reimburse you for the premiums, citing the extreme risk for you, your family, and the employer. Your employer could say no, yes, or offer to split the cost.

The cost of company benefits will vary with the company itself and the state in which the company is located. However, many of these benefits are negotiable. For example, if you are employed and sitting with your boss and the HR director for your annual review, do not hesitate to ask for any one of the above-listed benefits, like professional development education.

NEGOTIATING REMOTE WORKING CONDITIONS

The COVID pandemic brought to light something that both employers and employees have been grappling with for generations. Employers have claimed that most workers cannot be trusted to work away from the office. Workers have claimed they can be more productive working from a remote location, like their homes. There is research to prove that both sides are partly right and partly wrong. However, the research scales tip in favor of remote working as being more productive for a variety of reasons. Today, company executives and HR directors generally accept this and make a sincere effort to accommodate worker requests to work remotely.

If your potential employer does not have a remote working program, you may try to negotiate, citing the benefits for both worker and company:

> The company can save money by reducing the space and equipment needed to have all workers on premises.
> The company managers and directors can easily communicate with staff electronically, especially using the latest AI techniques.
> The worker can devote more time to accomplishing objectives remotely because there are fewer distractions.
> The worker can devote more time to the job because there is no commuting involved.

Remote work will always be a topic for discussion and negotiation. The COVID pandemic produced some untenable working conditions, one of which was 100 percent working remotely for everyone in the company except the executive staff. Today, many companies offer a hybrid model that requires some time in the office. A popular model is dividing the five-day workweek like this: two days in the office and three days working remotely, or vice versa.

BASIC RULES FOR NEGOTIATING SALARY, BENEFITS AND WORKING REMOTELY

Negotiating has an insidious connotation. It is usually thought of as being a hostile or confrontational procedure. To make your negotiations amicable and productive, remember the following rubrics:

- Be reasonable. Your employer has certain conditions to meet regarding salary ranges for workers in your prospective position. Find out what they are, and your negotiations will proceed amicably.
- Be friendly. Tell your future boss or hiring manager that you want to work with them to accomplish department and company objectives. Avoid being demanding. Remember not only that friends hire friends but also that friends help friends accomplish objectives.
- Be understanding. The person you are talking with has obligations and objectives to meet.
- Be trustworthy. Establish a sense of trust with the future boss. It is the foundation for all negotiations about salary, benefits, and working conditions.

KEY TAKEAWAYS

- Everything is negotiable except those benefits controlled by federal, state, or local governments.
- Negotiation is a standard part of the hiring procedure. You can negotiate for changes or additions to benefits and working conditions after you are on the job as well.
- Hiring managers and HR directors must abide by company-established limits on benefits and salaries.
- AI will have a serious effect on your job and the workplace in general. Stay informed.

PRINT AND DIGITAL RESOURCES

- One of the best sources for updates on workplace matters is the online source *Business Management Daily* (BusinessManagementDaily.com).
- "Beyond Salary: How to Negotiate Your Benefits Package" on CareerContessa.com

CHAPTER 10

HOW TO QUIT YOUR JOB GRACEFULLY

There will come a time when you decide to move on from your present employer. It could be six months or six years from now. There are many reasons why workers quit their jobs, and most are valid.

How do you leave your job when you decide to say goodbye? There are two methods of bowing out; one is done gracefully, and the other is done crudely.

THE PROCESS OF LEAVING YOUR JOB

Leaving gracefully means departing on friendly terms and observing the rules of business etiquette in the process. Before handing in your resignation, write down the reasons you are leaving and rehearse how you will break the news to your boss or the human resources director. You can submit your resignation verbally but accompanied by a written statement, which we recommend.

Your verbal resignation statement to the HR director should go something like this:

> Mrs. Petrocelli, I'm here to submit my resignation as marketing associate. This is not easy for me because

> there are many things I like about the company. However, in order to accomplish my career goal, which is becoming a vice president for marketing, I need to work as a marketing manager first. Ajax Security offered me that position, and I have accepted. Thank you for everything you have done for me during my employment here. This is my written resignation, which includes two weeks' notice.

Note the four essential characteristics of this resignation: 1) It is courteous; 2) it explains the reason why you are leaving; 3) it includes proper notice; and 4) the resignation is delivered verbally and in writing.

The written part of the process is essential but need not be lengthy or state the reason for leaving. The written notice could simply state that you are resigning and the date you are leaving the company. Here is a sample statement:

> To: Mrs. Mary Petrocelli, Human Resources Director
> From: Joseph Smith, Marketing Associate
> Re: Resignation
> Date: April 14, 2026
>
> I am resigning my position as marketing associate, effective April 28, 2026. Thank you for giving me the opportunity to work with the company for the past two years.
>
> Sincerely,
> Joseph Smith

Always give ample notice. Announcing your resignation on Thursday and leaving on Friday violates business courtesy. Two weeks' notice is standard for most jobs, but some require more notice. Some jobs, such as those in the medical profession, carry longer resignation-notice periods, which could be four to six weeks or more. Always consult your job contract or human resources guidelines before giving notice. Adhering to the company requirement will be a plus mark in your personnel file.

The resignation process applies to all jobs, not just those in the corporate arena. The process for resigning from your job as a carpenter for Toll Brothers Home Building Co. is the same as for a truck driver for FedEx or a high school biology teacher at King High School in Atlanta.

HOW NOT TO LEAVE YOUR JOB

The other way to leave your job is to vent your anger about the job or the company and do something stupid like walk into the HR director's office and say, "I've never really liked it here, and I'm leaving tomorrow. I've found something much better." This method of resigning will destroy any bridges to future employment with that company and with the HR director.

Another crude way to resign is the Johnny Paycheck way. Johnny was an American country music singer who in the 1970s released a hit song that stayed on the charts for several years. The lyrics frequently were quoted in jest. The title (and first line of the song) is "Take This Job and Shove It!"

Don't ever use this method of resigning . . . for obvious reasons. While Johnny was a colorful country guy, his advice for resigning is not appropriate.

TEN GOOD REASONS WHY WORKERS QUIT THEIR JOBS

There are trigger points for deciding to leave one's employer, and most are valid. Sometimes workers are criticized by outsiders for leaving what appears to be an ideal position. Don't worry about what others are saying. It's your life and your decision to make the best of it, even if it means leaving a job that pays well and is only a few minutes' drive from home. Here are the reasons cited most frequently by workers who leave their jobs:

1. The boss is the number one reason why workers leave their jobs, according to a recent Gallup poll of one million workers. The boss might be a micromanager, a gossip, a bully, untrustworthy, discriminatory, or just plain dumb. All are valid reasons for leaving your job.

2. The company has consistently missed its revenue goals. When this happens, it is time to seek alternative employment. If a company is not making money, reorganization will happen because a company cannot exist without being profitable. Along with the reorg, there will be mass firings. Guaranteed. Resign and move on before you get whacked.

3. The company has been acquired by one of its competitors. What usually follows is a complete reorganization where the acquiring company places its own workers in strategic jobs. It only makes good business sense to begin searching for an alternative career when the acquisition is announced—or before if you have access to that information.

4. Some workers resign because they just do not like their jobs. Taking the job was a mistake because it was not aligned with their qualifications and vision. If you do not find your job interesting or challenging and never see daylight ahead, move on.

5. Workers resign because of relationships with coworkers. The job itself may be fine, but the group you are working with is just not "your kind of people." It could be that they are potheads, heavy drinkers, or just behind you in intelligence and work ethic. Why continue working on a ship of fools? Move on.

6. Company culture is another reason why workers quit their jobs. It is difficult to determine the company culture until you are on the job. A difference in values is usually at the heart of it. Your idea of work may include a culture that is community conscious and reaches out in myriad ways, including monetary contributions to charitable causes. If there is a culture disconnect, move on and do a better job examining a potential employer's culture before signing on next time.

7. There is a disconnect between your lifestyle and working conditions. Assume you are a single mom or single dad with two kids in elementary school and you need flex hours to attend to their needs. The company does not permit flexing under any circumstances even though they told you during the interview that they are cognizant of family situations and make allowances. It's time to move on.

8. Workers quit because they no longer find "fulfillment" on the job. A job can't provide satisfaction and fulfillment every working minute. Much of work is routine and even boring, but some workers need the job to provide everything all the time. It is unrealistic, but still it is a reason why workers quit. We advise you to reexamine the meaning of work before resigning for this reason. If your job is nothing more than a paycheck at the end of the week, it's time to move on.

9. The company rarely promotes people from within. Instead, the company recruits outside workers for attractive jobs of higher rank. The candidate from within is rarely or ever promoted, despite meeting all requirements and goals. If this is your situation, move on.

10. The company rarely provides increases in compensation. This happens more frequently than one would think. Some workers meet all the requirements, are productive, are good team players, are loyal, but never receive recognition in the form of an increase in pay. A good employer will always reward its productive and faithful employees with something tangible, like more money in the paycheck. If this is where you are, turn in your resignation—after you have found an alternative employer.

This list of valid reasons why employees leave their jobs could go on forever, but the ten reasons listed above rank highest on the list.

At some time in your career, you will find a reason to resign your job and move on. It takes courage to quit! The easy thing to do is to just stay with your present employer as long as there is a paycheck. While this may be a valid strategy depending on your financial circumstances, long term it is not a good way to spend your working life. There are two rules that all workers, regardless of rank or compensation, should observe:

- Have another job before turning in your resignation. It is much easier to find alternative employment while you are still employed.
- Have enough money in the bank to provide for the basics during your transition to alternative employment.

KEY TAKEAWAYS

- Resign from your job respectfully and courteously.
- "Take This Job and Shove It" is a crude way to leave.
- Find another job before resigning.
- Resigning is a two-part process: 1) making a verbal resignation statement to your boss and the human

resources director; 2) submitting a written notice, which includes the date you are leaving, to your boss and the HR director.

DIGITAL RESOURCES

➤ "How To Know If It's Time to Quit Your Job" on BusinessNewsDaily.com

CHAPTER 11

STARTING YOUR OWN BUSINESS OR PURCHASING A FRANCHISE

The business of starting your own business does not have to be complicated. The beginning of any entrepreneurial adventure is planning and research, so I'll repeat a cardinal rule: Plan your work. Work your plan.

Owning a business requires your undivided attention and much time. However, if you like what you are doing, the time factor becomes insignificant. This oft-repeated advice also rings true: Do what you love, and you will never work a day in your life.

Becoming an entrepreneur requires intelligence, energy (physical and psychic), and passion. What could be more exciting than bypassing the corporate world and doing it your way? Bill Gates did it. Steve Jobs did it. So did Mark Zuckerburg. Elon Musk did it. So can you!

Join the thousands who have started their own businesses instead of working for someone else. Just because you have a wide array of skills learned in your previous jobs and a college degree does not mean that you are destined to work for a big corporation or a small business. Working for a company, particularly a large one, where the ground rules can be oppressive, may not be your idea of a good time. The alternative is to start your own business.

WHO STARTS A NEW BUSINESS?

What must you do before hanging out a sign with your name on it? Isn't it true that most business owners have money in the family and are mostly upper class? To clear up those misconceptions, here is the profile of people who start their own businesses, according to a November 13, 2012, infographic from *The Wall Street Journal* titled "How Entrepreneurs Measure Up": Less than 1 percent of people who start a business come from extremely rich or extremely poor backgrounds; 71.5 percent come from a middle-class background; 70 percent used their own savings as the source to fund their own business.[8]

Add to that general profile an interesting subset of business owners: military veterans. Veterans have an enviable record of success running their own businesses. According to Military.com and other corroborating sources, approximately 3.6 million veterans run their own show. That translates into 25 percent of the military veteran workforce.

As the workplace evolves, many workers are saying goodbye to the corporate world and starting out on their own. But this decision requires risk-taking and shouldering serious responsibilities. It requires learning about businesses that are potentially profitable and then pursuing one that is interesting and one that is affordable. New business owners often forget about the profit angle. For example, many people find the floral and gardening business interesting and relatively cheap to enter. What they do not realize is that the floral business has an extremely high risk of failure because it's a very low-profit business.

Starting your own business offers two important choices: 1) selecting a business that requires a physical location, like

---

8 "How Entrepreneurs Measure Up," *The Wall Street Journal*, November 13, 2012, https://www.wsj.com/articles/SB10001424052970204530504578 078952417071158.

a restaurant; 2) selecting a business that can be done from your home office, like a technology consulting business or an independent sales representative business. Both have advantages and disadvantages.

HOW TO GET STARTED

The rules of business entrepreneurship apply equally to everyone. Consider what Richard Branson, founder of Virgin Atlantic Airways, said in his first blog for LinkedIn, posted in 2012: "As LinkedIn is a business that started in a living room, much like Virgin began in a basement, I thought my first blog on the site should be about how to simply start a successful business."[9] Here are Branson's five top tips:

1. Listen more than you talk.
2. Keep it simple.
3. Take pride in your work.
4. Have fun; success will follow.
5. Rip it up and start again.

These are the steps that Richard Branson took when founding Virgin Atlantic, one of the most successful businesses on the planet. Branson has authored twelve books about starting businesses and how to run them. Go to LinkedIn periodically and read Branson's blogs to receive advice from one of the world's most successful business owners at a terrific price: free. You can learn much from him. He's been there, done that—without a college degree, without family money, and while working from a basement office. He planned his work and worked his plan. Success followed.

---

9   Richard Branson, "Five top tips to starting a successful business," LinkedIn, October 1, 2012, https://www.linkedin.com/pulse/20121002115242-204068115-five-top-tips-to-starting-a-successful-business/.

WHERE'S THE MONEY?

All entrepreneurs ask, "Where do I get the money to start a business?" It is a valid question. You can start some businesses with little money in your bank account; others require substantial funds. How much money you will need depends on what you intend to do. Let's get practical and explore how you can find the financial resources to start your business.

- Your personal savings. Some businesses do not cost much to begin operating. If you have only $1,000 saved, it could be enough to get you started.
- Family money. Many entrepreneurs find start-up money from parents and other family members. Tapping into family money comes with serious risk. Trust is involved. If you are exercising this option, prepare a detailed business plan and present it to your family members just as you would present it to a loan officer at a bank. There is one hard-and-fast rule about asking family members for money: Vow to repay every cent of the loan. You are not a charity case, and family members have their own lives to lead. Present a written statement for family members stating when you will begin repaying the loan and how much each payment will be.
- Banks. Local banks make money by lending money to entrepreneurs. You must create a detailed business plan to attract a banker's attention. There are online sources that give advice about preparing a credible business plan. Approach local banks in your area or a branch of a nationwide bank like Wells Fargo. Begin the process by learning the name of the bank loan officer and then make an appointment for a personal interview to present your business plan, résumé, and career profile. This is a no-nonsense deal, so dress accordingly. Remember that bankers make every effort to minimize risk.

- Angel funding sources. These are individuals or small organizations that provide seed money to entrepreneurs. Finding these sources takes time and research. You can find these sources online, by networking through social media like LinkedIn, or through loan officers at a local bank.
- Loans from government organizations. A variety of government sources provide loans for entrepreneurs. Learn who they are by reviewing the Small Business Administration (SBA) website, SBA.gov.
- Venture capital funding. Large companies that specialize in funding start-up businesses are known as venture capital firms. They generate revenue by lending money to start-up firms that have little downside risk. Usually, they seek businesses that are generating revenue and that require upward of $1 million to expand operations.

STARTING YOUR OWN BUSINESS AS A SOLE PROPRIETOR

Many small businesses are successful. Where are they? Take a walk down Main Street USA and talk with the owner of a storefront business, and you will get the answer. Here is an example of a small business founded by a worker who had a dream and ambition.

Gary's Story

I was looking for someone to wash the windows at our home in suburban Philadelphia. Fortunately, we found Gary through a referral from a neighbor. He did an excellent job washing our windows both inside and out while paying attention to details like washing the screens, cleaning the windowsills, and wiping down the hardware and window frames. The job took Gary about six hours, and we paid him $400, which translates to $66 per hour.

We have employed Gary for the past twelve years. He begins work at the appointed hour, supplies all window-cleaning products, and maintains a high quality of work. Recently, Gary added another service to his business: residential exterior power washing, which is a perfect complement to the window-washing business.

So, what is Gary's background? What kind of education do you need to start your own business? Here's the rest of the story. Gary graduated from Temple University in Philadelphia with a bachelor's degree in business administration and began working in the corporate world. One of his employers was General Electric, where he held a managerial position. He was not happy and decided to make it on his own. He researched several business possibilities and found there was no competition in the residential window-washing business.

I can hear the snickering now. Window washing with a college degree? You have to be kidding! Well, what if I told you that Gary's business generates a revenue stream comparable to that of a corporate manager, and he works only ten months of the year? (Gary works only ten months because inclement weather in January and February prevents him from working outside.) Now what do you think about the residential window-washing business? Compare that to a corporate job. An average mid-career corporate job will bring in about $125,000 per year. You will get three weeks' vacation, report to work each day at a specific time, and work in a corporate kennel, also called a cubicle. You will be on call twenty-four seven and have little time to call your own. Gary, on the other hand, makes an annual six-figure income, works on his own terms, and reports to a boss named Gary.

However, this is not the end of Gary's story. He has created the Window Business Startup Kit, which you will find on his website at WindowCleaningCash.com. This kit consists of a sixty-page manual, a thirty-five-minute video, and one year of phone and email support. The price is reasonable. Buy Gary's package and study what he has to say. It cuts through the hype written by MBAs selling you textbook promises. Gary explains the reality of starting your own business in the vernacular.

Gary's story is about how to make a living on your own terms. Owning and operating your own business is one of the most satisfying things you can do. Your business can provide a good income, the option to work on your own terms, and time to give back to the community by participating in your choice of outreach programs. The term "work" does not always mean putting in time with a Fortune 500 company.

STARTING A BUSINESS WITH A PARTNER

Another way to start your own business is with a partner who has interests and values similar to yours. Selecting the right partner is an important first step and requires a complete examination of that person's skills, energy, intelligence, passion for self-employment, ethics, values, and interest in the ideas you have for starting a business. Researching your potential partner is critical. If you select just a good friend instead of a good potential business friend who is compatible with you in every way, your business could turn into a nightmare. Many entrepreneurs have failed because they selected the wrong partner. Selecting the right partner will enhance the likelihood of creating a successful business that brings satisfaction and money to both partners.

STARTING A CONSULTING BUSINESS

Some workers start their own businesses as consultants by providing services in a particular industry. It is a quick and inexpensive way to leave the past behind and move forward in a new career you can call your own. If your past career focused on marketing in the publishing business, make that your consulting business. Starting a consulting business is not complicated. Here are the first steps.

1. Select your consulting focus.
2. Name your company.
3. Establish an email address.
4. Establish a working address.
5. Establish social media accounts.
6. Construct a website.
7. Purchase business cards and other means of contact.
8. Contact your former employer(s) to solicit business as an independent consultant.
9. Attend conferences and visit exhibit booths to find potential business contacts.

STARTING YOUR OWN BUSINESS WITH A FRANCHISE

Purchasing a franchise is intriguing but carries risk and serious funding. Franchises focus primarily on products and services related to the big three survival industries: food, shelter, and clothing. Some popular franchise businesses include fast-food restaurants, retail clothing, home and commercial cleaning services, residential real estate, and personal grooming.

The main franchise names that come to mind are McDonald's, Burger King, Starbucks, Dairy Queen, Chipotle, KFC, and Servpro Cleaning Services. Of course, there are many franchise opportunities in other businesses. The best way to explore them is by using the internet. In addition, talk to the owners of various franchises to learn how they work, how much they cost, and the profit potential.

How a Franchise Works

There are two entities involved in the franchise operation. First is the franchisor, which is the company that owns the brand name, like McDonald's. The other is the franchisee, the person who buys the product name and sells the franchisor's products at an individual store. The franchisor, the parent company, provides the location, training, marketing, sales support, advertising, and other requirements needed to operate a business. The company charges the individual store operator a franchise fee to begin the business and takes a percentage of the business revenue.

Purchasing a Franchise

There are hundreds of websites that provide information not only about cost but also about the process. One that I like is "Top 100 Franchises," found at FranchiseDirect.com. When I last checked this website, I found franchises in the $200,000 range, one of which is Servpro, a fire and water-damage cleaning and restoration business that has an excellent nationwide reputation for quality service. Another popular franchise is CertaPro Painters. Their recent franchise fee range is $155,000 to $215,000. If you want to purchase a McDonald's franchise, it will cost $1 to $2 million; $750,000 must be liquid capital (cash in the bank), and you must pay a franchise fee of $45,000.

You will find a list of popular and successful franchises and their approximate buy-in cost by reviewing the list of companies under "Digital Resources" at the end of this chapter.

WHAT KIND OF BUSINESS SHOULD I START?

There are many ways to start your own business that do not require a storefront or a serious amount of money. One of the least expensive ways to start working on your own is to become an independent sales representative. Independent sales reps usually carry products related to one specific industry. Take cutlery. Sales reps working in this narrow market niche might carry products for three or more different manufacturers, both domestic and foreign, and sell them to restaurants large and small, or to wholesalers—that is, companies that distribute and sell not only knives but also related products such as metal cooking pots and pans. I know of a man named Mickey, an independent sales representative in New Jersey, who sells cutlery to restaurants in the mid-Atlantic region. He's been doing that for more than twenty years and has an income exceeding that of a corporate vice president. His marketing slogan? "My knives are a cut above the rest."

For a list of the many industries in the US that you can explore for your entrepreneurial venture, consult *The Occupational Outlook Handbook* by the US Department of Labor's Bureau of Labor Statistics (BLS.gov/OOH).

The list of business ventures is endless, but a good place to start is in an industry whose products and services are in constant need and in which you have an interest. Some industries to explore are food, shelter, clothing, transportation, technology, insurance, education, and healthcare. These industries provide the products all people need regardless of age, gender, geography, race, or religion.

The next time you leave the house, look at the businesses on either side of Main Street. A majority of them will be stores focusing on food, shelter, clothing, and related products. The point is this: If you want to strike out on your own as an entrepreneur rather than work for someone else, just do it. Play to your passion. Do something that excites you every day.

KEY TAKEAWAYS

- Starting your own business requires intelligence, energy, and passion.
- Money to start your business is available from many sources.
- You can start a successful business as a sole proprietor or with a partner.
- Purchasing a franchise can cost serious money but yield very successful results.

DIGITAL RESOURCES

- Bright Hub (BrightHub.com)
- Franchise Business Review (FranchiseBusinessReview.com)
- Entrepreneur (Entrepreneur.com)
- Franchise Direct (FranchiseDirect.com)
- Franchise Opportunities (FranchiseOpportunities.com)
- Franchise Prospector (FranchiseProspector.com)
- "Top 100 Franchises" on FranchiseDirect.com
- VetFran (VetFran.com)
- The Small Business Administration (SBA.gov)

CHAPTER 12

GOVERNMENT JOBS

The American workplace is divided into the public sector and the private sector. The public sector consists of all elected and appointed government jobs at the federal, state, and local levels. Jobs at all government levels offer rewarding careers that pay well and provide attractive benefits and pension plans as well as work satisfaction. Workers seeking a new career path frequently overlook government jobs. Do not make that mistake.

According to the Bureau of Labor Statistics and other reliable sources, the public sector employs more than twenty-four million workers in jobs as diverse as president of the United States, state senator, governor, city building commissioner, and administrative assistant. Yes, you read that correctly: twenty-four million. Of that number, the federal government alone employs four million workers, including one million employed in military service. State governments employ six million. Local governments employ fourteen million.

By an overwhelming margin, local government is the largest employer in the US, far exceeding the largest private-sector employer globally, which is Walmart with 2.1 million workers.[10]

---

10 "Location Facts," Walmart, https://corporate.walmart.com/about/location-facts.

LOCAL GOVERNMENT JOBS

Fourteen million government jobs exist in towns, cities, and counties just around the corner from every worker looking for new career opportunities while still employed in the private sector. For those who have decided to explore a career in government or politics, the local level is a good place to start. Here at the grassroots level, you will learn how government works and the role you can play in it.

Former Massachusetts Congressman Tip O'Neill offered this sage advice for those seeking a career in government: "All politics is local." All successful government workers, including elected politicians, must first understand how it works on their own turf at the local level.

How do you get started? Begin by reviewing your local government website. For example, if you live in Stockton, California, visit StocktonCA.gov. You will find a list of both full-time salaried jobs and part-time hourly jobs.

Specific instructions govern applications for all government jobs, one of which is that you will need to apply online. If you see something appealing, complete the application and submit it, but don't just sit and wait for a response. Go to the next step, which is making a personal visit to the local government offices and asking to see the hiring manager personally. This person could be a mayor or a township borough manager. If this person is not available, ask to see the administrative assistant.

If you do not see a job posting for local government jobs, put on your business attire and, with your résumé in hand, make a personal visit to the government office and tell the receptionist you are there to see the mayor, or the highest-ranking official for that government entity, about job opportunities. If you cannot arrange a personal visit with the mayor, ask to see the mayor's administrative assistant and give them your résumé. Several days later, follow up by calling the mayor or the assistant to make sure they received your résumé. Remember to request a personal interview. Receptionists and administrative assistants may have more power than you suspect in the hiring process. You always want them on your side.

Government jobs—at any level—are sometimes awarded to those who know a prominent government official or businessperson. If you have family members or friends who work in government, use that person's name as the referral agent. Networking is often a key factor in obtaining a government job. Also, local government jobs could be posted with a local recruiter.

STATE GOVERNMENT JOBS

There are six million jobs at the state government level. To begin the process, visit your state government's website; if, for instance, you live in Florida, visit Florida.gov. Follow the instructions for seeking job opportunities and applying online. Next, personally visit the state government office closest to you and repeat the procedure you would use at the local level.

You cannot circumvent the application rules for government jobs, because legislation governs the employment process. Always try to use a referral source when applying for state government jobs, just as you would for jobs in the private sector.

FEDERAL GOVERNMENT JOBS

The federal government is the country's largest single employer and offers a variety of interesting jobs spanning every possible occupation. It employs four million workers, according to statistics released by the US Office of Personnel Management and the Bureau of Labor Statistics.

A common misconception is that federal government jobs are located primarily in Washington, DC. BLS statistics set us straight. Eighty-seven percent of federal government jobs are located outside of DC. There are federal government jobs in every state and in many foreign countries as well.

The processes for finding work with the federal government are sometimes complex and even contradictory. Go to the BLS website and read the article titled "How to Get a Job in the Federal Government" by Olivia Crosby. The information and instructions in this article will demystify the federal government employment process, save you time, and possibly lead to the promised land of employment. In addition, visit Dennis Damp's US government jobs website at FederalJobs.net to discover where they are, what's available, and how to complete a federal résumé.

Government political jobs such as senator, representative, or president are not permanent positions. They come and go with periodic elections. However, other jobs exist regardless of the political party in power. They are called civil service jobs and keep the wheels of government turning. These jobs offer attractive salaries and excellent benefits. To learn what positions are available, go to the website of the department that interests you. For example, if you are interested in health-related jobs, go to the website for the US Department of Health and Human Services (HHS.gov) and click on "Jobs."

Government jobs, political or civil service, in a country like the United States with a population of 340 million, offer the opportunity to do something meaningful and purposeful. Yes, one person can make a difference. It is not all partisan politics.

Resources for Exploring Federal Government Jobs

There are many sources of information for workers exploring or seeking employment with the federal government. Before you begin your exploration, carefully review all the sources listed below.

➤ USA Jobs (USAJobs.gov). This site is the federal government's official job site. It provides general information about working in a federal government job and specific advice about how to begin your search. In addition, this site provides location-specific federal government job postings. Enter your zip code to find any number of jobs in your immediate location.

- US Office of Personnel Management (OPM) (OPM.gov). Think of this as the human resources department for the federal government. It manages all hiring procedures, including recruiting, training, and benefits. In addition, it conducts background checks on all job candidates. If you are a military veteran, OPM is the place to go for job opportunities. Over the past several years, 40 percent of OPM hires were veterans, including 18 percent who were disabled.

- ***The Book of US Government Jobs.*** This book, authored by Dennis Damp, is in its eleventh edition, which tells you what a valuable resource it is. It has won numerous awards and is the best on the market for understanding how the federal government employment process works. The rules and regs for government employment can be onerous. This book will help you through the process and save you time.

- Federal Government Jobs (FederalJobs.net). Dennis Damp, the website creator and author of twenty-eight books, is a former federal government employee. He operates what is considered the most useful website for current information about federal government jobs. It includes instructions for applying for federal government jobs, government job listings, blogs written by staffing experts, résumé-writing instructions, and references to additional resources. Make this your first stop for learning about federal government jobs.

KEY TAKEAWAYS

- Government jobs pay well and provide attractive benefits.
- Most government jobs are not political.
- Applying for government jobs can be challenging. Allow extra time to learn the process.
- Not all government jobs are posted on internet job boards or with civilian recruiters.
- Government officials hold veterans in high esteem and will take extra measures to help them find employment.
- Eighty-seven percent of federal government jobs are outside of Washington, DC.
- Elected political jobs offer the opportunity to make a significant difference.
- Using a referral can be an important factor in winning government jobs.
- Prepare a special résumé for government jobs. Use the resources below for guidance.

DIGITAL RESOURCES

- FederalJobs.net
- USAJobs.gov
- Statista.com

CHAPTER 13

CAREER OBJECTIVES AND AI

It is unrealistic to believe that a job could provide everything a person wants and needs: money, a sense of self-esteem, recognition, purpose, lifelong security, satisfaction, and a positive impact on society. We would all like to do something that brings satisfaction and contributes to the common good. However, finding that kind of job eludes most of us and could be a contributing factor to the high rate of terminations and quitting, as we witnessed in 2022 and 2023 during the period called the Great Resignation. If you do not like what you are doing, interest in the job often wanes, cynicism sets in, and you cease contributing to the goals your employer expects you to achieve.

Most mid-career workers who have quit or have been terminated usually have been employed in one industry in similar departments, like sales or marketing, for the first half of their careers. For example, take mid-career worker Claudia, who had worked in the pharmaceutical industry since receiving her BS in biology. All her jobs were in sales or marketing. The money was good, but job satisfaction was zero. When she was let go in a reorganization, Claudia finally learned that she did not like working in sales and marketing and asked herself, *What's next? More of the same? How can I get out of this sales and marketing game and still make enough money to survive?* For workers like Claudia, being fired or laid off is often a blessing in disguise because it gives you time to pause, reflect, and reset before moving forward to another career.

THE REDEFINING PROCESS

While recruiting for a marketing director position, I reviewed the résumé of a mid-career worker that was astounding. Under professional employment, I saw "US Peace Corps, English teacher" for the past five years. Preceding that was a string of twelve jobs in different industries spanning twenty years. It was one year here, six months there, two years there, and so on.

When I interviewed this candidate, he said he had been fired from his last corporate job, as associate marketing manager for a publishing company. This was the catalyst that prompted him to enter an extended period of reflection to find his real self. The result was learning that he was driven not by status, power, and money as so many workers are. His motivation was to be instrumental in the lives of people studying to reach their full potential. He embarked on a mission to determine what he wanted to do next, which meant that he needed to define his objectives. After a period of introspection, he decided that the ideal job to accomplish that mission was teaching. He took online courses that awarded teaching certification and subsequently found work as a high school teacher. The job and benefits provided enough for him to be self-sufficient *and* gave him the sense of mission he had been seeking.

SEARCHING FOR CAREER OBJECTIVES

Just "looking for a new career" will yield nothing but grief and frustration. Begin by carefully defining your career goals and objectives.

Redefining your career goals is a process that you can accomplish in the classroom of your mind. You do not need multiple sessions with a shrink, nor do you need to attend every conference advertised by "Find Yourself in Three Easy Steps." You have the intelligence and energy to accomplish this mission on your own terms.

One way to begin the process is to use the NEXTERCISE from chapter 4 of this book. It will lead you to a company in an industry that is in sync with your interests, aptitudes, and skills. Let's assume that one of your objectives is to find work in the broadly defined field of environmental conservation but you have no idea where to begin looking for opportunities. There are several ways to begin the process.

Conduct a Google search and enter "companies with jobs in environmental conversation." When I did that, I found numerous employers active in such pursuits. Some of those were CWM Environmental, Watts Architectural and Engineering, North Cascades Institute, Packaging Corporation of America, and the State of North Carolina. For additional prompts on opportunities in the field of environmental conservation, consider federal government jobs, which are often overlooked by workers seeking new career goals. When I reviewed Dennis Damp's *The Book of US Government Jobs: Where They Are, What's Available, and How to Complete a Federal Resume*, I found an interesting reference to the Environmental and Natural Resources Division of the US Department of Justice. This division develops and enforces civil environmental laws that protect US natural resources.

Consult the online or print versions of the *Occupational Outlook Handbook*. Look for jobs focused on the environment. You will find them in the sections titled "Green Occupations," "Education," and "Life/Physical/Social Science." Each section lists related occupations, the forecast for such jobs, education and skill requirements, advancement opportunities, work environment, and average earnings. The immense *OOH* is a valuable resource for workers redefining their career objectives.

It is updated every two years. Have a copy on hand while exploring new careers.

Not every employed worker seeks a new career path. Many wish to continue working in their present careers but with an employer who provides opportunities for work–life balance, community outreach initiatives, and job satisfaction. Such workers can move directly to seeking potential job opportunities in their chosen industry. For example, a worker in the food industry who has had jobs in managerial positions with fast-food providers may now look for more health-conscious companies in the food industry, like Whole Foods or Wegmans.

Workers in the technology industry frequently reach a point where they need more than a big paycheck and less than a sixty-hour workweek. Take George as an example. He was fired from his tech company where he had nine direct reports and worked ridiculous hours. He wanted to remain in technology and used his downtime to find employers engaged in a socially conscious business. After almost a year of searching, he hit pay dirt with a national pharmacy company. His new job using AI is on the cutting edge of an industry utilizing robotic technology to fill prescriptions for people needing continuous refills of life-sustaining medications. He manages the entire process using his many technology skills and takes home more than the paycheck; he also earns job satisfaction from his work in a life-sustaining business using the latest in AI.

ARTIFICIAL INTELLIGENCE IS HERE

McDonald's is replacing thousands of jobs with AI. Apple is now building iPhones using AI, thus eliminating many workers in the process. Tech companies like Meta are investing billions of dollars in AI development; Meta will invest $65 billion in 2025 alone.[11] Going forward, AI will be dominating the workplace, so

---

11 Andrew Kessel, "Meta Plans to Spend as Much as $65B in 'Defining Year for AI' Says Zuckerberg," Investopedia, January 24, 2025, https://www.investopedia.com/meta-plans-to-spend-as-much-as-usd65b-in-defining-year-for-ai-says-zuckerberg-8780176.

be prepared. Study OpenAI, ChatGPT, and other AI initiatives. Also, learn about AI programs like AssemblyAI and Beautiful. AI. Recently, Forbes featured an article by Lisa Su, CEO of Advanced Micro Devices (AMD), where she said, "If you look out five years, you will see AI in every single product at AMD."[12]

Here are several AI companies and products that have made a serious impact on our worldwide workplace:

- ChatGPT, developed by OpenAI. Mark Zuckerberg, founder and CEO of Meta, told workers in 2025, just as AI was making a drastic change in the workplace: "I believe that open source is necessary for a positive AI future. AI has more potential than any other modern technology to increase human productivity, creativity, and quality of life—and to accelerate economic growth while unlocking progress in medical and scientific research. Open source will ensure . . . that power isn't concentrated in the hands of a small number of companies, and that the technology can be deployed more evenly and safely across society."[13] Zuckerberg's advice is an important message to all workers regardless of age or career as AI becomes a major force in the worldwide workplace.
- AssemblyAI. This California-based company provides three important initiatives for the workplace:
    - Speech-to-text transcription
    - Streaming speech-to-text
    - Speech understanding
- Beautiful.AI. This is an AI product that will enable you to make meaningful presentations. It's considered the leading presentation maker for the workplace.

---

12   Iain Martin and Richard Nieva, "Lisa Su Saved AMD. Now She Wants Nvidia's AI Crown," *Forbes*, May 31, 2023, https://www.forbes.com/sites/iainmartin/2023/05/31/lisa-su-saved-amd-now-she-wants-nvidias-ai-crown/

13   Mark Zuckerberg, "Open Source AI is the Path Forward," Meta, July 23. 2024, https://about.fb.com/news/2024/07/open-source-ai-is-the-path-forward/.

THE FEDERAL GOVERNMENT AND AI

In January 2025, the federal government set aside $500 billion to establish regional sites to develop AI infrastructure. The project, called Stargate, is expected to generate 100,000 new jobs.

Developing the program are OpenAI, SoftBank, Oracle, and MGX. Other federal AI initiatives are sure to follow.

WHERE AM I HEADED?

Based on our experience with workers trying to fulfill their career objectives, we predict that three to six months from now, you will be gainfully employed in one of four ways:

- Employment with a value company in an industry you like and that pays more than your present or previous position.
- Employment in a meaningful career using AI that gives personal satisfaction in addition to a good income.
- Employment as an entrepreneur, having decided to "go it alone" using your skills, your character, and your intelligence.
- Employment as a worker in an entirely different industry pursuing what you always wanted to do but could never before find the courage to try.

KEY TAKEAWAYS

- A meaningful career provides job satisfaction and purpose in addition to status and money.
- Workers can transfer work skills from one industry to another.
- There are multiple print and digital resources to help you through the redefining process.
- Learn as much as you can about using AI.
- You can redefine career objectives on your own terms.

Whatever you decide to do with your new perspective on work, stay the course. Success will follow.

PRINT AND DIGITAL RESOURCES

- *Occupational Outlook Handbook* (BLS.gov/OOH/)
- OpenSourceAI (AI.Meta.com/open)
- *The Book of US Government Jobs* by Dennis Damp
- Forbes (Forbes.com)
- AssemblyAI.com
- Beautiful.AI.com
- For information about the now and the future of AI, go to OpenAI.com.
- *The AI LEAD: Overcoming Data Drag to Accelerate Digital Dominance* by Brian Lambert, PhD

CHAPTER 14

DISCOVERING YOUR APTITUDE, IDENTITY, PERSONA, AND CHARACTER

Discovering your aptitude, identity, persona, and character will prepare you to move forward with confidence while finding your alternative career path. Keep an open mind to the many options for continuing the hunt or, as we say in the twenty-first century, *making a living*.

Workers who have quit their jobs to revise their career plans claim that the time off yields three benefits:

- It helps you discover your identity.
- It opens the door to examining and possibly reshaping your persona.
- It provides an opportunity to rebuild your character.

Before moving forward in your career, it is helpful to examine aptitude, identity, persona, and character.

YOUR APTITUDE

Much has been written about finding your aptitude—that in which you have an interest and ability. You can learn much about your aptitude by completing the NEXTERCISE in chapter 4.

Also, there are many online sources to explore. One of the best we have found is the Johnson O'Connor Research Foundation (JOCRF.org), which has been in business since 1922.

DISCOVERING YOUR IDENTITY

Who am I? You do not need to be a psychology or sociology major to learn who you think you are. This can be a laborious process filled with online and print research, but the most expeditious way to tackle the subject is to consult a source written in the vernacular, a source like the *Psychology Today* magazine or website. Here is a condensed version of what *Psychology Today* has to say about identity: "Personal identity is how we define ourselves as a son, daughter, mother, father, brother, or sister and beyond. Included in this personal identity are our personality traits, hobbies, interests, skills—all that defines who we are as individuals."

Social identity begins building when we take our first steps into society and start comparing ourselves with other human beings. Usually this begins when we go to school, even as early as preschool or kindergarten. Social identity becomes more complex as we climb up the school ladder and find ourselves in college or a trade school. Included in our social identity are gender, race, ethnicity, social class, political persuasion, and religion. Inclusion in one or more of these groups draws us close together with those of like kind. It's really basic sociology.

Work identity forms when we begin our first full-time job after college or high school and lasts over the three parts of our working lives: when we are employed; when we are fired or laid off; and when we are retired.

DISCOVERING YOUR PERSONA

The word "persona" derives from Latin, where it originally referred to a theatrical mask. In theatrical terms, it is an assumed personality. In today's world it refers to that part of your personality exposed to the public. It is the apparent "you" that people see, and it may be different from your character, the real you. It is you who created your persona, either consciously or subconsciously.

People in the public eye, such as TV personalities, actors, and politicians, frequently assume a persona that appeals to their target audience. Take politicians, for example. They want to be viewed as caring for the welfare of their constituents and the needs of the country as a whole. In reality, many use public office for personal gain. For example, the bitterly contentious 2016, 2020, and 2024 presidential election campaigns were all about persona and character, with trustworthiness being one of the key issues.

Persona in the private sector is similarly important. Take a minute to define your former bosses or company presidents. Were their public faces for real, or were they masks used for personal gain? Were the mask and the person behind the mask one and the same?

Let's review the persona of a well-known CEO, Steve Jobs, the now deceased cofounder and CEO of Apple Computer Company. When I worked with Apple in its early days, Steve's persona was that of the good, kind, caring, and generous boss. However, behind his mask, Steve could be a ruthless guy, one who might greet you in the morning and say a polite "Good morning" or look at you with fury in his eyes and say, "You're fired!" for no apparent reason. Nobody quite knew who Steve really was.

Bring this to a more personal level and look at your persona in the workplace, focusing on the role you play now in your present job or the role played in your last job. If you were in a leadership position, i.e., the boss, what was your persona? Was it in conflict with the real you? Did you think of yourself as the good, compassionate, helpful, caring boss dedicated to making the company great? Did you assume this persona, this mask, to hide your real motivation—to oust your boss and move up in rank and compensation? Could it have been the reason you were fired from your job as regional sales manager in a staged "reorganization," while your friend Mary, another regional sales manager, was kept on the payroll?

Before making the big move toward serious career revision, discover who you really are. Were you the one who used every chance to derail your boss? If your introspection reveals a difference between your persona and the real you, take measures to make these two competing entities one and the same. How do you begin? With honesty. If you have any doubts about how you are seen, ask your former boss and coworkers what they think of you, no holds barred. Also, think about what William Shakespeare had to say about persona: "All the world's a stage, and all the men and women merely players. They have their exits and their entrances, and one man in his time plays many parts."

DISCOVERING AND REBUILDING YOUR CHARACTER

Character is the aggregate of traits and features that form and identify the real you. Your character is the set of values and sense of ethics that you hold dear and determine not only what you say but also how you act.

While you are considering new careers, explore not only where you've been and where you want to go but also who you really are. Looking back, you might find that the real you became lost in the corporate culture or was disguised by a preoccupation with political correctness. On the job, you may have forgotten what you truly think or feel. It's time for a homecoming with yourself to find out who you are.

To begin the process of rebuilding character, we need a foundation upon which everything else rests. We like the foundation stones posited by Character Counts! (CharacterCounts.org), a nonprofit organization dedicated to character education. It provides online rubrics and workshops to accomplish the mission of character building. One of their constructs is the "Six Pillars of Character," which acts as the foundation for exploring character education and character building. These pillars are trustworthiness, fairness, respect, caring, citizenship, and responsibility.

The Rebuilding Process

The rebuilding process may be filled with doubts, maybes, should-haves, would-haves, and could-haves. However, the burdens of today are not what will drive you to distraction. Rather, what holds you back are the regrets over yesterday and the fear of tomorrow. Learn from the past, but do not accept past as prologue. Get rid of the two demons—regret and fear—that inhibit growth.

KEY TAKEAWAYS

- Persona is the face you present to the public at large.
- Character is who you really are.
- Persona and character must work in harmony for growth in your career.
- Regrets over the past and fear of the future are two demons that will inhibit your growth.
- Let go of regrets. Face the future with confidence and hope.
- Integrity and trust form the foundation for your character.

- Having good character means being who you are even when nobody is watching.
- Make time each day to define your identity.

PRINT AND DIGITAL RESOURCES
- *Psychology Today* (PsychologyToday.com)
- *Next! The Power of Reinvention in Life and Work* by Joanne Lipman
- *Reconfigurement: Reconfiguring Your Life at Any Stage and Planning Ahead* by E. Alan Fleischauer
- *The Road to Character* by David Brooks
- Character Counts! (CharacterCounts.org)
- Inspiring Character (Character.org)
- Johnson O'Connor Research Foundation (JOCRF.org)

CHAPTER 15

TWELVE TIPS FOR UNDERSTANDING THE WORLDWIDE WORKPLACE

While plunging into the practical details of career searching, let's use the following tips to help understand our workplace. These tips are useful not only for workers in the US but also for workers throughout the world.

Tip 1. The workplace is composed of industries, companies within those industries, and careers and jobs both corporate and entrepreneurial. For example, in the transportation industry there are automobile manufacturers like Ford, local automobile dealers who sell Ford cars, mechanics who repair Ford cars, and thousands of workers around the world making hundreds of Ford components like tires, semiconductor chips, windshield wipers, and radios. The worldwide workplace is truly interdependent.

Tip 2. According to recent data from multiple sources, there are 1.5 billion people in India, 1.3 billion in China, 340 million in the United States, 263 million in Indonesia, and 209 million in Brazil. The United States workforce, numbering 160 million workers, makes the US workplace alone one of the largest "countries" in the world and a fertile ground for job opportunities.

Tip 3. The purpose of work, no matter where in the world you live, is to make money to purchase the "basic three" for survival. They are food, clothing, and shelter, with an emphasis on food. It has been that way since hominids began hunting four million years ago. There are additional subbasics we have invented to deal with the complexities of modern-day living. Some of these are AI, education, transportation, technology products, and insurance.

Tip 4. The workplace does not discriminate by gender, race, ethnicity, or religion. Employers the world over hire workers with the best qualifications for a specific job. Diversity? Equity? Inclusion? Cracking glass ceilings? Forget it. Despite what the media and politicians shout, employers hire workers with required skill sets, required education, and job-specific expertise and experience.

Tip 5. Work provides meaning in one's life, like the pride tradespeople derive from constructing a beautiful commercial office building in Tokyo. Likewise, IT workers derive meaning and purpose from inventing new technology products to facilitate our personal and work responsibilities. Consider the satisfaction, pride, and sense of purpose experienced by a physician who has worked in America and abroad. And let's remember our active military personnel. Data from the Department of Defense reveals that there are 70,000 women in the US Navy. Recently one of them, a jet fighter pilot, said that her military career gave purpose to her life.

Tip 6. Employers are in business to make money in order to expand their business and pay their workers by producing products and providing services for customers throughout the world. Their employees produce these products and services while working in traditional work settings or remote locations throughout the world.

Tip 7. In developed countries like the United States, there are enough jobs for everyone, both native-born workers and immigrants. Recent data tells us that the US employs more than 160 million workers, making it the job basket of the world. And contrary to media hype, employers in developed countries like the United States, England, and Japan continue to hire even in stressful times, like during the global COVID-19 pandemic.

Tip 8. Artificial intelligence and robotics are changing the workplace forever. The worldwide workplace will continue to evolve every day because of AI. The job you have today could be gone tomorrow. Be prepared.

Tip 9. In all countries workers are fired and laid off every day. For example, data from the Bureau of Labor Statistics tells us that 55,000 workers are fired or laid off in the United States every day. That's approximately 20 million each year! And workers in America change careers an average of six times from first job to retirement. Because of this constant churning, workers are always searching for identity to give meaning to their lives.

Tip 10. Many jobs in every country originate in small companies and entrepreneurial businesses rather than multibillion-dollar and multinational companies like Apple and Toyota. For example, in the United States 46 percent of all private-sector workers are employed by companies with 500 or fewer workers.[14]

Tip 11. Employment contracts and termination agreements are legally enforceable. Workers must carefully read the agreement provided by the employer to fully understand workplace policy, obligations, privileges, and restrictions. The smart thing to do in today's workplace is to have an attorney review all hiring and termination agreements before signing.

Tip 12. All workers have two unique traits, persona and character. Persona is that which we show to the public. It is that part of ourselves that we put onstage for the world to see. Character is who we really are, our inner core that defines what we hold dear. Workplace problems frequently arise when there is a conflict between persona and character. To find meaning in employment, workers should make certain that their persona and character are in sync. Employers, too, have a persona and character that frequently are in conflict and cause workers to quit their jobs for better opportunities where employer persona and character are simpatico.

The workplace is constantly changing, and workers must consult the data and research to maintain understanding. In addition, workers must begin planning and saving for the time when they are terminated and when they retire. Here are some references to get you started.

---

14 "Frequently Asked Questions About Small Business, 2024," US Small Business Administration Office of Advocacy, July 23, 2024, https://advocacy.sba.gov/2024/07/23/frequently-asked-questions-about-small-business-2024/.

- Access social media focusing on careers, like LinkedIn.
- View TV programs like the Bloomberg channel, CNBC, and Jim Cramer.
- Read *The Wall Street Journal*, published daily.
- Read *Barron's* financial magazine, published on Sundays only.
- Attend trade shows and conferences held at major conference centers, like the Javits Center in NYC and McCormick Place in Chicago, the largest convention center in North America.

PART 2

FIRED!

SEARCHING FOR UNDERSTANDING, MEANING, PURPOSE, AND IDENTITY WHEN FIRED OR LAID OFF

CHAPTER 16

TERMINATED! WHY ME?

It happens when you least expect it, like on a Friday afternoon at 4 p.m. while you are thinking about plans for the coming weekend. It can happen to anybody regardless of age, race, ethnicity, gender, rank, tenure, or record of achievement. It happens to presidents, sales representatives, editors, managers, directors, teachers, doctors, nurses, truck drivers, lawyers, and tradespeople. It happens in America, Poland, Spain, Japan, Mexico, South Africa, Brazil, and every country in between—in short, to any worker, in any country, at any time.

This dreaded event is being terminated from your job. In America it happens to 55,000 workers each day, according to data from the Bureau of Labor Statistics. That's 20 million workers per year getting the axe. It's not a pretty picture, and all workers must prepare for this event because it's not a matter of if it will happen; it's a matter of when it will happen.

When it happens, the outcry can go something like this.

- "We'll settle this in court."
- "They will not get away with this!"
- "If I'm let go, it's gender discrimination!"
- "If you fire me, that's racial discrimination!"
- "If you let me go, that's ageism!"
- "You can't fire me! That's ethnic discrimination!"

We understand the angst, but it is what it is. When your employer decides you must be let go, for whatever reason, you are gone. Finished. Out of work. No paycheck. No benefits. And for most workers, one devastating effect is the shattering of their identity. Before being let go, a worker might take pride in saying, "I'm Kelsey DeLuca, VP marketing with Big Tech." That title and company affiliation defined her identity. After being let go, she are just plain . . . Kelsey. This troublesome event cuts to one's inner core and can send workers into a deep depression, even pushing them to suicide. Some terminated workers are so disturbed that they turn to revenge against their former employer. We've all heard about disgruntled terminated workers returning to the workplace with a gun and killing their former boss and others.

Layoffs in America and throughout the world are nothing new. They can be caused by something unexpected like the COVID-19 pandemic, which saw the unemployment rate in America rise from an unprecedented low of 3.5 percent in January 2020 to 15.8 percent in May 2020. Layoffs, even mass layoffs, can happen at any time. Let's backtrack to the beginning of 2012. At that time, the Bank of America (BoA) employed 247,000 workers. BoA was one of the most highly regarded employers in the US. Many BoA workers thought that working there was a lifetime proposition. However, as the economy began to deteriorate, BoA laid off thousands of workers. At the end of that calendar year, BoA had let go 14,000 workers for a variety of reasons, and the slaughter continued into 2013.

The unexpected happened again in 2015 with another company, the technology icon Hewlett Packard. The company decided to break into two separate functioning parts, and the layoffs began. When the transition was complete, over 30,000 unsuspecting workers were terminated.

And in February 2021, Best Buy let go 5,000 full-time

workers in a massive reorganization and downsizing. (Ironically, Best Buy hired 2,000 part-time workers while the mass layoffs were taking place.) Preceding this turn of events, Best Buy had already "furloughed" 51,000 workers in April 2020, blaming the COVID-19 pandemic. At the bottom of all this hiring and firing was an attempt by Best Buy to save money and survive. Mass terminations will continue to happen at any time for any number of reasons, not just because of a pandemic.

These real-life stories illustrate what can happen to one's career regardless of rank, position, or dedication. Also, they illustrate the alarming trend of employers disregarding the human rights of their employees. Workers must understand how it works and how to move forward and rebuild their careers.

The termination mayhem continues to this very day. It is happening right now as you read this book. Check it out in the print or digital *Wall Street Journal* or watch it every day on CNBC. It will not go away, so it behooves all workers to remain vigilant and craft an action plan to implement when it happens. One of the most serious mistakes workers can make is to assume that being terminated only happens to someone else. Think again.

TERMINOLOGY

There are specific terms employers use to describe this event. The term "fired" is used when a worker is let go for cause. An example is a salesperson failing to meet a stipulated revenue goal. "Laid off" is the term used when a worker is terminated for reasons unrelated to personal performance. For example, company A merges with company B, and the VP of sales for company A is let go. The new company does not need two workers in that position.

"Let go" is commonly used for all terminations because it avoids the emotional impact delivered to unsuspecting workers when they are terminated. It's a gentler way of delivering the axe. And it could avoid costly lawsuits against the employer.

For example, an employer may terminate workers because of a decline in business revenue. In this instance, it's usually called downsizing. Some workers may be terminated because of a radical change in company structure called a reorganization. Reducing staff because of a drop in revenue is sometimes called rightsizing. But whatever it is called today, the word "fired" is the term most frequently used . . . as it is in this book.

LAWSUITS ON THE RISE

Many fired workers hire lawyers and seek legal remedies. In order to understand your legal workplace rights, particularly during times of workplace stress caused by events such as the COVID-19 pandemic, stay on top of the situation by reading information, in print or online, such as from the HR Specialist (TheHRSpecialist.com).

According to an article in the July 2021 *Employment Law* newsletter from the HR Specialist, "The COVID-19 employee lawsuits: Top 5 threats," questionable terminations during the pandemic period resulted in steep increases in legal action against former employers.[15] The following list details the percentage of specific worker claims, many of which resulted in lawsuits.

- ➤ Wrongful discharge: 40 percent
- ➤ Unsafe working conditions: 23 percent
- ➤ Disability discrimination: 15 percent
- ➤ FMLA legal offenses: 12 percent
- ➤ Wage and hour offenses: 6 percent
- ➤ Other: 4 percent

---

15 The HR Specialist, "The COVID-19 employee lawsuits: Top 5 threats," *Employment Law*, July 2021, https://www.thehrspecialist.com/res/issues/yatl/Sample.pdf.

HIRE A LAWYER TO PROTECT YOUR WORKPLACE RIGHTS

When hired, you enter into a contractual agreement, written or oral, with your employer that gives both you and your employer certain legal rights. Frequently, workers forget that and believe the employer is holding all the aces. There is an entire body of workplace law in every country delineating both employer and worker rights. Protect your legal rights by seeking advice from lawyers specializing in workplace law. Find such lawyers in your location and contact them while you are employed to establish a professional relationship.

When your boss or the HR director terminates your employment, your first and only response should be "I'll contact my attorney about this. Before I leave work today, please give me your official notice in writing stating the specific reasons why you are letting me go. My lawyer will contact you as soon as she reviews your actions against me."

When you leave the work site, be it an office building or an automobile dealership, take out your cell phone and call your lawyer. Explain what has transpired and ask for advice.

The terminated worker confronts a host of perplexing challenges that involve income, reputation, family matters, and more. It's important to understand how this complex process works and how you can sort it out. Why? Because it could very well happen again.

KEY TAKEAWAYS

- You can find an employment lawyer in your area by googling "employment lawyer in my area."
- Always contact a lawyer after being let go, no matter how friendly the termination is presented by your employer. Don't be taken in by warm and fuzzy talk.
- Understanding completely why you were terminated is

necessary to move forward with the task of rebuilding your career.
- The two most devastating results of being let go are loss of identity and loss of income.
- Employment is a contractual relationship. You have defined legal rights. Do not forfeit them for any reason.

CHAPTER 17

OVERCOMING GRIEF AND DEPRESSION

Everyone goes through a period of grieving after a significant loss, which could be the death of a loved one, loss of a spouse through divorce, loss of physical function through permanent injury, and loss of a job. Losing a job frequently triggers a period of grieving as severe as that caused by death or divorce. For verification, ask anyone who has been fired or laid off.

The severity of the grieving process caused by job loss is proportionate to the separated worker's rank, compensation, and age. Mid-career workers usually suffer the most because they have the most to lose in terms of money, status, and rank. They are likely to have significant mortgage or rental payments, automobile payments, credit card payments, childcare expenses, college tuition payments, insurance payments, and more. Being forced to deal with all those responsibilities will throw most laid-off workers into the classic stages of the grieving process.

THE GRIEVING PROCESS

Swiss psychiatrist Elisabeth Kübler-Ross worked with terminally ill patients and their loved ones. In one of her books, she states that there are five stages in the grieving process: denial, anger, bargaining, depression, acceptance.

Some terminated workers move through the grieving process using their own resources, but others require professional help from a psychologist, psychiatrist, clergy member, or career counselor.

In my work as an executive recruiter, I have seen laid-off workers go through a prolonged grieving process. For others the process is abbreviated because they quickly become preoccupied with finding another job, a time-consuming process that pushes the worker through the grieving process. I have noted the following, only slightly modified stages of grief when counseling, and consoling, job candidates who have lost their jobs, especially those in mid-career.

Denial

After hearing those torturous words from the boss or the HR director—"We have to let you go"—most workers say aloud or silently, "This can't be happening to me. I've given my blood, sweat, and tears to this company, and there is no reason I should be laid off." Many workers refuse to believe they are being asked to leave the premises and petition the boss and HR director for reinstatement. If that does not work, they persist in seeking reasons for dismissal that make sense. They want more than "We're having a reorganization." Some take it to the next level and demand to see their boss's boss or the president or CEO. Usually, the appeal to a higher authority bears no fruit, and the laid-off worker leaves the premises dejected but still in denial.

After leaving the workplace, some workers seek help from a colleague in the company. Some ask a company friend to intercede with the boss or human resources director to reinstate their jobs. Others seek the help of a lawyer to have their employment reinstated. These initiatives rarely are successful except in cases where the company violated a provision in the employment contract or violated current state or federal workplace laws, which are always changing.

Humiliation

A person who has just been terminated feels a great sense of humiliation. When it happens, it seems that the eyes of all coworkers are on you. You feel that they know you were sacked. Word travels fast. The most humiliating event is being walked out of the workplace accompanied by a security officer as though you committed a crime. It hurts like nothing else and sets you up for the next stage, anger.

Anger

A worker enters the anger stage of the grieving process when attempts to become reinstated have failed and when the humiliation continues as more workers become aware of the termination. The anger is usually directed at three sources: the company, the boss, and the HR director, the one who frequently delivers the bad news. If not resolved quickly, the anger stage will prevent the fired worker from thinking clearly and planning the next step: rebuilding their career.

Workers in the anger stage have been known to hurl epithets at the boss, the company, and anyone who will listen. Some will curse. Some will lose it completely and resort to violence by physically injuring the HR director or the boss. I'm sure we all recall several instances covered in the media when laid-off postal workers returned to their former place of employment and shot the boss and former coworkers, leading to the term "going postal." When you find yourself in a prolonged stage of anger, do everything possible to move forward, like seeking counseling from a psychologist, a career coach, or a clergy member.

Depression

Many terminated workers lose the sense of professional identity that sets them apart from the rest of the pack. When employed, you might have been Tom Jones, director of marketing for ABC Inc. When you are fired, you become plain-vanilla Tom Jones. This is a traumatic event and triggers emotional changes. Frequently, laid-off workers enter a stage of pessimism, inadequacy, helplessness, and despondency. Some enter a state of depression that requires clinical help from a psychiatrist. One can work through this stage of the grieving process by activating a network of family and friends for support and encouragement.

Acceptance

Acceptance is the final stage of the grieving process. In previous stages, you may have tried to resolve the problem to no avail. You are not going to be rehired. Period. You must put the past behind you. Acceptance is liberating. It closes the grieving cycle and enables you to move forward to rebuild not only your career but also your entire life on your own terms. In a sense, being fired or laid off might be one of the best things that has ever happened to you. When you accept your situation, you can take total ownership of your future.

Transitioning to the acceptance stage of the grieving process is a prerequisite for defining a new you, independent of job rank or title. However, it is important to evaluate your financial situation to make sure that you can meet obligations related to your personal well-being and that of your family and your dependents. Those who have children know this better than anyone else. Children are at the front of the line when it comes to allocating family finances, like college tuition payments, which seem to rise every semester.

FIVE SOLUTIONS FOR WORKING THROUGH THE GRIEVING PROCESS

Workers at every rank can move through the grieving process using these resources: the internet, print and digital books and magazines, a career coach, a friend or family member, a cleric, an outplacement service, and common sense. I have witnessed fired workers use some or all of these resources to move forward successfully. Here are five initiatives to hasten your trip through the grieving process.

Take a Break

The first thing most laid-off workers do is plunge into the job-hunting process, a huge mistake. Instead, take a well-deserved break. Consider beginning the process by going to an upscale restaurant or pub, preferably with a trusted friend. Go out and let loose. Have a good time. Lift your glass and get it off your chest, shouting the line made famous by country singer Johnny Paycheck: "Take this job and shove it!" Pay in cash and leave a generous tip. While you are at dinner, begin planning the next step: leaving the house and having more fun.

The day following your night on the town, make a written list of activities for the next seven days, activities that you can do alone or with a close friend. Do not include anything work related. You will have time for that later. Include in your list all those things you could not do when you were working because your job sapped your time and energy. (Remember those irritating text messages at 10 p.m. on a Saturday night?) Plan to leave the house each day to participate in activities like visiting museums and art galleries, playing golf, swimming, hiking, skiing, biking, mountain climbing, and exploring locations that arouse your curiosity. Make sure they take place away from home. At the conclusion of this week of physical activity, move forward to the next portion of "taking a break": leaving town.

If you have enough discretionary income, leave town for a week alone or with a close friend, to a faraway national or international destination. Attractive and reasonably priced travel deals can be found with a bit of research. For example, a reputable travel agency, Gate One Travel (GateOneTravel.com), offers a number of fly/drive tours and escorted tours to national and international destinations for under $1,500. How would you like six days in Ireland, six days in London, or seven days in Thailand? How about nine days touring the Grand Canyon, Sedona, Monument Valley, or Bryce and Zion National Parks? Getting out of town is the best remedy I know to forget about the past, particularly about that nasty employer who had the temerity to let you go. The hell with them! Move on. You can live without them. Truth be told, you never liked working there. Other jobs are out there, just waiting for you to discover them.

Conduct a Personal Inventory

Make a list of all the good things you still have, such as your spouse or partner, children, family members, friends, intelligence, job skills, energy, and education. Your former employer cannot take that away from you. In addition, record the personal possessions that your work has enabled you to acquire, i.e., the best of the basic three. While millions in the world will go to bed hungry tonight, you will not. Be thankful for what you have and remember that you are among the most fortunate people in the world, a worker in the United States or an economically developed country. While millions of people around the world are banging on the door of America to get a job, you are already here. Best of all, you still have your attitudes and opinions, which you will use moving forward.

Study the Numbers

When you are out of a job, there is a tendency to hear only the bad news. Tune out the media babble about the dire state of the economy and conduct your own research. Study the numbers from the Bureau of Labor Statistics (BLS.gov), the Department of Commerce (Commerce.gov), and the Pew Research Center (Pew.org). Look at our employment rate (as opposed to the unemployment rate) in America and other countries.

Evaluate Your Work–Life Balance

What did you usually do after work? In your last job were there any "after-work hours," or were work and personal life one and the same? Define and write down what brings you pleasure and satisfaction in your life outside of work. In your last job, how much time did you devote to those pursuits? One hour each day? Maybe a few hours on the weekend after the usual household chores? Vow to never again permit an employer to control your life. This is your life. Define it on your own terms.

Evaluate Your Work History

Did you really like your last job, or did you go there every day solely for the money? Do you want to continue working in your specialty, or would you be happy moving on to something else? For example, assume that your work life to this point has been in sales, first as a territory sales rep, then as a district manager, and most recently as a regional sales manager. You were on the road more than 50 percent of the time, rushing from one airport and hotel to another. You were constantly making pipeline reports and evaluations of your subordinates. Did you really enjoy that? If not, define and write down your five ideal jobs after completing the NEXTERCISE in chapter 4 of this book.

KEY TAKEAWAYS

- All let-go workers experience a period of grieving.
- Accepting the fact that you were laid off and have no chance of your job being reinstated is a liberating experience.
- The numbers will tell you much about the US economy and your place in it.
- Put away the regrets of the past.
- Forget your fears of the future.
- Move forward to another career in America, the job basket of the world where jobs are always available for those who know how and where to find them.

DIGITAL RESOURCES

- Gate One Travel offers a number of independent tours and escorted tours to domestic and world destinations at reasonable prices (GateOneTravel.com).
- The Bureau of Labor Statistics (BLS.gov)
- The Department of Commerce (Commerce.gov)
- The Pew Research Center (Pew.org)
- "8 Steps to Bouncing Back After Getting Fired" on TheMuse.com

CHAPTER 18

SEVERANCE AND YOUR RIGHTS UNDER EMPLOYMENT LAW

Terminated workers under shock frequently ask, "Do I have any legal rights now that I've been terminated?" The short answer is a resounding yes. There are numerous state and federal legal rights that you have when your employment is terminated. They may or may not be listed in your termination document, so you must exercise diligence and carefully read this document. Furthermore, you should always consult an employment lawyer to read the fine print to make sure you are being treated fairly.

Here is a list of your legal recourses related to insurance and workers' rights when you are terminated.

Consolidated Omnibus Budget Reconciliation Act (COBRA)

COBRA is a federal government program that enables workers to continue their medical insurance coverage after being let go.

There are strict rules governing its application. For example, workers who are let go for cause, i.e., fired for gross misconduct, are not eligible to receive COBRA benefits. The charges may or may not be accurate, because they are put in writing by your boss and the HR director. If you are denied COBRA, consult your lawyer.

While COBRA is a helpful risk-lowering federal medical insurance plan, you must pay the entire cost of the plan plus an administrative fee when you are laid off. If your company's annual group medical insurance premium was $5,000 and split between you and your employer, you are now responsible for paying the entire premium plus a 2 percent administrative fee. Generally, you must apply for COBRA benefits within sixty days of being separated. Benefits will last for eighteen months and will cover you, your spouse, and children. However, as with all government programs, the rules and regulations are constantly changing, so act immediately if you elect to choose COBRA benefits. For other rules and regulations regarding COBRA, review the Department of Labor website (DoL.gov). Caution! Do not assume that you will quickly find another job with medical insurance benefits and pass up the chance to use COBRA. Your period of unemployment could go on for six months or more, and you cannot be without medical insurance for that long.

Affordable Care Act (ACA)

The Affordable Care Act is sometimes called Obamacare because this federal law was enacted during President Obama's administration. The ACA contains comprehensive health insurance reforms and tax provisions that affect individuals, families, businesses, insurers, tax-exempt organizations, and government entities. These tax provisions affect how individuals and families file their taxes. ACA provisions have changed frequently since being enacted, so review the ACA website. Being fired and losing health insurance through your employer could be a "qualifying life event" that allows you to sign up outside the typical November enrollment period.

Unemployment Compensation

Sometimes called unemployment insurance, this is a joint

federal and state program that provides cash benefits to eligible workers. To be eligible, your termination must be for reasons other than gross misconduct. All states follow a certain set of guidelines established by federal law, but each state administers a separate unemployment insurance program with different guidelines and requirements. For example, New Jersey allows a maximum of $830 per week for twenty-six weeks based on meeting certain requirements. Consult your HR director for state-specific information. For verification, check online by googling your state's unemployment compensation benefits website.

The Worker Adjustment and Retraining Notification Act (WARN)

WARN is a federal law that protects workers and their families by requiring employers with 100 or more employees to provide notification sixty calendar days in advance of plant closings and mass layoffs. This worker right is frequently overlooked, sometimes intentionally, by employers. Its administration can be complicated, so consult your lawyer for guidance.

Your legal rights may be extended by provisions of your local and state governments. Before accepting a severance package, always check with your HR director, your state and local employment offices, and with your employment lawyer.

SEVERANCE AGREEMENTS

Employers are eager to clear the books when terminating workers individually or in mass layoffs. They may ask you to sign immediately. Usually, the HR director will present you with a written severance package during the exit interview and tell you that termination benefits will not be offered if you wait to sign.

Under no circumstances should you sign a severance package agreement before walking out the door. You need time to review the document and consult with your employment lawyer. In fact, under federal laws, if you're forty or older, you must be given at least forty-five days to sign in a group termination and twenty-one days to sign if your layoff is not part of a mass layoff. In either case, if you accept the offer, you also must be given a seven-day period afterward to change your mind. Each state may have its own requirements in addition to the federal minimum requirements. Check your state's labor department site to see what its specific requirements are.

What Should a Severance Agreement Contain?

Severance agreements are not all the same, but here are the basic provisions that should be addressed:

- Salary continuation for an agreed-upon period
- Benefits continuation
- Stock options
- Unused vacation time
- Unused sick leave
- Outplacement services
- Nondisclosure provisions
- Employer references
- A lump sum of money beyond salary continuation based on time served and position
- At-will and noncompete provisions

Severance Agreements Are Negotiable

Terminated workers frequently assume that the terms of the severance package are final. However, like all agreements, the package is negotiable. If the agreement provides twelve weeks of salary, ask for what you feel is appropriate. That may be twenty-four weeks or even a year or more. Do not be intimidated. If you can't bring yourself to negotiate the money or other terms in the agreement, have your lawyer negotiate for you.

Severance is a career-altering agreement that should be handled with utmost care. For a comprehensive summary about how to proceed, go to Indeed at Indeed.com/career-advice/severance. Remember to consult your employment lawyer for advice if you have any doubts about the provisions in the severance package.

KEY TAKEAWAYS

- We rarely expect to be terminated. Getting fired is what happens to the worker in the cubicle next door . . . we assume. But with twenty million workers per year being fired, it pays to be prepared. Why? Because it could happen to you without warning.
- Severance will affect your work life going forward. Make sure you understand the provisions.
- Severance provisions are negotiable.
- The severance package is written by employers with their own interests in mind.
- Always consult a lawyer about severance provisions before signing.

DIGITAL RESOURCES

- Find advice about severance at Indeed.com/career-advice/severance.
- Affordable Care Act information on HHS.gov

CHAPTER 19

PROTECTING YOUR FINANCIAL SECURITY

When the paychecks stop, there might be a knee-jerk reaction to begin liquidating savings and other assets in order to continue your lifestyle as though you were still on the payroll. Nothing could be riskier. Even though you are out of work and have no regular paycheck, it is important to evaluate, monitor, and preserve the financial gains you have made. Make this a priority. The paycheck will return in about six months, the average length of time it takes to move forward with another job. Evaluate your assets and decide how to preserve them. When you have been terminated, follow every step in this chapter to survive financially.

PROTECTING AND MAINTAINING YOUR SAVINGS, INVESTMENTS, AND IRA

An investment is anything that has monetary value: savings accounts, individual retirement accounts, non-IRA brokerage accounts, credit cards, mutual funds, real estate holdings, and personal possessions. Financial investments should be monitored constantly because of the cyclical nature of our economy. The last thing you need is to see your investments lose significant value overnight. It happened in the Great

Recession of 2008 and the COVID pandemic of 2020 to 2023. It can happen again. Two consecutive quarters of negative GDP herald a recession, a time to move your money to a safe haven like cash, which can be reinvested when the economy emerges from the recession. (You can learn more about how to monitor the economy by viewing financial TV channels like CNBC, Fox Business, and Bloomberg Business.)

Protecting Your Cash Savings

According to a 2023 study conducted by the Financial Industry Regulatory Authority (FINRA), only about half of all workers have enough in their cash accounts to cover three months of necessary expenses.[16] Alarmingly, a study by Forbes reveals that 28 percent of Americans have less than $1,000 in their savings account.[17] This borders on a national tragedy and reveals that the majority of adult workers have not learned the basics of money management. Every worker, regardless of income level, should keep enough money in a cash account to cover three to six months of expenses. My recommendation is to keep an extra margin for safety and make it six months during your working years.

Establishing a Six-Month Cash Emergency Fund

To determine where you stand financially after losing your job, make a list of all necessary monthly expenses. Do not include money that you would spend on items like going out to dinner, going to concerts, ball games, or shows; purchasing the latest fashion items advertised on TV, the latest clothing, digital apps

---

16   "Economic Well-Being of U.S. Households in 2023," The Financial Industry Regulatory Authority, May 2024, https://www.federalreserve.gov/publications/files/2023-report-economic-well-being-us-households-202405.pdf.

17   Jamela Adam, "American Savings by Generation: How Balances and Goals Vary By Age," *Forbes*, August 15, 2024, https://www.forbes.com/advisor/banking/savings/average-american-savings/.

for the children, new cell phones, new pets, and new furniture. Include on your list only those items that are absolutely necessary, such as mortgage payments, car payments, children's tuition, insurance premiums, utility bills, tax payments, food, and critical clothing needs for yourself and family members.

After determining your monthly expenses, multiply by six to learn what you will need to carry you through a six-month period of unemployment. If you do not have a sufficient amount in your money market or savings account to cover necessary expenses for six months, the maximum length of time it should take to find a new good employment opportunity, establish an emergency fund. Do this by transferring money from other sources, like your personal investment portfolio. Transfer only what you need to cover six months' expenses. For example, if you determined that expenses are going to be $24,000 and you have just $15,000 in ready cash, transfer only $9,000 from your personal investments. This might require selling favorite equities or mutual funds. Protect your newly created cash emergency fund by resisting the temptation to buy unnecessary items. When you find another job, rebuild your emergency fund to the $24,000 level. Your newly created cash emergency account will build the confidence you need to make the right employment choices moving forward.

Protecting Your IRA

This is an opportune time to reevaluate your entire financial position. If you were enrolled in a company-sponsored 401(k) with your previous employer, you had a certain amount withdrawn from your paycheck and invested in the 401(k), usually in a mutual fund. Most workers believe the company and the fund looked after your best interests, but did they? Now is the time to evaluate the funds in your 401(k). What funds are they in? Bond funds? Equity funds? Exchange-traded funds?

Money market funds? Domestic funds? International funds? How much does the mutual fund company charge in annual fees? How much does it charge for making changes to your account? A 1 percent fee could add up to thousands of dollars over the life of your retirement fund. You do not have to leave your 401(k) with the company used by your former employer. You can transfer it to another company during employment or after unemployment.

If you decide to move your 401(k) to another company, you can do so easily. The move is transparent, and you lose nothing in the process. There are many reputable companies to consider for your retirement fund. Two of the most popular are Vanguard (Vanguard.com) and Fidelity (Fidelity.com). Both have very low administrative fees and buy/sell fees. Most of their funds do not have a front-end load, which is a fee assessed for buying into a specific mutual fund.

If you have dependent children, consider establishing a 529 College Savings Account, a plan that offers many advantages. Your provider, like Vanguard or Fidelity, will help you online or by phone to establish the 529.

Moving forward to the time when you are employed again, assume total control over your 401(k) rather than permitting your employer to make the decision for you. Evaluate all your options and select the company and fund that meet your objectives.

MONITORING THE COST FOR NECESSITIES WHILE UNEMPLOYED

Those who believe that their next job will be forever should think again. Fact: The majority of workers change jobs six times during their working years. Fact: 55,000 workers lose their jobs every day. Your next job could be an executive-level management job with an American icon like General Electric, which could provide you with a false sense of security. But this job might come crashing down six months later when your GE division in the US moves operations to India and you are out of a job. And let's remember Ford in June 2023 when they made massive layoffs to reduce their debt. Nobody saw it coming. "Prepare" is the watchword.

This is an ideal time to make an objective review of all your basic necessities. Begin by making a written inventory of everything you own and need. Place a value beside each item. Decide if it is a short-term item that you can modify downward or live without.

Food

The cost of food can be a stealth expense. Usually, we go to the supermarket and load our basket with things we like regardless of cost. You can save a bundle by evaluating every item you place in your basket. Take the traditional box of cornflakes. Recently I went to my local supermarket and purchased an eighteen-ounce box of cereal. I had two choices: the Kellogg brand or the store brand. I selected the store brand at a substantial savings. Multiple savings on food purchases over time will save thousands.

In 2024 and 2025, the cost of certain food items seemed out of control. For example, large or jumbo eggs were selling for over $7 a dozen. When it happens, ask yourself this question and act accordingly: "Do I really need to have eggs at this price?"

Another stealth expense can be food purchased at fast-food restaurants. For example, the cost of a burger and fries and a beverage can be $30. Do that five times a week, and you spend $150; for a month it's $600, a lot of money for a load of cholesterol. The same applies to eating upscale. Go to a medium-grade restaurant, and the average price for just an entrée can be $28. Add beverages, an appetizer, and a dessert, and you are looking at $60. Do that four times a month, and you've spent $240. Over six months, the average length of time you could be out of work, your restaurant bill will be $1,200. When you are out of work, you do not need to eat out every day or every week. If you do, allot a certain amount of money for your meal before looking at the menu.

Shelter

Next, consider the item that has become a national obsession: housing. Why is it that we spend so much of our money on shelter? Why are we constantly "moving up" the shelter chain to something larger and more luxurious? Do we really need that 3,000-square-foot house or apartment we live in now? How much money could we save by downsizing? And what about all those accoutrements filling the house? Do we need that new $5,000 sofa advertised on QVC? Do we really need a Persian rug in every room? And what about those impressionist paintings gracing the walls? Do we need all of them? They make our house more attractive, but could we get by with six instead of fifteen?

Clothing

The cost of clothing is huge. The next time you are dressed in business attire, add up the cost of everything on your person, from underwear to jewelry. For men the cost could be $500. For women it might be higher when the cost of jewelry is added. If you have children, make the same cost inventory.

Clothing is a stealth cost because we go online to purchase much of it. It is so easy to do. A skirt from Talbots. Shoes from Nordstrom. Nike shoes for the kids from Amazon. We charge these online purchases to credit cards like Visa, MasterCard, American Express, and others. When we receive the bill at the end of the month, we are shocked at the total. When we had a paycheck on a regular basis, we thought nothing of paying that bill online. In the entire process we never touch money, paper or coin. When we spend money in the cloud, we lose track of value.

While unemployed, set a strict budget for clothing. Buy only what you need for yourself and family members. Go back to brick-and-mortar stores and pay for clothing using real money, not credit cards. The high cost of this basic necessity will once again become a reality and enable you to control your clothing costs.

Transportation

Have you considered whether you really need a $75,000 Mercedes to transport you from point A to point B? After all, a Ford, Honda, Toyota, or Chevrolet sedan could accomplish the same objective and save you a bundle. If you live in the middle of the city, maybe a car is unnecessary because you can walk or take public transportation to and from work. If you want to leave town on weekends, you can always rent a car. Choosing this option will save thousands of dollars in car cost, insurance, parking, and maintenance.

Education

What can you do to cut expenses if you have children moving toward college? A year at a middle-ranked college could cost $40,000 per year. An Ivy League will likely set you back at least $70,000 per year. Even your state college might cost $25,000 per year. Why send your kids off to a high-priced college when they might not have the slightest clue about what they would like to do with the rest of their lives?

So how do you keep college costs from putting you in long-term debt—say, for ten years after your child graduates with a BA? There are two viable alternatives:

> ➤ Have your child take a year or two off after high school—gap years, as they are called—and work in any kind of

job to learn what this world is all about. After that, send your child genius to a community college for two years to learn what a college degree can do to focus their career goals. It may be that your child/student will discover that a hands-on job like carpentry or photography is more in line with their interests and aptitude.
- Another alternative is studying for an online degree while working part-time. We are slowly learning that the traditional four-year college immediately following high school makes little sense for many teenagers.

The bottom line is this: As you proceed with your career change, the most important thing to do is conserve your assets in anticipation of the next crisis, which could include being let go again from a future job, suffering a health setback like cancer, losing a sizable percentage of your financial assets because of events beyond your control, or taking care of an aging parent with Alzheimer's or some other incurable disease. Living is dangerous and unpredictable, whether you are employed or unemployed. Plan accordingly.

KEY TAKEAWAYS
- Always keep six months of expense money in cash reserves.
- Constantly monitor your expenses and financial assets.
- Take total control of your 401(k).
- Your possessions are investments. Evaluate their usefulness and cut back if they are expendable.
- Prepare for the next crisis, which may be losing your job again.

PRINT AND DIGITAL RESOURCES

- CNBC TV Financial News
- Fox TV Business News
- Bloomberg Business News TV
- *Mad Money* with Jim Cramer, CNBC TV
- Job Openings and Labor Turnover Summary from the Bureau of Labor Statistics (BLS.gov)
- *Rich Dad Poor Dad* by Robert Kiyosaki

CHAPTER 20

INSURANCE PROTECTION

Most people consider insurance a boring topic to be avoided at all costs. The unexpected illness or accident always happens to someone else. Don't fool yourself. In today's world you cannot live without insurance. Most workers do not like to talk about insurance. They avoid the topic, except when they are sued for negligence and the verdict exceeds their coverage.

Insurance matters are of great importance, and all fired workers must address them as soon as practicable. Life goes on after you lose your job, and so do the risks you face every day. Unpleasant events never get laid off or take a vacation. On any given day you could contract a life-threatening disease like pancreatic cancer, a long-term debilitating virus like COVID-19, or a costly illness like Lyme disease, or have a car accident resulting in serious personal injury and substantial property damage.

Your house or apartment is at risk, too. A hidden electrical malfunction could burn your dwelling to the ground and destroy all your personal possessions in the process. And wildfire risk like Los Angeles residents experienced in 2025 is always present. Risk is omnipresent, and insurance is the only way to hedge against it. So while insurance matters may be boring, when it comes to reducing risk, boring is good. In today's world insurance has become a necessity along with food, shelter, and clothing.

MEDICAL INSURANCE

Every person, regardless of social status or employment status, needs protection that insurance offers. The most important classes of insurance are medical, dental, life, long-term disability, automobile, and homeowners. Medical situations rank at the top of our risk ladder. We'll examine each classification, beginning with medical insurance, but first a word about COBRA.

COBRA is a federal government program that enables workers to continue their medical insurance coverage after being let go. However, there are strict rules governing its implementation. For example, workers who are fired for gross misconduct are not eligible. Also, companies that employ fewer than twenty workers cannot participate in the plan. Read more about COBRA in chapter 18.

When you are terminated from a qualifying company, most likely you will be offered COBRA. If you chose not to accept it, or if your previous employer was not eligible to offer COBRA, your most important post-termination action is to purchase medical insurance through a private insurer like Blue Cross, Cigna, or Aetna. The time to plan your medical insurance is not after you are fired but while you are still employed.

The ACA, also covered in chapter 18, provides an array of choices for individuals seeking medical insurance. Your options are contingent upon your income and state of residence. This controversial government program is highly political and subject to modification at any time. Cost is critical when assessing what to do about medical insurance after leaving the company. Learn what a medical insurance policy offered by ACA would cost and compare it with the cost of medical insurance outside of ACA. For information and updates on the Affordable Care Act in your state, go to Healthcare.gov.

Medicare is a federal government health insurance program for people over sixty-five. For information about its provisions and how to sign up, visit the official website, Medicare.gov. Also, see chapter 32 in this book for a comprehensive review of Medicare.

Medicaid is a federal and state program that provides healthcare coverage to qualified individuals. People who are eligible for Medicaid include the following:

- Pregnant women with low income
- Children from low-income families
- Children in foster care
- People with disabilities
- Seniors with low income
- Parents or caregivers with low income

Medicaid programs are state administered. For additional information go to Medicaid.gov.

DENTAL INSURANCE

I speak from personal experience on this matter. One fine day I was taking an early-morning bike ride, wearing my helmet, when I unexpectedly hit a patch of damp road. Down I went, striking my face on the pavement. The result? Two front teeth were cracked beyond repair and had to be replaced with dental implants. The cost? Five thousand dollars. I had no dental insurance!

Dental problems can arise without notice on any given day. We are always at risk for infections that require costly root canals and for teeth damaged by accidents. For a realistic account of what can happen unexpectedly, talk with your dentist.

If you had dental coverage in your last job, by all means try to extend coverage while you are out of work. If you did not have it, go online and look for reasonably priced dental insurance. Most dental plans are limited to group coverage through an employer, but there are a handful of dental insurance companies offering individual plans. Delta Dental is one of them and is noted for its generous coverage at modest cost. Check it out at DeltaDental.com. To explore other dental insurance plans for your location, go to DentalPlans.com.

HOMEOWNERS INSURANCE

When out of work, many workers try to minimize expenses by cutting insurance coverage on their homes or apartments. They say, "It will never happen to me. I'll cut my coverage while unemployed and pick it up after I get another job." Don't buy into that narrative. Homeowners carrying a mortgage do not have a choice, because the lender requires coverage and it is factored into the monthly mortgage payment. However, if you own your property outright or live in an apartment, coverage is optional. Do not eliminate this coverage. On any given day your residence could burn to the ground and take all your belongings with it. On another given day, someone could trip and fall in your apartment and incur serious personal injury. You will be held liable. Purchase at least $500,000 in personal liability coverage and replacement value for your house.

AUTOMOBILE INSURANCE

Automobile insurance is required if your car is financed. The premium is usually built into your monthly payment. In all states, proof of financial responsibility, i.e., automobile insurance, is required. You must present proof of coverage when you apply for or renew your license plates. Do not even think about skirting the rules and discontinuing premium payments, believing that you will never get into an accident if you drive extra carefully. Once again, risk is with you twenty-four seven. Automobile insurance is a necessity. See chapter 32 for more about automobile insurance.

LIFE INSURANCE

"Why life insurance?" you might ask. "I'm in the prime of my life and I'm not going to die in the foreseeable future." Think again. Your life could end at any time, day or night, regardless of your age, leaving your dependents or extended family with expenses that could reach beyond their means. Burial expenses come to mind. Today, the average cost of a funeral, including the cemetery grave plot and headstone, ranges between $7,000 and $15,000 depending on your location. Add some upgrades like a fancy coffin and elaborate headstone, and the cost of your goodbye will run closer to $20,000.

There are several forms of life insurance. The most common, and the lowest in price, is called term life insurance, which is what most employers provide for their employees. It terminates as soon as you are fired. Purchasing term life insurance should be a priority for all let-go workers. It is readily available from any number of life insurance companies at reasonable cost. Conduct an online search for low-cost term life insurance and purchase it immediately. Dying is not cheap. Death never takes a vacation. Plan accordingly.

The following story illustrates how risky life is.

Linda's Story

I recruited Linda for a job as a reading consultant with an educational publisher where I was regional sales manager for the Northeastern United States. Linda excelled in her job and was sought after by school districts implementing their new reading programs.

Linda belonged to a number of fine and performing arts organizations in Boston. She was an officer in the Junior League and performed volunteer work for the Museum of Fine Arts. Her teenage daughter was her pride and joy and attended only the best private schools.

As Linda entered mid-career, she and her husband frequently took skiing trips to Aspen and Vail in addition to vacations in Europe and the Caribbean. Life was good for Linda. One February, they went on a five-day ski trip to Vail and returned home tired and happy. However, Linda seemed more tired than usual and scheduled an appointment with her doctor to see if she needed a dose of vitamins to keep up her energy level. As a precaution, Linda's doctor ordered lab tests and an abdominal CT scan. He called them "routine." However, the "routine" tests indicated that Linda had pancreatic cancer. Surgery followed, and so did death, seven weeks after diagnosis. Linda possessed intelligence, energy, and passion beyond the ordinary, but death does not play favorites. To this day, Linda is missed by her husband, daughter, friends, and coworkers. They still ask, "How could she have died in the prime of her life without warning?" Rest in peace, Linda.

LONG-TERM DISABILITY INSURANCE (LTD)

The thinking goes something like this: "I don't need LTD insurance, because 'it' will never happen to me." Most of us delude ourselves into thinking that accidents resulting in long-term or permanent disability only happen to the other guy. I fell into this trap in mid-career, too, and but for the guidance of an extraordinary insurance saleswoman, I would not have survived financially. Here's my story.

My Story (Chicken Man)

It was a beautiful early-autumn morning, and I was riding my bike through a rural area in suburban Philadelphia. The area was dotted with small farms, some of which raised chickens. While riding past a farmhouse with chicken coops nearly reaching the road, a bantam chicken darted from weeds growing along the shoulder and ran into the front wheel of my bike. I had no time to outmaneuver this fast-moving beast, and down I went. I suffered a fractured pelvis, a torn rotator cuff, a concussion (despite wearing a helmet), and multiple lacerations, contusions, and abrasions. I was partially disabled for eight months following fourteen days in the hospital, surgery, and intensive physical therapy. During that time, I had no income or disability payments from my employer. The expenses, however, continued as usual. I was responsible for home mortgage payments, car payments, insurance payments, food, clothing, medicine, and more. You get the picture.

Here is how the insurance industry rescued "Chicken Man," as a TV reporter who put my story on the 11 p.m. Philadelphia news called me. I would have defaulted on the mortgage and car loan but for an LTD insurance policy that I had purchased from Northwestern Mutual Insurance Co. and which had become effective only three days before the accident. That policy covered almost 100 percent of my expenses during my disability. Without it, I could not have survived financially. Here's the rest of the story:

Joanne, my insurance agent who sold me life insurance and homeowners insurance, had been after me for months to buy an LTD insurance policy because my employer did not provide it. I told her that I was in good health and did not participate in dangerous pursuits like mountain climbing or skydiving, so my chance of ever needing LTD insurance was minimal.

"Wrong," she said. "On any given day, you could be hit by a truck and become incapacitated for the rest of your life. Long-term disability is more important than life insurance for individuals with family responsibilities. Chances of incurring long-term disability for a middle-aged person are much greater than dying." I refused to listen to Joanne, but she kept after me until in a moment of frustration I said, "Okay, Joanne. Get off my case! Write up the policy and don't bug me anymore." She did just that, and three days after it went into effect, I was hit not by the proverbial truck but by the chicken. To this day, I thank Joanne for taking the time to educate me about the risks we face every day . . . like getting hit by a chicken.

Many insurers provide LTD coverage, but most are for group plans through employers. Two companies that provide individual LTD insurance are Northwestern Mutual (NorthwesternMutual.com) and Unum (Unum.com). Go online and check out their LTD options and prices.

KEY TAKEAWAYS

- Apply for COBRA medical insurance immediately after being separated from your company.
- Consider an Obamacare or private medical insurance policy as an alternative to COBRA.
- Death takes no holidays.
- According to the National Highway Traffic Administration, an automobile accident occurs every sixty seconds.
- LTD and life insurance are equally important for all workers regardless of age.

PRINT AND DIGITAL RESOURCES

- For detailed information on COBRA, visit COBRAinsurance.com.
- The United States Bureau of Labor Statistics (BLS.gov)
- For information about the costs associated with your funeral, go to Parting.com.
- For information about funeral insurance, visit

FuneralWise.com/plan/costs.
- For current information about disability insurance policies, go to Insure.com/disability-insurance.
- For information and updates about the Affordable Care Act, go to Healthcare.gov.
- For information about dental insurance, go to DentalPlans.com.
- "Life Insurance: What It Is, How it Works, and How to Buy a Policy" on Investopedia.com

CHAPTER 21

FAMILY MATTERS DO MATTER

Our workforce is almost evenly divided between men and women, and contrary to popular opinion, women and men lose their jobs at the same rate. When employers need to shed personnel, gender, race, and ethnicity are not a determining issue.

Women and men face similar challenges after being let go. As they finish the grieving process and begin moving forward to a new career, they encounter hurdles involving childcare, aging parent care, separation or divorce, and education. Adding these issues to the mix makes the process of career hunting very challenging. Working in a job with required regular hours, say eight to five, leaves little time to address family responsibilities, continue professional development, and enjoy personal pursuits. One alternative is to seek part-time job opportunities with companies catering to workers who need flexible hours. Other alternatives include working in sales positions focused on insurance, real estate, or automobiles, all of which offer flexible hours. And let's not forget about jobs that can be worked from home. Remote work has benefits for both employers and employees. Many workers find this attractive. In fact, Stanford economist Nicholas Bloom revealed that the average worker values working from home and is willing to give up about 8 percent of their wages to exercise this option.[18]

Let's examine each challenge and explore solutions.

THE CHILDCARE CHALLENGE

When a worker is laid off, the family income stream is severed, in whole or in part. Though there might be a continuing income stream from a spouse's job, something has to give. Expenses across the board must be adjusted. Usually, the person at home, the one unemployed, picks up the slack. Adding these responsibilities to the process of finding another job is frustrating because there are only so many hours in a day. Not fair? Sorry. That's just the way it is, so let's move forward and deal with it.

With children at the K–12 level, the challenges revolve around getting them to and from school, making sure they complete homework assignments, meeting with teachers to discuss the children's progress or problems, and transporting them to and from recreational events. All these responsibilities exist in addition to caring for the children's day-to-day physical and emotional needs. Working women and men can share these responsibilities or outsource them, but that is a costly proposition.

The Childcare Solution

Nothing happens without a plan. Your first initiative should be crafting an hourly written plan that you can refer to every day. Block out those hours you will spend seeking new employment, even if it means letting household chores take a back seat. (It is too easy to become distracted by household matters that shout for attention.) If your spouse has concerns about how you care for the kids while career hunting, construct a plan to pick up

---

18   Daniel de Visé, "How much is that remote job worth to you? Americans will part with pay to work from home," *USA Today*, October 16, 2023, https://www.usatoday.com/story/money/2023/10/16/americans-save-money-by-working-from-home/71140252007/.

the slack. One or the other might not like doing some routine childcare chores, but you are in this together.

During this unemployment hiatus, you can't possibly do it all yourself. What happens when you are going to a trade show or meeting with a network contact, or when you go to an interview? Again, you go back to the plan. When it is necessary to leave the house, you will need a backup to handle the childcare responsibilities. The key is to plan for these outside-the-home events in advance, even while you are still employed. Line up help from your spouse, neighbors, friends, parents, or grandparents. Most people, including your spouse, are willing to lend a hand to someone in need as long as the request for help is timely. When you need help, say so.

If you can't resolve the childcare issues with "free" help, sit down with your spouse and make a financial plan that includes paying for outside help with the children. This could mean a reallocation of discretionary dollars to childcare dollars, which may be uncomfortable, but remember that this is temporary. When you find another job, you can reconstruct your budget to include formal childcare payments.

THE AGING PARENT CHALLENGE

All of us can cite examples where a mid-career worker is faced with caring for an aging parent or a parent who has contracted a debilitating illness such as Alzheimer's. This is a serious challenge for everyone. Unfortunately, illness has no respect for your time or the fact that you are temporarily unemployed.

The Aging Parent Solution

If the parent in need is at home and needs periodic nurse visits or transportation to and from the doctor or hospital, build that into your plan. If your parent-care schedule conflicts with your eighth grader's basketball schedule, the child will need to make an exception for the grandparent in need. Bring children into the picture by prioritizing events in order of importance. Counsel them that caring for a family member comes before a basketball game, no exceptions.

When the aging parent situation becomes severe, some opt to seek only part-time employment. As an alternative to seeking another full-time job, consider part-time work to make all the moving parts—parent care, childcare, income stream, and work–life balance—work together.

THE MARITAL DIVORCE OR SEPARATION CHALLENGE

While exiting an unhappy marriage can be a liberating experience, it can pose a challenge for anyone who has been fired. When this event occurs, two factors come into play: finances and responsibilities. Some studies show that job loss adds to divorce challenges. What all of this means is that the divorced spouse now has to deal with both the trauma accompanying divorce and the trauma of losing a job. It's a challenging situation, but there are solutions.

The Marital Divorce or Separation Solution

The most pressing challenge for those divorced is to maintain self-confidence. All need to reaffirm their ability to move forward and rebuild their career into something that will provide income, job satisfaction, and work–life balance, all while trying to sort out the divorce or separation. Many workers in this situation opt to sit at home, firing off résumés to everywhere, expecting that job interviews and job offers will follow. That is the least productive method for finding a job and soon leads to depression. There is an alternative.

The best way to find a new career, and avoid depression, is to leave the house and attend trade shows at nearby convention centers. There you will find hundreds of potential employers under one roof and opportunities to make new friends, build your professional network, and expand your work horizons. Even if the trade show is not focusing on your area of expertise or interest, attend just the same. A new environment frequently reveals interests and abilities never before imagined. You will find a nationwide list of convention centers in the appendix of this book.

But what about the divorce? Dealing with a double whammy is a real bummer, and both are calling for your attention. We suggest focusing on the job first because in our culture, a job confers self-esteem, a sense of identity, respect, dignity, and financial independence, all of which are invaluable in resolving uncomfortable issues. When you have a job, even a job that is not exactly what you would like, you will be able to work through the divorce or separation with more confidence and resolve. When you are out of work, you are just plain-vanilla Bob Jones. When you have a job, you could be Bob Jones, director of marketing for Ajax Software. There is a world of difference.

THE EDUCATION CHALLENGE

It happens like this. You graduated from college with an AA, BA, or MA and proceed to an entry-level job. You work with this employer for five years and receive two promotions. Now you are working at the managerial level. Unexpectedly, one of your competitors comes to you with a job offer for a senior management–level position and an increase in compensation that puts you in the low six-figure income bracket. *Nice*, you think. *Getting that college degree was a smart move on my part.* So far, so good. You get married and have two children whose care takes up all your nonworking hours. Ten years later you are still at the same company and have been promoted to a director-level position. Now you are making an annual base salary of $135,000 plus benefits, bonus, and eligibility for the company profit-sharing program. Life is good. Then one ordinary day, it happens. Your company is purchased by a competitor, and your position is eliminated.

Now you are out looking and have had only two interviews after three months of job searching. During an interview the hiring manager tells you that your education background, especially in technology applications and AI, is very weak compared to other candidates. She asks if you have taken any professional development courses recently. Your negative answer seals your fate. It is not that you were unaware of changes taking place in the workplace. You saw it coming but just did not have the time to update your skills. How could you? After all, the non-working spouse still has responsibility for taking care of the kids. Not fair? That's just the way it is. Suck it up and move forward.

The Education Solution

Much has changed since you received your last college degree, especially on the technology front. Younger and less experienced candidates have education credentials reflecting the change in workplace requirements. Before being let go, begin taking certified online courses to bridge the gap, particularly in the technology area focusing on AI. Make sure that your coursework provides written certification that you can present to potential employers. You can find certified courses by conducting an online search.

In my recruiting business, I have noted that many employers are requiring candidates for senior-level management positions to have project management professional training (PMP). PMP training is available online from many sources. One is the Project Management Institute (PMI.org), the world's largest source for training. It boasts 500,000 members and 280 local chapters. Another online source for certification is Villanova University (VillanovaU.com/PMP).

KEY TAKEAWAYS

➤ There are many part-time job opportunities for working mothers and fathers.
➤ Attending trade shows is the best job-hunting strategy for rebuilding careers.
➤ Education skills must be updated continually, especially technology skills.
➤ The workplace is changing fast because of the use of AI.
➤ Sales jobs frequently offer flexible hours and work schedules.
➤ Plan your work. Work your plan.

PRINT AND DIGITAL RESOURCES

➤ *Fortune* magazine (Fortune.com)
➤ "Best Companies for Working Mothers" on WorkingMothers.com
➤ *The Book of Federal Government Jobs: Where They Are, What's Available, and How to Complete a Federal Resume* by Dennis Damp
➤ *Occupational Outlook Handbook* by the US Department of Labor (DoL.gov)

CHAPTER 22

RÉSUMÉS, INTERVIEWS, AND AI

Terminated workers frequently worry about preparing a new résumé and preparing for an interview. The basic rules for the résumé and interview are virtually the same whether you are employed or unemployed and seeking new opportunities.

When pursuing a career while unemployed, use the same rubrics for résumés and interviews that you would use if employed. You will find them in chapters 6 and 7 of this book. Assuming that you have selected an industry you like, you will find an employer with a career offering made just for you. Remember that the US is the job basket of the world. It does not get better than that . . . even after you have been terminated.

THE RÉSUMÉ

To learn how to craft your résumé, go to chapter 6, "Crafting a Résumé and Digital Profile While Employed." Here you will learn how to prepare a résumé that will get you in the door for an interview.

There are two additional items to add when unemployed:
- Be honest.
- You do not need to state your reason for being terminated. You will handle that in the interview.

THE INTERVIEW

The interview is the most important part of your search for a new career. Prepare for it by following the rubrics in chapter 7, "Conquering the Interview While Employed."

Some additional considerations for preparing for an interview after being fired:

- ➤ The interviewer will ask why you were fired or laid off. Answer truthfully. Do not skirt the issue.
- ➤ Do not disparage your previous employer (s).

CHAPTER 23

OVERCOMING OPPOSITION TO YOUR CANDIDACY

Job candidates who have been fired or laid off report that potential employers frequently voice three objections to their candidacy:

- "Sorry! You are overqualified."
- "Sorry! You are lacking education requirements."
- "Sorry! Your compensation requirements are too high."

Sometimes these are unrealistic or perceptual objections. Sometimes they are accurate. Whatever the case, you must be prepared to deal with these objections in your virtual or personal interviews. Let's do some background work to see why these objections are raised.

Workers who have been let go often have attained the rank of manager, director, vice president, or president. Moving forward, they assume the next job should be equal to or above their last job in title, rank, and compensation. This appears to make good sense, but it does not always happen that way.

Here's an example from my personal experience when I was working on the corporate side. I was an editor with a Philadelphia publishing company. The job seemed promising, but after six months I learned that the company was dysfunctional and heading toward bankruptcy. I decided to leave the company and found an attractive opportunity with another publisher that was a step below a lateral move. I truly liked the company, the job, and the hiring manager who would be my boss. However, he raised the overqualified objection, and I was rejected.

The hiring manager said he could not "risk" hiring me. I probed for his reasons. He feared that I was willing to move down a notch only to get out of a bad situation, and that as soon as something better came about, I would leave. When I tried to overcome this objection, he stood firm in his decision not to hire me. My job hunting continued, and soon I connected with an employer that did not have that objection. A footnote to my story: The publisher I left filed for bankruptcy six months later, and all employees were let go. My story illustrates what can happen to any worker regardless of previous employment status.

SORRY! YOU ARE OVERQUALIFIED

The overqualified objection usually is raised during the personal interview. Most candidates never see it coming. They assume that the hiring manager would be delighted to have an experienced candidate who could be productive on day one.

A typical situation finds the candidate, a let-go worker at the mid-management level, interviewing for a job titled "director." It seems to be a lateral move, and the candidate feels confident that this will work. Toward the end of the interview the hiring manager says, "Mary, you have all the qualifications listed in the job description, and there is no doubt you can do the job. However, you have more experience than we need for this job. In short, I think you are overqualified." This jarring statement leaves you scrambling for a lucid response. Here are possible responses you can offer to the hiring manager when this happens to you.

Responses to the Overqualified Objection

Your first reaction might be disappointment accompanied by a sharp verbal response with negative body language: "That's ridiculous. My twenty years of experience in this industry should put me at the top of your list." Such a reaction will seal your fate: disqualification. Here are responses that might overcome the overqualified objection and keep the conversation moving forward.

- "Thank you for recognizing my background and experience. Moving forward, I think the depth and breadth of my experience would be valuable to your cause. I could help take some of the pressure from your job and make your life easier. Combine your knowledge of the company culture and operations with my depth and breadth of experience, and together we could take this department to a higher level. I think we would make a great team."
- "I understand why you might feel that I'm overqualified. I'm flattered that you have given that much thought to my candidacy. However, rest assured that I will not use my experience to steamroll your status and authority in the department. I'm not after your job. I'm looking for work–life balance and believe that I can find that here. I think we would make a great team."
- "I might bring more to the table than you need right now, but I assure you that I'm not looking for just another paycheck until I find something better. I've targeted your company for its stability, profitability, and employee-friendly culture. I think we would make a great team."
- "I'm looking for more than a paycheck and job title. You could use my experience to your advantage. In addition, I like you personally, and I think we would make a great team."

> "I can understand why you might feel that way. However, my qualifications, particularly in the technology sphere and AI, could be of value to the company going forward. AI is moving at lightning speed, and I can help the company keep up with the rest of the pack. In addition, I reviewed your profile on LinkedIn and believe our tech skills are complementary. I think we would make a great team."

You may have noticed that each of the responses was positive and included a statement about working together as a team. When a potential boss is confronted by a candidate whose background, experience, and qualifications exceed theirs, the survival instinct kicks in. They could see you as a competitor for their job. Human beings are in survival mode every waking hour without even realizing it.

The best way to allay the fears of your potential boss is to learn their background and experience to find common and complementary attributes and interests. Articulate that at the beginning of the interview to begin building a friendly relationship. Remember one of the cardinal rules of *Hired! Fired! Retired!*: Friends hire friends.

SORRY! YOU ARE LACKING EDUCATION REQUIREMENTS

Most job descriptions include education requirements, like a college degree, but that should not stop you from applying. Many job descriptions are written by HR directors and not hiring managers, who want to know your skills and achievements.

The Education Solution

In today's workplace, your skills and experience are more

important than having a college degree, unless the job requires very specific knowledge in topics like engineering and medicine to get the job done. I've noticed that many job descriptions now state "college degree or *equivalent*." Employers recognize that your job skills and experience are more important than a BA after your name.

On your résumé and in your interview, state your specific formal education plus all your online and informal education experience. Emphasize technology education, especially AI experience. The hiring manager is forward-looking and will not disqualify you if your education does not include a BA you received twenty years ago.

For more information on education requirements, review the material in chapter 21, "Family Matters Do Matter."

SORRY! YOUR COMPENSATION REQUIREMENTS EXCEED OUR BUDGET

Compensation is a serious issue for workers searching for a new job. The expectation is that you should get what you made in your last job, or more. Assume the base salary in your last job, business development manager, was $95,000 a year plus benefits. Going forward into job-hunting mode, that is the number you have in mind when you begin talking with potential employers. However, is this a realistic expectation?

Research indicates that salary expectations are related to several factors, one being age. Workers under forty, those in early mid-career, are more optimistic than older workers that they will find acceptable compensation packages. Younger workers usually have lower daily expenses and can afford to take a lower salary. Their tendency to take less makes their candidacy more appealing to potential employers. Workers over forty have more expenses and require more compensation to meet their needs.

For laid-off or fired workers seeking new employment, there is another factor at play: their ego. Being let go is a devastating event, and terminated workers subconsciously make every effort to salvage their self-respect. For example, when Ed is laid off from his manager-level job paying a base of $110,000, his pride might not permit him to accept a job paying $95,000.

Responses to the Compensation Objection

Facing reality will save much time and angst and hasten the job-hunting process. There is nothing that will delay finding employment more than the entitled belief *I will not take less than $105,000, no matter what. That's what I made in my last job, and that's what I should get in my next job.* That is not reality in our workplace. What follows is a true-life example of what can happen if you are delusional about compensation.

George's Story

One day in early January, George, a mid-career worker from Philadelphia, came to my office. He was well dressed, articulate, and exuded an air of confidence. After pleasant introductory remarks, he said that he had been working for a software company as an outbound sales representative for the past ten years and thought that he had earned a ticket to lifetime employment. However, one afternoon the human resources director called George in for a chat. He told George the company was being purchased by a competitor. It was an asset acquisition, and therefore his job was being eliminated. George was laid off that day and never saw it coming.

Now he was on the street looking for another sales position. His annual base salary was $100,000, and commissions averaged $80,000 per year, total compensation $180,000. George asked me to keep him on my list for job opportunities in a sales position in the technology industry. I asked him about compensation expectations, and George told me he would not accept a penny less than his previous package. He expected a base of $100,000 and commissions that would average $80,000 per year.

Knowing compensation numbers for such a position with companies in the area, I told George that his expectation was unrealistic; positions of that type were paying an average base of $80,000, and commission plans varied greatly. George did not like what I said and gave me a litany of reasons for his expectations. Four months later, George called to see what was happening. I told him that I did not have anything meeting his expectations and urged him to become more reasonable. In December of that same year, he came to my office again to inquire about job opportunities. It had been almost a full year since he had been laid off, and he was still unemployed. Once again, I told him what the market was paying, but once again, he would not lower compensation demands. Talking reason with George was unsuccessful. After implying that I did not know my job, he left the office in a huff. George from Philadelphia was still unemployed after almost a year of job hunting because he was delusional about his worth in the job market at that time.

George's story illustrates two points: Workers must be prepared to make compromises on compensation based on market conditions, and workers must do their homework about compensation levels for their type of job. What George forgot is that the job market had changed over the past ten years.

Here are three compensation rubrics for all let-go workers to follow as they enter job-hunting mode.

➤ Be open to compromise on compensation. We do not live in an entitlement business culture.
➤ There is no guarantee that you will exceed rank, title, and compensation once you have reached a certain

point in your career. It does not work that way in the US or other countries.
- Research compensation levels for job categories, remembering that compensation frequently varies by geography. A managerial position might average $150,000 per year in California, where the cost of living is very high, and $120,000 in Maine, where the cost of living is much lower.

KEY TAKEAWAYS
- Before having your first virtual or personal interview, plan how you will deal with the three most frequently encountered issues: overqualification, education, and compensation.
- Overqualification is frequently a matter of perception on the part of the hiring manager.
- Additional education, especially in AI, will help meet or exceed education requirements.
- Compensation is a matter of negotiation.
- Verify everything, especially money matters.

PRINT AND DIGITAL RESOURCES
- Project Management Institute (PMI.org)
- Bureau of Labor Statistics (BLS.gov)
- The United States Census Bureau (Census.gov)
- *The Occupational Outlook Handbook* by the US Department of Labor

CHAPTER 24

FINDING EMPLOYMENT AT JOB FAIRS, CONVENTIONS, TRADE SHOWS, OFFICE PARKS, AND ONLINE

Finding employers in your chosen field is a task that will prove interesting and successful if you use tried-and-true strategies. The best way is to attend trade shows, conferences, and job fairs. Additional methods include using online digital technology and personally visiting business, industrial, and office parks.

FINDING EMPLOYERS AT JOB FAIRS

Attending job fairs is an excellent way to meet potential employers and their hiring managers. There are hundreds of fairs available throughout the year, some at locations within driving distance of your home. Some job fairs are general in nature, and others are industry specific, job specific, and candidate specific. For example, some job fairs are exclusively for military veterans. Select your area of interest and attend.

The managers you meet at job fairs have one objective in mind: To find the best candidates for their company job openings. It is all business, so you must go prepared, just as you would when attending a trade show. That means bringing a dozen résumés and a hundred calling cards and dressing appropriately in business attire. No jeans and a sweatshirt! How you dress could take you to the top of the heap or put you in the trash can.

FINDING EMPLOYERS AT CONFERENCES AND TRADE SHOWS

The best places to find potential employers in the flesh are convention centers where trade shows are held. Here you will find a multitude of potential employers, all under one roof. I know from firsthand experience that many candidates have met their potential employers on the floor of a convention center; in fact, candidates have even been hired on the floor. You will not find a more productive use of your job-hunting time and effort.

What Is a Trade Show?

A trade show is a gathering of workers from companies in a specific industry. The purpose of a trade show is to give companies an opportunity to display their products and advertise their services in exhibit booths.

Trade shows go by different names: conventions, conferences, exhibits, expos, trade fairs, or trade exhibitions. All mean the same thing. Usually, they are held at convention centers, which are located in cities. Sometimes they meet in hotels or resorts that have large rooms for hosting exhibits and smaller rooms to host "breakout sessions," where industry experts present new products or discuss research and industry trends. Industry organizations sponsor these shows, which can be very costly. Some of those costs are defrayed by member dues and by conference attendance fees, which can be found on the website for the conference in question.

Attending trade shows is the most productive strategy for job hunting, but it is a process. Do you know where to go and what to do once you find yourself in a convention hall?

Preparation Checklist for Attending a Trade Show

One does not just show up at a trade show and expect miracles to happen. To reap maximum benefits, plan for it in advance. Here are some notes and suggestions for planning purposes.

- Many shows hold exhibits only on specific days and at specific hours. For example, the dates listed for the Consumer Electronics Show (CES), the technology conference in Las Vegas, may be January 10 to 16, but the exhibits could be open only on January 11 to 15, from 10 a.m. to 6 p.m. You can find this information online or by calling the conference center or the organization hosting the show. This is important because your primary goal is to visit exhibit booths, where you will find hiring managers.
- The organization sponsoring the conference will publish the list of companies in attendance in the printed conference program. Frequently the directory will include the names of the representatives who will be attending, along with their contact information, and these might be key executives and hiring managers. Obtain this list either online or at the conference center.
- Bring at least a hundred business cards and twenty résumés to the show each day. The exchange of business cards is still an acceptable way to build your list of networking contacts.
- When you enter the conference center to attend the show, first go to the registration desk to pay the exhibit fee, obtain your name tag, and pick up the conference program, which is usually tucked in a tote bag. Make sure you get the conference program. Always wear your name tag while walking the convention floor.
- Almost all shows charge a fee for attendance. Many large trade shows, which are open to the public, charge

very low entrance fees, in the $25 to $50 range. Fees may vary with the number of days you will attend, your affiliation, and your work status. Sometimes there is a steep discount for veterans and students. Ask for this discount at the registration desk.

- If you are coming from a distance and plan to stay overnight near the conference center, make hotel reservations well in advance. If the conference center is in a large city like Chicago, local hotel rates will be quite steep. Find a hotel or motel just out of town at a more reasonable room rate and then drive or Uber to the conference center each day. In addition, some conference organizations negotiate lower room rates with hotels and motels in the area, so always check this online several months in advance.
- Dress at trade shows is usually upscale casual, but as a job candidate you should always be dressed as though you were going for an interview. You are there to sell your candidacy and should dress with that in mind.

What You Do at a Trade Show

Are you ready for a bit of fun? Here you can have a good time in a very relaxed environment and meet hundreds of full-time company workers, many of whom will be hiring managers. They typically conduct business in a pleasant way. People working in the various exhibit booths will often be dressed informally, wearing a casual shirt bearing the name of the company and the company logo. Remember, however, that you are not a worker here, and you should be in casual business attire.

After you register and get your name tag, enter the exhibit hall and begin visiting each booth. You might start your booth visits in the first aisle and proceed around the hall until you have stopped at each booth. If there are hundreds of exhibits, this may take two or even three days. Exhibit halls are crowded with customers who are there to get product information and to visit company representatives.

What to Say After You Say Hello

When you enter an exhibit booth, view the products on display and ask one of the representatives to explain what the company does. Establish a personal relationship by learning what the person's job is and how they like working for the company. After you establish the relationship, tell the person you are job hunting and ask to speak with a hiring manager. If you are interested in marketing and the director of marketing is not there for some reason, ask for that person's name and contact information, and follow up with a phone call or email when you return to your home office.

If all of this is new to you, below is a script you might use to break the ice and get in the game, remembering that workers are eager to help a person looking for a job. Establish the relationship by addressing the worker by name, which is always on the name tag.

Script for Talking with a Company Representative at a Trade Show

The premise: You are visiting a booth at a conference, and you initiate a conversation with a representative named Tom. Here's how you might proceed:

"Hello, Tom. My name is Olga, and I'm here for two reasons and would appreciate your help. First, I would like to know more about your company and what you do. Second, I'm seeking employment and would like to see the hiring manager for marketing if this person is attending the conference. If not, would you please write their name and contact information on the back of your business card for me? Also, could you give me the name and contact information for the company human resources director? Thanks, Tom."

Before you leave the exhibit booth, give your business card to your new contact and write on the back, "Seeking employment and would appreciate your help."

If the hiring manager you want to see is in the booth, request a few minutes for an informal interview and give that person your résumé. The way to get this moving without feeling awkward is to say something like this: "Mary, here's my résumé, and if you have the time now, maybe you could take a minute to review it. I'm looking for a job opportunity in marketing, and being in mid-career, I have a wealth of experience. If you don't have time now, could we make an appointment to chat for a few minutes, maybe over a cup of coffee or lunch? My treat, of course."

Where the Hiring Managers and Recruiters Hang Out

The big guys, the hiring managers, always attend trade shows and conventions in order to meet their key customers, to keep up with industry trends, and to recruit workers for all levels of employment. Recruiters, too, often attend these shows to prospect for new clients, workers for open positions, or qualified candidates to place in their database for future reference. I have attended hundreds of conferences to recruit job candidates and seek new clients. I have never been disappointed. In the job-hunting world, trade shows and exhibits are the promised land. Visiting these shows is the best way to search for a new job as you rebuild your career after being fired or laid off.

How to Recognize a Hiring Manager

In exhibit booths and on the convention center floor, you will see people dressed in formal business attire or upscale casual attire. Often, these are the company executives, the people you need to meet. Lacking an introduction, you just have to wing it.

Walk up to that person and say something like "I can tell by the way you're dressed that you must be running the show here. My name is John, and I'm here job hunting. I'm looking for a sales position. Could you steer me in the right direction? I would really appreciate your help."

This person will appreciate your sense of humor and the subtle note of respect and recognition. The odds of getting a positive response are in your favor because business execs remember when they were in your position and are willing to lend a hand to a worker seeking new opportunities.

Lunch Is a Time for Networking

On the convention center floor, there will be formal restaurants, kiosks selling hot dogs and soft drinks, and sometimes bars selling alcoholic drinks. This is another place to meet people. After you buy a burger and a Coke, find a table that is partially occupied. Take a seat, introduce yourself to the person next to you, and go into your sales pitch. Lunch is not just lunch; it is a networking opportunity. Never select an empty table, whip out your smartphone, and begin texting and tweeting. Never. Why waste your time and money tweeting when you could be meeting potential employers?

Thirsty for a Cold Beer?

Convention center restaurants frequently sell alcoholic drinks. Never buy them. Do not even think about it. A cardinal rule is never to drink anything alcoholic while job hunting, even if others around you are. You are there on business, not to throw down a beer or a malbec. Hiring managers could be sizing up your personal habits. Company managers do not hire candidates who drink while job hunting. The same rules apply to using any form of controlled substance.

TOP CONVENTION CENTERS AND TRADE SHOWS

There are hundreds of convention centers across the US, at least one in every state. Some are well-known centers like McCormick Place in Chicago and the Moscone Center in San Francisco. In addition, large hotels like the Marriott in Philadelphia often serve as convention centers.

Go online for a listing of trade shows that will convene at a specific center. For example, I reviewed the website for the Javits Center in New York and found the dates for the New York Travel Show and the New York Boat Show, both of which attract thousands of visitors. There are hundreds of exhibit booths at the travel show alone, each hosting a company that is a potential employer. If you are interested in the travel or boating industry, these two trade shows could be your pipeline to job opportunities found nowhere else.

Finding Jobs with Convention Centers

When you review the conference center website, always check out the center's career postings. Convention centers like McCormick Place are profit-making organizations and employ many workers across all specialties. These are good full-time jobs in sales, marketing, technology, finance, and human resources. When attending a conference, go to the conference center offices and inquire about job opportunities.

Hotels that habitually host trade shows often have built-in conference facilities and similar job openings. The most popular hotels hosting conventions are the Sheraton, Hyatt, Marriott, and Hilton.

A complete list of major convention centers, and their contact information, appears in the appendix of this book. Be sure to check it out.

Having attended hundreds of trade shows across the country, I know the top sites and trade shows and would like to share them with you. A number of state convention centers and trade shows deserve special attention because of their strategic locations and the important conferences they attract. Here are my faves.

In California

The Moscone Center (Moscone.com), located in the heart of San Francisco, hosts some of the largest conventions. In recent years it attracted the National Auto Dealers Association, the Molecular Medicine Convention, the RSA Cybersecurity show, and numerous "green" conferences dealing with environmental products and services.

In Florida

The Orange County Convention Center (OCCC.net) in Orlando is one of busiest convention centers in the world, hosting national and international conferences. There are two separate facilities a block apart, and each can accommodate tens of thousands of visitors at one time. The convention halls are massive, so be prepared for a lot of walking. Conventions to attend here are the Orlando Home Show, the Florida Educational Technology Conference, and the PGA Golf Industry Show. The Golf Industry Show attracts hundreds of companies, each a potential employer and all gathered under one roof. Attendance usually runs over 50,000. Do you like the sporting industry? Attend the golf show.

The Tampa Convention Center (TampaConventionCenter.com) is one of the premier conference centers in the Southeast. It accommodates medium-sized conferences that attract hundreds of companies exhibiting their products and services. Its location is on the waterfront in Downtown Tampa.

The Miami Beach Convention Center (MiamiBeachConvention.com) hosts the largest jewelry show in the Americas each year. It is sponsored by the Jewelers International Showcase and features three shows annually that attract thousands of exhibitors and thousands of attendees from fifty countries in the Caribbean, Latin America, and North America. A recent show had approximately 1,200 exhibit booths! If you like gold, silver, diamonds, rubies, and pearls, this is the place to find a job in the jewelry industry.

In Georgia

The Atlanta Convention Center (AtlConventionCenter.com) facility, at more than 800,000 square feet, attracts many national and international trade shows each year, including the franchise trade show and the women's beauty and fashion trade show called CASA.

In Hawaii

The Hawaii Convention Center (MeetHawaii.com) is a one-million-square-foot center just down the street from the famed Waikiki beach and is one of the best of its kind in the world. It holds many large and small conferences throughout the year, many of them with exhibitions staffed by key employees, like hiring managers.

The convention center itself employs full-time sales reps, a complete staff of IT workers, and an active marketing department. Check out the careers, listed under "Jobs," on their website.

Ready for some sun, surf, and a luau on weekends after convention hours? That's working in Hawaii. Does it get any better than that?

In Illinois

McCormick Place (McCormickPlace.com), located on the shore of Lake Michigan in Chicago, is the largest convention facility in North America. This convention center is one of the most popular in the country because of its central location. Some of the shows it has hosted are the Progressive Insurance Boat Show, the International Home and Housewares Show, and the National Restaurant Show.

Go to the website and click on the show title, and it will take you to that particular website. You will find all the information you need, including the names and addresses of hundreds of companies that will be exhibiting.

In Indiana

The Indianapolis Convention Center (ICCLOS.com) hosts many national and regional conferences representing all industries. Its central location and reasonable attendance fees make it a popular destination.

One of the most important regional conferences held here is the Indiana Bankers Association Annual Convention. I checked out a recent conference, and it listed all the attending banks, many of which were national financial institutions. And it listed the names of the attendees from each bank. Pay dirt!

In Iowa

The Iowa Events Center (IowaEventsCenter.com) brings together under one roof manufacturers and dealers of farming equipment and agricultural products, all of which are potential job targets. If you are interested in agribusiness, where better to find a job than in Iowa?

When I reviewed the Iowa Events Center website, I found an interesting array of job opportunities in marketing, sales, events management, and food/beverage operations.

In New York

The Javits Convention Center, (JavitsCenter.com) is one of the best-known convention centers in the world and attracts an impressive array of important conventions. Companies that exhibit here always send their executives and hiring managers, making the Javits one of the best venues for job hunting.

The largest and one of the most interesting trade shows in the US is NY NOW, a retailers and designers trade show focusing on home and lifestyle companies from all over the world. Attending this conference is not only a good job-hunting experience but also an interesting learning experience.

In Washington, DC

The Walter E. Washington Convention Center (EventsDC.com) is one of the most frequently used convention centers for regional and national trade shows and exhibits. It hosts annual events such as the National Book Festival and the USA Science and Engineering Festival. Check the website frequently because conventions in Washington draw copious vendors and attendees. Hiring managers and top-level executives of major companies attend DC conventions.

In addition, many large DC hotels, such as the Marriott, Holiday Inn, and Hilton, host trade shows, and I suggest checking their websites for conference information. If you cannot find information online, call the hotel and ask to speak with the conference manager.

BEST TRADE SHOWS FOR JOB HUNTING BY INDUSTRY

The following list of annual trade shows by industry could be your ticket to finding a new career path after being fired or laid off. Check out the show nearest to your location or those focused on a particular area of interest.

To get you started, I'm focusing on only eight industries:

food, clothing, shelter, education, insurance, healthcare, transportation, and technology.

Food

This huge industry includes everything imaginable, including fast foods, beverages, restaurants, online grocery shopping, and hospitality. There are many local, regional, and national conventions catering to the food industry. Here are two you may want to explore:

At the International Restaurant and Food Service Show (InternationalRestaurantNY.com), held at the Javits Center in New York, you can meet 16,000 workers representing 500 exhibiting companies. The convention is the best in this market niche.

The National Restaurant Association (NationalRestaurant Show.org) meets at McCormick Place in Chicago each year. How can you beat a convention with 2,000 exhibitors (all potential employers) and 45,000 attendees? If your interest is the restaurant niche, plan to attend this conference. For general information about this part of the food industry, contact the National Restaurant Association or visit their website (Restaurant.org).

Clothing

This industry includes various specialties, like children's clothing, sportswear, women's fashion apparel, textile manufacturing, footwear, and exercise gear, to name a few. There are no national conventions catering to the clothing industry as a whole. The best way to find trade shows in a specialty of the clothing industry is to conduct an online search for your area of interest. One of the best and largest shows for women's accessories is the Apparel Sourcing show held annually at the Javits Center in New York City. Go to 10Times.com/ApparelSourcing for more information.

Shelter

You might recall that one of the three necessities for survival is shelter. Therefore, it is not surprising that there are many home and commercial building shows throughout the US that attract thousands of companies exhibiting their products. Each one is a potential employer. These are found at conference centers throughout the country. If you live in or near the Chicago area, for instance, there are several home shows in different area locations hosting many hundreds of exhibitors. To learn more, visit ChicagoHomeShow.net.

There are so many home shows that it would take many pages to list all of them here. An easy route to find these conferences is to google "home trade shows" in your local area. Sometimes these shows combine home building and improvement companies with garden and horticulture organizations. As an example of what you will find, I'll highlight just two.

The National Association of Home Builders (NAHB) (NAHB.com) runs an annual convention called the NAHB International Builders Show. At this show, you will find approximately 1,000 exhibiting companies, all potential employers. If the shelter part of survival intrigues you, attend this show and other home shows that take place in major cities. In addition to providing an opportunity to meet hiring managers or workers who can lead you to them, this show will provide an education about how the shelter industry works in the US. Attend this show or other regional home shows, and your knowledge of the housing industry will increase exponentially.

The Philly Home and Garden Show (PhillyHomeShow.com) takes place in Philly each February and hosts hundreds of exhibitors. Most are local companies, but some are national. While you are there, remember to have one of those famous Philly cheesesteak sandwiches. Also, visit the Philadelphia Art Museum, where you can have your picture taken beside the famous bronze of Rocky. And remember to save a day to visit Independence Hall and the Liberty Bell.

Education

The education industry is truly worker friendly. Many people work in this industry due to a sense of mission, job satisfaction, and attractive compensation. When you attend an education conference, you will meet hiring managers working for companies like College Board, Educational Testing Service, Scholastic, McGraw-Hill, Texas Instruments, and Pearson. Here are some of the best:

Hundreds of companies exhibit at the American Association of School Administrators (AASA.org) show to display their products to school superintendents and other high-level school administrators. The companies attending this convention are publishers and producers of instructional materials, school supply companies, bus companies, insurance companies, security companies, and more.

The American Library Association (ALA.org) conference focuses on books and digital products related to public and school libraries and online education. It is a fascinating show with hundreds of exhibitors from the education, publishing, and online learning industries. When you are on this website, click on "Education and Careers" for job opportunities with the organization.

The International Society for Technology in Education (ISTE.org) show focuses on products and services related to educational technology and meets each June at a different location. If you are interested in an industry that makes a difference, this one is for you. Do not miss it, because here you will find hundreds of exhibitors under one roof. Each is a potential employer.

In addition, there are many curriculum-related education conferences held annually in different locations and sponsored

by the following professional curriculum organizations:
- National Association of Biology Teachers (NABT.org)
- National Council for the Social Studies (NCSS.org)
- National Council for Teachers of English (NCTE.org)
- National Council of Teachers of Mathematics (NCTM.org)
- National Science Teachers Association (NSTA.org)

International Education Book Fairs

There are several international publishing conventions each year. Attending are companies from across the world hosting exhibits staffed by workers who will tell you about job opportunities and provide the names and contact information for hiring managers. Foreign companies may be looking for workers to represent their interests in America, and you might be the one for such a job. Here are some of the best international trade fairs in the publishing industry.

- Frankfurt Book Fair (Buchmesse.de/en). Exhibitors from around the world gather at this largest of all international book fairs, which meets in Frankfurt, Germany, every October. Can you imagine 7,000 exhibitors, each one a potential employer, gathered in one place?
- The London Book Fair (LondonBookFair.co.uk). This major bookseller event meets in London, England, each spring. It attracts close to 1,000 exhibitors, ranging from retail booksellers to educational publishers and communications companies.
- Bologna Children's Book Fair (BolognaChildrensBookFair.com/en/home/878.html). This interesting book fair focuses on products related to elementary school education. Hundreds of companies publishing books and offering digital products exhibit here. Bologna, Italy, is the host city for this annual conference. Check it out if you happen to be in Italy in spring.

Insurance

Insurance of every type is necessary to live as a self-sufficient human being. Like it or not, you need insurance. Many insurance companies have been in business continuously for more than a hundred years and are attractive places for long-term employment. The industry hosts many conventions throughout the calendar year in many different cities.

One of the largest conferences in the industry is sponsored by the National Association of Mutual Insurance Companies (NAMIC.org) at a different location each year. Recent conferences were held at the Gaylord National Resort and Conference Center in National Harbour, Maryland, and at the San Diego Convention Center.

The best place for information about insurance trade shows is the *Insurance Journal*. Visit the website at InsuranceJournal.com.

Healthcare

Under the broadly defined label of "healthcare," there are numerous subgroups: pharmaceuticals, physicians, radiologists, certified nurse midwives, medical equipment producers, physical therapy, medicinal packaging, and the like. There is no large catch-all convention, but there are many small conventions serving segments of the healthcare industry. Many of these conventions are local or regional in scope. Here are some of the professional healthcare organizations sponsoring the larger national conventions:

- Nurse Practitioners in Women's Healthcare (NPWH.org)
- Radiological Society of North America (RSNA.org)
- Healthcare Information and Management Systems Society (HIMSS.org)

- American Society of Clinical Oncology (ASCO.org)
- International Society for Pharmaceutical Engineering, which sponsors the annual Pharma Expo conference (PharmaExpo.com)
- American College of Nurse Midwives (ACNM.org)
- American Physical Therapy Association (APTA.org)

Transportation

Transportation is one of the basics for modern-day living. The transportation industry conducts hundreds of conventions each year in locations throughout the country. Google "auto shows" and add the largest city close to home, and you will find all the information you need. One major transportation show is the New York International Auto Show (AutoShowNY.com). This conference is one of the largest auto shows in the world and hosts hundreds of companies on the floor of the Javits Center. Attend this conference and you will find potential job opportunities in the automobile industry. Guaranteed.

Technology and AI

The world's largest technology show is the CES, which convenes every January at the Las Vegas Convention Center. Attendance at this show can exceed 200,000, including many people from foreign countries. More than 1,000 companies attend and host exhibits at CES. Can you imagine 1,000 potential employers gathered together? If you are interested in technology, including AI, you cannot afford to miss CES. For more information and to register for the next show, visit ConsumerElectronicsShow.com.

AI matters are frequently incorporated into most conferences regardless of industry.

HOW TO FIND A TRADE SHOW CATERING TO A PARTICULAR INTEREST

There are many sources to find conventions matching your interests: industry journals, both print and digital; local newspapers; and convention center schedules. In addition, you will find a trade show directory on the website of Events in America, EventsinAmerica.com/tradeshows. This organization tracks and publicizes the names and locations of industry trade shows across the country.

GOING ONLINE TO FIND EMPLOYERS

Using online resources creatively can yield positive results, but proceed with caution, because online job hunting can steal your time like nothing else.

The best digital employment networking site is LinkedIn.com. For those not familiar with LinkedIn, here is an example of how it works: If you are interested in the broadly defined area of information technology, enter that term in the LinkedIn search box, and you will find the names and contact information for many people in that field. I did that just now by entering "sales managers" and came up with the names of 134 contacts, all of them networking sources and some of them hiring managers. Even better, enter the job title and a company name. For example, "marketing director for Texas Instruments."

Online Job Sites

The most popular online job sites are as follows:
- Indeed (Indeed.com)
- ZipRecruiter (ZipRecruiter.com)
- Career Builder (CareerBuilder.com)
- Monster (Monster.com)
- Simply Hired (SimplyHired.com)
- Robert Half (RobertHalf.com)

- Korn Ferry (KornFerry.com)

Corporate Websites

To learn what's happening at a particular company, like Proctor and Gamble, review their website and check out their career pages. However, do not assume that all available jobs are posted on company websites. Many jobs from entry level to mid-level and up are posted elsewhere or given to recruiters.

When you do respond to a company career-page listing, make sure that you respond to a named person with a title. Sending it to "Employment Manager" is a waste of time. To find the name and contact information for an HR director or department head like the VP of sales, call customer service.

FINDING EMPLOYERS AT OFFICE AND INDUSTRIAL PARKS

In every metropolitan area, you will find office, business, and industrial parks, places where hundreds of companies locate their local offices, regional offices, or home offices. Some parks specialize in one particular industry, while others host companies from different industries. For example, an industrial park in Langhorne, Pennsylvania, specializes in medical offices for both physicians and dentists. An industrial park in Portland, Maine, hosts a diversified group of companies, including J. Weston Walch Publishing Company, a 100-year-old educational publisher.

How do you contact companies in a business or industrial park? Easy. You leave the house at 8 a.m. in your business attire and armed with business cards and a dozen résumés to distribute to hiring managers and human resources directors. You go door-to-door and request a personal meeting with the hiring manager in charge of your field of interest.

One might ask, "Do I make a cold call on every business in the business park?" If you are job hunting for any kind of job regardless of industry or position, the answer is yes. If you are interested only in positions with insurance companies as an underwriter, sales representative, or claims adjuster, narrow the cold calls to insurance companies. You learn who these companies are by reviewing the online directories for that business or office park.

Use the Internet or AI to Find Business Parks

There are many business, office, and industrial parks in every area of the country, and the best way to find out where they are is to google or use ChatGPT to find "business, office, and industrial parks" in your local area. For example, I googled "industrial parks in Houston, Texas" and found the Beltway Industrial Park, where small manufacturing companies are located. Industrial parks in other locations host large manufacturers as well as warehouses and regional offices. If manufacturing is your thing, you can't go wrong by cold-calling companies in an industrial park dedicated to manufacturers.

No matter where you live in the US, you will find office parks and industrial parks located near your home. Does it get any easier?

KEY TAKEAWAYS

- The best place to meet hiring managers and key executives is at conferences, trade shows, and job fairs. Trade shows convene every week in large metropolitan areas.
- Access convention center websites for a list of upcoming trade shows. A list appears in the appendix.
- Dress in business attire while attending trade shows.
- Never drink alcoholic beverages or use controlled substances while job hunting. Never!
- Look for jobs in the "Help Wanted" sections of your local print or online newspapers. They still exist.
- Use AI to look for jobs.

PRINT AND DIGITAL RESOURCES

- Events in America (EventsinAmerica.com/tradeshows)
- Employment Crossing (EmploymentCrossing.com)
- *Hired! Fired! Retired!* appendix. Here you will find a list of major convention centers.

CHAPTER 25

REBUILDING YOUR CAREER BY STARTING YOUR OWN BUSINESS

For most workers seeking a new beginning, the thought of starting a business is intriguing. But how do you toss the first pitch in this ball game? Street talk elevates stories of entrepreneurs who dropped out of college, locked themselves in a garage for a couple of years, and then emerged with a business called Apple Computer, Microsoft, or Virgin Air.

Continue listening to the street, and you hear that it can only happen if you are rich or famous or have significant family connections. Reality is far different. All workers with intelligence, energy, and passion can start their own businesses by following a few simple rules from successful entrepreneurs like Steve Jobs and Steve Wozniak, founders of Apple; Elon Musk, founder and CEO of SpaceX and cofounder of Tesla; and Richard Branson, founder of Virgin Air.

As you begin exploring this initiative, make your first stop the US Small Business Administration (SBA.gov). The SBA provides information in nontechnical language about how to start and operate your own business and make money in the process.

GETTING STARTED

So, you have been terminated along with 55,000 workers in the US who lost their jobs today. How could this have happened? This sort of thing only happens to workers who have serious issues at work. When it happens to you, it's devastating, and you enter the grieving period, needing time to recover and move forward.

Assuming you have recovered from grieving, it's time to begin exploring your options. One is to find a similar job with a similar company in the same industry. Another is to reevaluate your career using the NEXTERCISE in chapter 4 of this book. Another is to say goodbye to corporate life because this business of being terminated could happen again and again. And another is to start your own business as an entrepreneur as thousands of other terminated workers have. But how and where do you start? Do you start from absolute scratch, or do you purchase a franchise? Do you start a business that requires a physical presence like running a restaurant, or do you start a business that can be operated from home, like a consulting business? And do you start a business as a sole proprietor, or should you have a partner? There are many options.

Becoming an entrepreneur is a process that begins with a thoughtful written plan. You can't just wing it by conversing with a friend or relative. Beginning your own business requires much thought, much time, and money.

FAMOUS ENTREPRENEURS

If you explore how other entrepreneurs founded their businesses, their stories will be similar to that of Bill Gates, founder of Microsoft. He dropped out of Harvard after his sophomore year and founded Microsoft. He had no family money and a middle-class background. Steve Jobs and Steve Wozniak both dropped out of college after their first year and founded Apple Computer, working out of a garage.

Then we have Larry Ellison, founder and CEO of Oracle, who bypassed college altogether and founded one of the world's largest software companies. His net worth is in the $100 billion range. What does he do with his money? For starters he purchased the entire island of Lanai in the Hawaiian Islands. Yes, the entire thing, not just a few acres. He still has plenty of money left over, much of which he donates to charities.

Mark Zuckerberg, founder and CEO of Facebook (now called Meta Platforms), is another person with big dreams and little appetite for continuing his education at Harvard. He dropped out of college and founded Facebook. Mark is in mid-career, and his start-up is now a publicly held company. Mark's net worth is in the $85 billion range, much of which he donates to charitable causes.

And let's not forget the world's richest person, Elon Musk. He needs no introduction. His story is too lengthy to recite here. To learn how Elon did it, just google his name.

We have constructed a comprehensive chapter in *Hired! Fired! Retired!* devoted entirely to starting your own business or purchasing a franchise. It is chapter 11, "Starting Your Own Business or Purchasing a Franchise." Here you will learn everything you need to know about saying goodbye to future employers and starting your own business.

CHAPTER 26

CONNECTING WITH CAREER COACHES AND COUNSELORS, OUTPLACEMENT SERVICES, AND RECRUITERS

Employing a career coach/counselor or an outplacement firm is a serious business decision as you begin your search for a new career. Finding the right provider—one with whom you connect personally and professionally—is key to a successful outcome. It requires a commitment not only of time and money but also to implementing the strategies you learned in order to become successful in navigating your career.

There are times when workers find themselves walking in a dark cloud of anxiety or even depression after being fired or laid off. They look for a sliver of daylight but find nothing but more darkness. The universe seems unresponsive. They do not want much, maybe just a sign that says: We understand where you are. Just take my hand, and I'll help you out of this mess. The person holding that sign may be a career coach, career counselor, or an outplacement service.

Reaching out to a career-care provider takes courage, understanding, and a good deal of common sense. First, what's the difference between a career coach and a career counselor? Where do you find them? What do their services cost? What are their qualifications? And what do these outplacement services really do? All are valid concerns. Let's deal with career coaches and counselors first.

CAREER COACHES AND CAREER COUNSELORS

Go online and search "career coach and counselor," and you will get thousands of hits. It makes one wonder how to sort it out. Some are named Joe Smith, life coach; Mary Jones, executive career counselor; and Robert Brown, PhD, career coach. Read their credentials, and you might be even more confused. Who are the successful ones? Who are the pretenders? Let's look for answers to help you see daylight, to find a break in the dark cloud.

Career Coaches

Career coaches are solution oriented. They focus on helping clients define career objectives, like finding an industry that includes nonprofit companies where passion for the mission is as important as the bottom line. They exude a spirit of optimism, educate you about the job market, and show you how to navigate the world of work. Most will help you craft a résumé and provide job-hunting rubrics. Some are former human resources directors or executive recruiters. Almost all have experience working in the corporate world.

Career Counselors

Career counselors perform many of the same services as career coaches but extend their efforts to uncovering emotional, behavioral, or psychological barriers that might impede your search for meaning and purpose in work. Some are certified psychologists or former human resources directors or both. Many hold an MA in counseling and are certified by the National Board of Certified Counselors. They can help you solve complex issues, like why you always have issues with authority figures like your boss.

Fees for Services

All coaches and counselors charge a fee for their services. Their charges can range from $75 to $500 for a forty-five- or sixty-minute session. Some offer package deals that contain a certain number of sessions spread out over a certain amount of time. Others offer their services on an as-needed basis. Personal sessions will cost more than virtual sessions.

Specialized sessions will cost more than general sessions. For example, some providers work only with executive-level clients, like former presidents, CIOs, CFOs, or CEOs, whose career searches target positions of like kind. Fees for such clients will be considerably higher.

Few coaches and counselors will advertise their fees online, which means that everything is negotiable. Do not hesitate to negotiate a mutually acceptable fee with a provider. Do not be intimidated by a fancy shingle like Dr. Aldus Geronimo, Certified Career Counselor. Everyone is open to negotiating fees . . . even PhDs.

Career counseling services provided by a certified psychologist or psychiatrist may be covered by your medical insurance.

Assessing Provider Credentials

The background and experience of coaches and counselors vary widely. Some have no formal training, while others have had training at brick-and-mortar institutions. Many have completed online certification programs. The most reputable coaches and counselors have certifications for successfully completing coaching and counseling programs.

COACHING ORGANIZATIONS

Here are some of the more reputable training organizations for career coaches and counselors. All provide written certifications for successful completion of training courses.

- International Coaching Federation (ICF) (Coaching Federation.org): This highly regarded coaching organization based in Lexington, Kentucky, provides online certification courses for coaches. Access this site for information about the coaching business generally and about suggestions for finding the right coach or counselor to meet your needs.
- National Career Development Association (NCDA) (NCDA.org): This respected organization, based in Broken Arrow, Oklahoma, dates back to 1913 and provides not only credentialed programs for coaches but also assistance for those seeking help in a particular location. Those who successfully complete the NCDA career coaching program receive the global career development facilitator certificate and a GCDF after their name. When you are interviewing prospective coaches, always ask if they have this certification.
- Professional Association of Résumé Writers and Career Coaches (PARWCC) (PARWCC.com): This organization provides intensive career coaching training and awards those who successfully complete the course with the certified professional career coach credential, designated by a CPCC after the name. In addition, PARWCC offers credentials to coaches who complete training for interviewing techniques and for résumé writing, and it offers help for those starting their own businesses. Importantly, it will refer you to a professional in your location.

- AARP (AARP.org): Formerly the American Association of Retired People, this organization is no longer focused exclusively on retired workers. For a low membership fee of $16 per year, workers fifty and over can enjoy many AARP benefits. One of them is career counseling for unemployed workers or for workers making a career change.

HOW TO SELECT A CAREER COACH OR CAREER COUNSELOR

The ICF recommends that you ask these questions when you are evaluating and selecting a prospective coach:

- What is your coaching experience (number of individuals coached, years of experience, types of coaching situations, etc.)?
- What is your coach-specific training? Is it an ICF-accredited training program or other coach-specific training?
- What is your coaching specialty or area in which you most often work?
- What types of businesses do you work with most often? And at what levels: executives, upper management, middle management?
- What is your philosophy about coaching?
- What types of assessments are you certified to deliver?
- What are some of your coaching success stories (specific examples of individuals who have succeeded as a result of coaching)?
- Are you a member of ICF?
- Do you hold an ICF credential?

Noomii: The Professional Coach Directory (Noomii.com) recommends coaches based on your stated goals. Noomii offers an interesting approach. After completing a questionnaire, you are provided with a list of certified coaches whose expertise is aligned with your profile and goals. We suggest that you review their services. We like the cost: free.

Kathy Caprino (KathyCaprino.com), a women's career coach and leadership trainer, is one of the most celebrated career coaches in the world. She was laid off in mid-career and after much soul-searching started her own business focusing on career training and coaching. She offers a free subscription to her weekly newsletter and valuable rubrics for moving forward in your career. Be sure to read her article, "The Top Five Regrets of Mid-Career Professionals."[19] She believes they are . . .

- "I wish I hadn't listened to other people about what I should study and pursue."
- "I wish I hadn't worked so hard and missed out on so much."
- "I wish I hadn't let my fears stop me from making change."
- "I wish I had learned how to address toxic situations and people."
- "I wish I hadn't let myself become so trapped around money."

WORKING WITH AN OUTPLACEMENT SERVICE

Outplacement is not a mom-and-pop business; rather it is a large industry unto itself with national or multinational companies in its fold. Employers frequently provide brick-and-mortar or virtual outplacement services, at their own cost, for workers they let go. This service is expensive and costs the employer upward of $5,000 per terminated employee. For high-level

---

19 Kathy Caprino, "The Top 5 Regrets Of Mid-Career Professionals," *Forbes*, October 16, 2016, https://www.forbes.com/sites/kathycaprino/2016/10/16/the-top-5-regrets-of-mid-career-professionals/#3dfdeaee7dd2.

executives, outplacement services could cost the employer as much as $25,000 per executive. If your employer did not include outplacement in your severance package, you can purchase it as an individual. However, you can try to negotiate this into your severance package.

The traditional outplacement service consisting of group sessions in an office setting has changed, unfortunately. Previously, weekly or semimonthly group sessions at an office location and spearheaded by an experienced leader/teacher offered much-needed support for laid-off or fired workers. A spirit of mutual support and assistance were invaluable aids to the person still working through the grieving period. It was reassuring to know that you were not alone in this battle. I myself can attest to the effectiveness of this model, having attended group outplacement on location in Philadelphia after having been laid off from a technology consulting firm. Try to find an outplacement service that still offers this kind of personal service.

Most outplacement now is rendered online, by email, phone, Zoom, or a combination of all options. Individual attention is what the current model advertises. Services included in most packages are general career counseling, résumé preparation, interviewing techniques, industry and company evaluations, cover-letter and follow-up-letter writing, and referrals to recruiters or human resources directors. Most outplacement companies advertise one-on-one sessions focused on the items you selected.

There are mixed reviews for outplacement services. They appear to work best for top-level executives whose companies included personal on-location outplacement services in their severance packages.

Outplacement Resources

There seems to be little difference between the services of an outplacement company and an individual career coach/

counselor. Use the same evaluation techniques that you would use for evaluating a career coach.

Go online, making sure to localize your search. If you live in New York, you want to find a service in the NY Metro area, not in San Diego. Here are two references to get you started:

- Quest Outplacement (QuestOutplacement.com): Quest offers a variety of one-on-one outplacement packages to individual fired workers. The cost varies depending on the length of time and the support items offered. Their support is through phone and online tools. They do not provide an office location.
- Lee Hecht Harrison (LHH.com): LHH is a multinational recruiting and outplacement firm with 300 offices scattered throughout the United States and abroad. Home offices are in Woodcliff Lake, New Jersey. The company has been in business for fifty years and has a sterling reputation for quality service. It enjoys a 3.9 out of 4 rating from Glassdoor. When you access their website, enter "outplacement services" and your location in the search bar.

CHURCHES, COLLEGES, AND UNIVERSITIES

Many churches, regardless of denomination, provide counseling for their members by the pastor or a member of the congregation. Many have previous experience counseling workers with problems of all kinds. They are compassionate, supportive, and nonjudgmental. Reach out to them personally after a Sunday church service or at their offices at any time of the week.

The same can be said for counseling services provided by colleges and universities throughout the country. Many provide counseling services by faculty members at minimal cost or at no cost at all. Review your local college/university website to learn about these services. Remember to include community colleges as well.

BEYOND THE TEMPORAL

An increasing number of workers are incorporating prayer into their daily lives. Prayers to God usually fall into two categories: thanksgiving and solicitation. For example, workers who are preparing for an interview may ask their God for help. This kind of prayer does not have to be in biblical terms. It can be in the vernacular. It could be as simple, but sincere, as saying: *Hey God, I have an important interview coming soon and I ask that you be on my side as I prepare and sit for the interview. Thanks, God.*

KEY TAKEAWAYS

- Selecting a career-care provider is a business decision.
- Always check and verify the credentials of a career care provider.
- Local providers offer the most effective services.
- Craft a plan defining your needs and goals before employing any services.
- Working with a career coach or outplacement firm will keep you focused on your objectives and provide direction to find your way out of the dark cloud of unemployment.
- The priest or minister at your local church may provide career counseling.
- Pray to your God for success in your career search.

PRINT AND DIGITAL RESOURCES

- *What Color is Your Parachute* by Richard Bolles
- *The Career Coaching Handbook* by Julia Yeates

- Glassdoor (Glassdoor.com): This site provides free reviews for everything job related, including coaching and outplacement services.
- Monster (Monster.com)
- *Psychology Today* (PsychologyToday.com): This resource is available as a print or online magazine. It offers a special section titled "Work."
- *AARP* print magazine or online at AARP.org
- Lee Hecht Harrison (LHH.com)

CHAPTER 27

BUILDING AND MAINTAINING YOUR IDENTITY

Identity is not something you were taught in school. It was something that you yourself began to form when you were a child, and it continues to the present day. We are always asking, subconsciously, *Who am I?*

As mentioned in the first part of this book, each of us has three identities according to psychologists and counselors:

- Personal identity: what we think of ourselves as a family member.
- Social identity: how we view ourselves in relation to others in the community.
- Work identity: how we see ourselves on the job.

BUILDING IDENTITY ON THE JOB

We spend at least ten hours each working day in an environment that supports or challenges our identity. Most workers are overtly conscious of their work identity and continue to build it as their careers move forward. Here is how it works.

Mary Jones's Story

Mary Jones enters the world of work as an office-bound sales rep talking to clients via phone or Zoom for Big Tech Inc. Her job title is sales representative, her name is listed on the company website, and Mary has paper or virtual calling cards stating her name, work title, phone number, email address, and company name. Mary is proud to present her calling card in person when attending a local trade show or virtually to customers when working with them on the phone or Zoom. After three years of successful sales and meeting her annual sales goal, Mary is promoted to regional sales representative. Now she leaves her office to meet customers personally at their offices or at trade shows. Now she is Mary Jones, regional sales representative. Her identity is building, and she is proud to tell family and friends about her success and maybe even how much money she made last year, let's say $75,000 base and another $25,000 in commissions, a total of $100,000 plus benefits, not bad for a person just three years out of college.

Life continues and Mary's confidence builds each year along with her identity as she is recognized by her boss at company meetings as a sales rep who has exceeded her sales goal three years in a row. She receives many congratulations from colleagues, family, and friends. Now her boss advises that she take for-credit courses in artificial intelligence, all tuition reimbursed by the company, which she does on weekends and evenings.

Three years later Mary is promoted to regional sales manager, and once more her identity climbs because now she is Mary Jones, regional sales manager for Big Tech Inc. She has ten sales reps reporting to, and her compensation is $130,000 a year plus benefits, including a 401(k) retirement plan. Another happy occasion comes about on the personal side when Mary is married and has beautiful twin daughters three years later.

Mary is especially proud when attending a reception at a trade show and meets a stranger who asks her name and makes small talk in an effort to establish a relationship. After the introductory chatter this person asks, "What do you do, Mary?" She proudly answers, "I'm regional sales manager for the Midwest for Big Tech Inc. and have ten sales reps reporting to me. It's really a neat job." *How much better does it get?* Mary thinks. Well, Mary is in for a pleasant surprise when the president calls her in for a chat and says, "Mary, our vice president for sales is leaving the company, and we're looking for a replacement. You have done a marvelous job for us these past ten years, and we believe you are the one to become our new VP. Congratulations, Mary."

Mary can't believe her good fortune. She is vice president for a tech company beginning to use AI extensively. She manages a sales staff of fifty reps and six regional sales managers with Big Tech Inc. Her compensation totals $300,000. Her identity is firmly established. She enjoys going to work every day. She has reliable help with the twins, and her husband is supportive in every way.

Mary and her husband like (and need) her compensation because they have a home mortgage with a monthly payment of $3,000, $1,500 per month for property taxes, insurances with monthly premiums of $2,000, good food for the family of four totaling $2,000 each month, car loan payments of $1,800 per month, household maintenance totaling $500 each month, a nanny for the kids totaling $1,500 each month, clothing for all the family averaging $300 each month, credit card payments of $300 per month, $5,000 per month for her 401(k) contribution, and $400 each month for fun and games and eating out. A lot of expenses, one might say, but Mary can afford it. After all, she is vice president of sales for Big Tech Inc. And what might be next—executive vice president or maybe even president?

Five years pass, and Mary could not be happier. She excels in her job, is frequently quoted in regional and national newspapers, and has had several live interviews with national TV business programs. In addition, Mary has written two articles published in *The Wall Street Journal*. When she attends trade show receptions, everyone knows who she is and what she does. Nobody asks, "Mary, what do you do?"

Twenty years pass, and Mary's work identity is firmly established, so much so that she never has to wonder, *Who am I?* She is in mid-career; her family life could not be better, and she sees herself as future president of a big technology company. But something has been happening in the technology industry that Mary has dismissed as just part of the business environment. Consolidation is taking place. There is an increase in mergers and acquisitions, particularly in technology because of the rapid increase in the use of AI.

Then it happens one Monday morning. Mary and the other six company vice presidents are told to attend a board of directors meeting on Tuesday at 7:30 a.m. She is surprised when she enters the boardroom and sees not only her own company executives and board members but three other persons whom she has never seen before. Mary is both curious and perplexed. What's going on? The CEO of Big Tech Inc. begins the meeting with a ten-minute introduction and then reveals the names of the visitors and their corporate titles. They are the CEO, CFO, and COO of a relatively new competitor being financed by two of the biggest banks in the US. Now Mary is beginning to sweat because she can guess what's coming.

The CEO of Big Tech Inc. then discloses the reason for the meeting. The upstart company has made an offer for Mary's company, which was accepted. The CEO of the new company then takes the floor to announce what's going to happen. He says that this is an asset acquisition, which means that the new company is not taking on any of the present employees, like Mary, but just the company's physical assets and infrastructure. When the meeting concludes at 8:30, Mary does not have a job. Mary has been terminated, laid off—just plain fired!

Now, at 8:30 a.m. on an ordinary Tuesday, here's what

Mary has lost: salary, bonus and benefits, company perks, and her work identity. She is no longer Mary Jones, vice president of sales, Big Tech Inc. She is now just plain Mary Jones.

HOW TO MAINTAIN YOUR IDENTITY AFTER BEING TERMINATED

I have interviewed many workers who lost their jobs, and each has their own tale of woe. Some are shocked about their loss of income, especially those with family obligations. Being married and having children to support is a costly operation. Loss of insurance, especially health insurance, is frightening. Seeking a new career is time consuming and often confusing. Negotiating fair severance is a nightmare. Overcoming grief is a huge psychological hurdle.

However, for all workers who have been terminated, loss of identity is at the top of the list for trauma. The sooner you overcome this loss, the sooner you will be able to proceed with a career search to rebuild your work identity. Here are strategies for maintaining and rebuilding your work identity.

- Ask yourself, *What am I now?* Well, you are not just plain-vanilla So-and-So. You are a human being who applied intelligence, energy, and passion to win a job. You will always carry that job title and identity with you. It may be past tense, but you can be rightfully proud of what you have accomplished. Do not hesitate to keep that identity and tell others about it, even though you are temporarily out of work. You worked hard for that job and title, and as we all know, hard work equals success.
- Fall back on your personal identity as son, daughter, husband, wife, grandparent. Your loss of work identity can never take away these attributes that define who you always are.

- Blend activity into your social identity. Join groups specializing in what you identify with. If you derive satisfaction from doing charitable work for the poor, rekindle that interest and activity while you are career seeking. This might include becoming active with members of your political party. Campaigning for a political candidate can confer identity and give your life a sense of purpose.
- Put aside the temptation to take the easy way out: sitting and grieving about your loss of a job and the identity it conferred. Become introspective and begin to ask questions: *Did I really like my last job? Did it give me the kind of identity I was proud to mention to family and friends and coworkers?*

KEY TAKEAWAYS

- Identity is something that you build on your own. It is not taught.
- There are three types of identity: personal, social, and work.
- Activate your personal and social identity when terminated.
- Maintain your work identity even though it may be past tense.

PRINT AND DIGITAL RESOURCES

- *Job Loss, Identity, and Mental Health* by Dawn R. Norris
- "When You Lose Your Job—and It's Your Whole Identity" by Rebecca Zucker, *Harvard Business Review* (HBR.org) (Google the title of this article for easy access.)
- *Psychology Today*, print and online at PsychologyToday.com

CHAPTER 28

TWELVE TIPS FOR REBUILDING YOUR CAREER AFTER BEING FIRED OR LAID OFF

Tip 1. Plan your work digitally or handwritten. Work your plan. Just talking about your next move will get you nowhere. You must establish objectives and the time frame for achieving them.

Tip 2. Decide your career path using the NEXTERCISE in chapter 4. To reach the promised land, you need to discover your prime interest and your skills and then match them with the industry you love and the companies within that industry.

Tip 3. After being terminated, take time off from career searching and do the things you always wanted to do but could not because work took all your time. Use your time-out to become reacquainted with yourself and the world.

Tip 4. Finding a job requires personally meeting hiring managers at trade shows, conferences, and job fairs.

Tip 5. Do not just dust off your ten-year-old résumé. Craft a new résumé that incorporates the current style and key words.

Tip 6. Interviews, both in person and Zoom, should be conversations, not just Q and A sessions. Wear business attire and follow the rules for body language.

Tip 7. Hire an employment lawyer to review your severance package and a new job offer. Employment laws are made at the local, state, and federal levels and change constantly.

Tip 8. Craft a budget to protect your financial security. Make this a written document and share it with the entire family. Paste it on the refrigerator door so it is always on view.

Tip 9. Do not drop any insurance policies, especially health insurance. The temptation to drop certain insurances can be overwhelming, but resist at all costs. Insurance can be boring, but when it comes to avoiding risk, boring is good.

Tip 10. Purchase long-term disability insurance as soon as possible. A sudden illness or a debilitating accident can happen to you on any day. Ideally, purchase it while you are still employed.

Tip 11. Explore opening your own business or purchasing a franchise. Remember that AI is growing and will be part of any business. Prepare!

Tip 12. Learn who you really are by exploring your personal, social, and work identities. Work identity is critical, and when lost because of termination, it can cause anxiety and even depression. Consult a career coach or counselor to help you through this challenge.

PART 3
RETIRED!

SEARCHING FOR UNDERSTANDING, MEANING, PURPOSE, AND IDENTITY IN RETIREMENT

CHAPTER 29

RETIREMENT PLANNING

The third and final phase of your career in the worldwide workplace is retirement. For most workers this is a happy and productive time to pursue long-delayed ambitions, be it alone or with a spouse or partner, friends, or family members. If today's retiree has planned accordingly, this will be the ultimate good time because there is so much to do, so many places to explore, and so many opportunities to give back to the community after rendering fifty or more years of service to various employers. Now you can do whatever you want on your terms. No more reporting to a boss. No more signing in. No more pipeline reports. No more weekly and monthly productivity reports. No more sales quotas. No more annual productivity meetings with the human resources director. No more texts from your boss at 9:30 p.m. on a Saturday evening. Freedom at last!

Retirement is the most misunderstood phase of the work cycle. Preparation for it should begin on the day you begin work. But we're not going to let you sit and wonder how you can solve retirement challenges and dilemmas. We'll not leave you crying about regrets of the past and fear of the future. And we'll help you win three games retirees play constantly. They are "shoulda," "woulda," and "coulda."

However, before we become too giddy about retirement, we must understand that the concept and practice of retirement is changing in the worldwide workplace. The traditional meaning of retirement was ceasing active work altogether and paying for living expenses from Social Security funds and employer pension plans. Now it varies, factoring in age, employer and government benefits, pensions, encore careers, Social Security benefits, IRAs, and annuities. It is no longer one size fits all.

For example, in the UK, retirement age for collecting government benefits is sixty-five and will increase to sixty-seven in 2028, and to sixty-eight in 2037. In France, retirement age has been raised to sixty-four from sixty-two amid hostile nationwide protests in 2023. Contrast that with America, where workers can begin collecting Social Security benefits at age sixty-two, but with a discount. To collect full Social Security benefits in America, workers must be sixty-seven, but they will get a bonus if they delay taking benefits until age seventy. Social Security benefits are related to both age and years of employment. Go to the Social Security website (SSA.gov) for clarification or consult with your HR director. Unfortunately, Social Security has become politicized, and benefits and requirements could change at any time.

With all these variables in the workplace and the political landscape, advance planning is key to crafting a happy retirement.

THE NUMBERS TELL THE TALE

Today, retirement planning requires changes in attitude and behavior. Numbers from the US Census Bureau, the Pew Research Center, and the US Department of Labor are enlightening. They send a clear message to the worldwide workplace generally and the American workplace in particular: Retirement is an ever-changing dynamic. Workers must constantly review the data and plan accordingly using the latest in AI.

Approximately 66 million retirees receive monthly Social Security benefits. Each day in America, 10,000 workers retire from their jobs at an average age of sixty-one, but the numbers are increasing. According to the Census Bureau, nearly 12,000 workers will retire each day in 2030. The average lifespan for American workers is seventy-nine.

According to Fidelity, the average amount of money American workers have in their individual retirement accounts at age sixty-five is $257,000, a pittance considering the money one needs to survive until death.[20] Latest statistics reveal that the retired sixty-five-year-old American worker needs an average of $52,000 per year to pay for all expenses.[21] If you live to age eighty, you will need a minimum of $750,000.

Let's examine Social Security benefits using 2023 as an example but remembering that these benefits will change with the number of years you paid into the Social Security system. Here are present-day maximum benefits for workers who meet the required number of payment years:

- Age sixty-two: $2,572 per month
- Age sixty-seven, which is considered full retirement age (FRA): $3,627 per month
- Age seventy: $4,555

These numbers will change in each succeeding year. They will be different in 2024, 2025, 2026, etc. That is why it is critical to begin planning for retirement before you set your retirement date. You can't decide to retire next month based on the current payment schedule. Social Security benefits will change each year.

---

20 "How do your retirement savings stack up?" Fidelity Viewpoints, March 3, 2025, https://www.fidelity.com/learning-center/personal-finance/average-retirement-savings.
21 Christian Simmons, "Average Retirement Spending in 2025: Typical Expenses + Budgeting Tips," Retire Guide, updated March 21, 2025, https://www.retireguide.com/retirement-planning/average-spending/.

How Much Do I Need to Retire Comfortably?

To determine how much you will need to retire without financial stress, create a simple accounting spreadsheet with a handwritten list of your expenses, or use an Excel spreadsheet. Include what you will need for the big three, food, shelter, and clothing. Add the cost of insurance premiums, property taxes, rent, mortgage payments, utilities, medical needs like prescriptions and doctor visits, transportation costs, and gifts for family and friends. Toss in a limited amount for recreation like playing pickleball, golf, or tennis, and eating out. Total all your expenses per month and per year. In another column, total all your income and see if it is adequate to cover your expenses. But there is more to this equation.

The annual amount of money the average American retired worker needs to live a middle-class life varies greatly with location. If you live in a high cost of living area like New York City instead of a lower cost of living area like Montana, how do make up the difference?

It must come from your IRA, a company or government pension plan, an annuity, dividends from an investment portfolio, an encore career, or from accumulated cash. For the average retiree nationwide, Citizens Bank recommends that you have about ten times your last annual salary. For example, if your income at retirement was $80,000, you will need $800,000 in savings to live comfortably in retirement.

Workers planning for retirement might want to consider relocating to a state with a low annual income requirement. You can find this information for each state online. Those workers considering retirement should use this data to chart a meaningful course of action for their final years in the work cycle, those years inappropriately named "retirement."

THE TWO BIG CHALLENGES FOR EVERY RETIREE

The big two challenges for all retirees are 1) loss of income and 2) loss of identity.

So how does the newbie retiree handle these two challenges for the remaining years of life on earth? Everyone needs a sense of identity, but how does one make that happen without a job title and company affiliation? And how does one budget Social Security income plus income from a possible retirement account against daily survival expenses for the basic necessities? And how do you budget for additional expenses, including insurance premiums, costs for transportation, recreation, and other unforeseen expenses like replacing the heating furnace in Minneapolis that breaks during the coldest months of the year or replacing the air-conditioning unit in Chicago when the August temp is ninety-eight in the shade with relative humidity at 90 percent? These challenges will be addressed in detail in chapters 31, 32 ,33.

WHEN AND HOW TO BEGIN RETIREMENT PLANNING

The appropriate time to begin retirement planning is when you begin your first job. Adjustments should be made each succeeding year until retirement as your income and benefits change and as changes occur in government benefits. Don't be caught off guard as millions are each year when they plan to retire but can't because their financial and insurance benefits are insufficient.

There are a multitude of print and digital resources offering advice for meaningful retirement planning. One of the best online articles is offered by the US Department of Labor (DoL.gov), titled "Top 10 Ways to Prepare for Retirement." They are as follows:

- Start saving. Keep saving. Stick to your goals.
- Know your retirement needs.
- Contribute to your employer's retirement savings plan.
- Learn about your employer's pension plan.
- Consider basic investment principles using AI.
- Don't touch your retirement savings.
- Ask your employer to start a plan for you.
- Put money into an individual retirement account (IRA).
- Learn about your Social Security benefits.
- Question your employer, bank, union, financial adviser, and AI.

Local Retirement Planning Resources

Every state, and most counties within each state, has a retirement and financial planning department where you can have a personal counselor provide advice on retirement planning and retirement implementation. To gain access and arrange an appointment, google your state and county plus "retirement planning."

KEY TAKEAWAYS

- Money can be the cause of grief or happiness in retirement.
- If you can't retire with enough income to cover expenses, keep working.
- The cost of living is much lower in rural areas of the world. Consider relocating.
- You are not going to live forever, but you might still be alive at ninety-five. Prepare for it.
- Your retirement identity independent of a job title is key to emotional well-being.

PRINT AND DIGITAL RESOURCES

- US Department of Labor (DoL.gov)
- Bureau of Labor Statistics (BLS.gov)
- Search "Retirement planning, what to do, Vanguard" (Vanguard.com)
- "Women and Money" and "Retirement Planning and Strategies" by Suze Orman (SuzeOrman.com)
- "Plan for the Retirement You Want" on AARP.org

CHAPTER 30

WHEN, WHY, AND HOW WORKERS RETIRE

When, why, and how do workers retire? Usually, it comes down to having sufficient money, which is a challenge needing insight and rubrics. You will find solutions to financial challenges in chapter 31 of this book.

WHEN WORKERS RETIRE

The *when* of retirement is a very personal decision for workers in the private sector and for some in the public sector as well.

Mandatory Retirement

Mandatory retirement in the US is unlawful except for in certain government-related jobs, such as those in military service and federal police agencies like the Federal Bureau of Investigation, airline pilots, and air traffic controllers. The age at which a person retires is for most workers a personal choice.

The Age Discrimination in Employment Act (ADEA) of 1967 and its revision in 1986 prohibits employers from establishing a mandatory retirement age for all workers over forty. Prior to that, there was a federal mandatory retirement age of sixty-five, which became law in 1935 when President Roosevelt established the Social Security Act. Of course, only 60 percent of Americans lived that long in 1935. Like so many other federal mandates, retirement age appears to be politically driven.

Private-Sector Retirement

To understand age-required retirement, we must look at this from a historical point of view. Prior to ADEA, most employers set a mandatory retirement age for all of their workers, usually the age at which workers were eligible to receive Social Security benefits. Once you turned sixty-five, you were given a retirement party and a retirement benefits package, and you vacated the premises. For many workers in so-called white-collar jobs, this was traumatic.

It was similar for hands-on workers like those in the building trades, but they did have one advantage: They could continue their trade as individual workers. For example, a carpenter could continue working jobs in the local neighborhood but at a wage lower than that received from the general contractor.

Public-Sector Retirement

The retirement age for government workers at the federal level needs explanations from experts because there are so many requirements. One size does not fit all. There are two types of government retirement systems, referred to as FERS and CSRS. Here is a brief summary from the country's foremost government jobs and retirement expert, Dennis Damp.[22]

> Many feds retire early, including those working in law enforcement, fire fighters, and air traffic control. Because of the physical demands, this early retirement system allows employees to retire with just 20 years of service. It

---

22   Dennis Damp, "Should I Stay or Should I Go Now? Leaving the Federal Government for the Private Sector," Clearance Jobs, January 11, 2022, https://news.clearancejobs.com/2022/01/11/should-i-stay-or-should-i-go-now-leaving-the-federal-government-for-the-private-sector/.

also includes a mandatory retirement when the employee reaches a designated age or years of service.

Federal employees working under the Federal Employees Retirement System (FERS) are eligible to retire when they reach their Minimum Retirement Age (MRA) of between 55 to 57, depending on the year they were born, and have 30 years of service. Other options include retiring at age 60 with at least 20 years or at 62 with as little as 5 years of service. A reduced retirement is available for those who reached their MRA and have 10 years of service. Lots of options if you are seeking a change and want to move to the private sector.

Civil Service Retirement System (CSRS) employees can take an immediate retirement if they have at least 30 years of service and are 55 years of age, 60 with 20 years of service, and at age 62 with as little as 5 years of service.

What to Do Now

In today's world, with the help of federal laws regarding retirement, workers over age sixty-five are still employed, enjoy working, and enjoy living. Stay healthy physically and mentally, and you can work well into your senior years—and in fact you need productive work to remain healthy. When you work, you learn. Stop working, and you stop learning. Stop learning, and you stop growing. Stop productive work, and your life begins to decelerate to the point where rising from bed each morning is a chore.

Retirement is at the discretion of the worker, and for many it is the best of the three phases of the work cycle. Most support for children and other family members is over, and workers can plan enjoyable social events.

WHY WORKERS RETIRE

There is no general reason why workers retire. It's a personal thing based on factors both planned and unexpected, like health issues or family needs. Here are some of the most common circumstances that drive workers to retirement, many of which align with reasons why workers leave jobs at any age:

- An overdemanding and unfair boss.
- Career dissatisfaction.
- The company has become unprofitable.
- The company has been reorganized or purchased.
- Your job was terminated by AI.
- Personal health reasons.
- Family health reasons, like caring for a loved one.
- You have enough money in savings to finance your retirement.
- The employer does not respect older workers.

HOW WORKERS RETIRE

When you are firm in your desire to retire, select an exact date when you will leave the company. Make sure this date aligns with federal, state, and local government requirements and benefits. When these chores are completed, prepare a written retirement statement giving the exact date you will leave the company and present it to both your boss and the HR director. Make sure it is in writing, text, and email. You want to have verifiable proof of your retirement date and verifiable proof that you retired and were not terminated. State the exact date you will be leaving the company.

Trust but Verify

When you hand in your retirement notice, the employer will issue a retirement package, stating conditions and benefits. Review this against your employment contract to make sure you are getting what was promised and that it's legally enforceable. Do not sign the retirement agreement until you are sure it is fair. Don't hesitate to question certain items that seem vague, and don't hesitate to negotiate for better retirement benefits, like a period of extended salary or greater insurance benefits like long-term disability insurance. If you need advice, check with online retirement resources and the employer's HR director and legal department.

The next step is to hire an employment lawyer to review the retirement document. Do not sign any retirement document until it is reviewed by your lawyer. Retirement is the third and final phase in your career, and you must get it right because it will affect the rest of your retirement years. Most likely your employer will assure you that the document is fair and routine and that you should just sign and begin your retirement. It may be difficult to resist because you want to make your exit an enjoyable occasion, but remember the words made famous by one of our presidents: Trust but verify.

You may need advice about benefits and finances. You may find counseling from your HR director, but that advice likely favors the employer, not you. Retirement has many sides, and there are times when retiring workers need professional advice. Unfortunately, the retirement proposition has become politicized, and it takes time and talent to keep up with the changes.

To make sure you are doing the right thing, seek advice from financial advisers, insurance advisers, lawyers, and the Social Security Administration. Here are several resources to consider:

- Financial advisers like Vanguard, the top pick for online retirement advice by Consumer Affairs (Vanguard.com)
- US Department of Labor (DoL.gov)
- The Social Security Administration (SSA.gov)

Winding Down

A recent survey indicates that many workers prepare for retirement in defined increments. They either, with employer approval, begin to reduce hours gradually for the last five years of work but at a reduced salary; or they change to a job with their employer that is less stressful, also at a lower salary.

Required Retirement Benefits

With the popularity of the 401(k) as a company benefit, one would think this benefit would be mandatory. However, there is no federal retirement plan, and only ten states have legal retirement requirements:

- California
- Colorado
- Connecticut
- Illinois
- Maine
- Maryland
- New Jersey
- New York
- Oregon
- Virginia

The Employee Retirement Income Security Act of 1974 (ERISA) is a federal law that sets minimum standards for most voluntarily established retirement and health plans in private industry. ERISA does not require an employer to establish a retirement plan; it only requires that those who establish plans must meet certain standards. The law generally does not specify how much money a participant must be paid as a benefit.

These are the only required benefits provided to all employed workers, whether by the government or the company: Medicare, Social Security, unemployment insurance, workers' compensation, health insurance, and family and medical leave. When you retire, the only benefits you are entitled to are those in your employment contract, what may be contained in ERISA, and Social Security.

KEY TAKEAWAYS

- Planning for retirement should begin with your first job.
- Always consider local, state, and federal laws when retirement planning.
- Always ask for advice from retirement planners, HR directors, and lawyers.
- Have your lawyer review the company retirement package before signing.

PRINT AND DIGITAL RESOURCES

- Retirement counseling with training specialist Tammy Flanagan (RetireFederal.com)
- FederalRetirement.net, run by Dennis Damp
- FederalJobs.net, run by Dennis Damp
- The Office of Personnel Management is the HR department for the federal government. Federal workers should contact Retire@OPM.gov for retirement information.

CHAPTER 31

FINANCIAL PLANNING AND WILL PREPARATION

FINANCIAL PLANNING MATTERS

Financial matters can be relatively easy to handle as you prepare for retirement because they involve tangible items that intelligent human beings can manage with planning. You can make progress solving this challenge using a simple accounting exercise: Prepare a list of your expenses and a list of your income sources. If your projected expenses exceed your projected retirement income, you will need to find another job or another source of income when you retire. Many workers have done just that to remain self-sufficient during retirement. In fact, a large percentage of retirees continue working in another full-time or part-time job after "retiring." Let's cite a familiar example of how money rules retirement using a retiree named Ed.

Ed's Story

After the retirement party, the traditional pat on the back for service rendered, plus the award of a trophy or an Apple Watch or the latest technology gadget, a serious challenge faces our example retiree, Ed from Chicago. He was marketing director for an upscale retail store on Michigan Avenue and retired at sixty-five, believing his monthly Social Security check would cover expenses. But let's take a closer look.

Ed had a monthly paycheck of $6,000 for a total of $72,000 per year, which ceased after his retirement party. Annual living expenses for retirees in Chicago total approximately $50,000. To meet that number, Ed collects Social Security payments of $2,500 a month, $30,000 per year. In addition, he can take $15,000 in required minimum distribution (RMD) from his IRA, giving him an additional $1,250 per month. The total amount in his 401(k) is $142,000. Now Ed has a pretax annual income of $45,000. Subtract federal and state taxes of $9,000 (20 percent), and Ed has only $36,000 a year. Where is Ed going to find another $14,000 to meet annual expenses? But that's not all. Let's take this to another step.

Ed is sixty-five and has about fourteen more years to live. Multiply his annual living expenses, $50,000, times his remaining fourteen years on earth, and you get $700,000, the amount of money Ed will require to avoid going on welfare or moving in with relatives, neither a pleasant option. To stay even, he will need to find an encore career—not a pro bono "community outreach" venture but one that will pay him for services rendered. Good luck, Ed. Too bad you did not start saving for retirement when you began your first job.

PLANNING FOR ADEQUATE RETIREMENT INCOME WITH A 401(K), IRA, SEP, CD, AND ANNUITY

Ed's experience is repeated across the US every day by Marilyn, Dick, Harry, Sally, Jane, and Bob. Why? It seems like a simple eighth-grade math problem that every working adult of any age should be able to solve: In order to pay for your expenses, you must have a comparable amount of income.

The main reason why retirees face the income challenge is that they did not follow common sense advice: Begin planning for retirement when you begin your first job. It's not difficult. You place a certain amount of your salary in your employer's 401(k) or your own IRA. You determine the amount you will need for retirement based on the yearly requirement for retirement living based on your geographical location and multiply by the number of years you have until you retire. If you are twenty-five and plan to retire at sixty-five, you have forty years to acquire retirement income. If you are forty-five, you have only twenty years to make it happen. If your employer does not offer a retirement plan, establish your own IRA with an asset management firm like Vanguard or Fidelity. Take money from your monthly paycheck and put it in a total stock market index fund.

The 401(k) Retirement Plan

The best place to put your retirement savings is in an employer-sponsored 401(k). Employers usually offer several places to implement the 401(k). It may be with Vanguard, Fidelity, Prudential, Schwab, or some other company. There are certain limits to the amount you can put into the plan drawing from your monthly paycheck. Also, the employer may offer to match your amount in whole or in part. For example, if you put $500 per month into your 401(k), the employer may contribute another $500 or a lesser amount, contingent upon company policy. At the end of one year, you will have $12,000 in your 401(k). (This is an important benefit a company uses to attract job candidates.) Do not hesitate to accept the maximum amount your employer offers. It really is "free money."

You have the right to place your money into several 401(k) accounts, like a money market, a CD, individual stocks, or an index fund. The company 401(k) adviser will recommend the best place depending on several factors, like your financial goals and the state of the economy, but the final choice is yours. When you are saving for the long term, most advisers recommend placing your money in an index fund, such as the Vanguard Total Stock Market Index Fund, the Vanguard 500 Index Fund, or the Vanguard Balanced Index Fund. Periodically you can move your money from one fund to another. Long term, these funds have averaged an 8 to 10 percent annual yield. You may begin withdrawals from the 401(k) at age fifty-nine and a half, but that can change. Keep abreast by checking periodically with your adviser.

The Internal Revenue Service (IRS) places restrictions on 401(k) plans. For example, in 2023 an employee could contribute a maximum of $25,000 per year. There are other IRS restrictions which can change without notice, so every worker should consult with a financial adviser, HR director, or the IRS (IRS.gov) directly to stay updated.

The Roth Retirement Plan

The Roth is nothing more than a variation on the 401(k). Vanguard defines a Roth IRA as an individual retirement account that offers tax-free growth and tax-free withdrawals in retirement. Roth IRA rules dictate that as long as you've owned your account for five years and you are age fifty-nine and a half or older, you can withdraw your money when you want to and you won't owe any federal taxes, regardless of your employment status. The Roth plan does not have RMD withdrawals during the lifetime of the owner.

The Individual Retirement Account (IRA) Plan

An IRA, or individual retirement account, is an account that enables you to delay paying taxes until the money is withdrawn. It's similar to a 401(k). However, instead of the account being managed by your employer, you select the account and manage it by yourself. You may begin withdrawals at age fifty-nine and a half.

If your employer does not offer a 401(k), immediately establish an IRA with an asset management firm like Vanguard, Prudential, or Fidelity. Remember that this is your retirement account, and you will need to draw from it when you retire. There are restrictions and conditions for an IRA established by the IRS. Go to the IRS website and your financial management firm for advice and guidance.

Where do you deposit your money? The best places for long-term growth are index funds incorporating stocks from the total stock market or only from stocks in the S&P 500.

The Simplified Employee Pension (SEP) Plan

A (SEP) plan is for small business owners, enabling them to contribute to their own retirement. It's similar to a 401(k) plan. Business owners can make substantial contributions to the SEP and begin RMD withdrawals at age fifty-nine and a half. You can adjust the amount of your contributions periodically. The SEP is a must-have for small business owners.

Annuities for Retirement

Annuities are advertised as retirement savings accounts that can't fail. They are products issued by insurance companies that give you monthly payments that can be in the 7 to 10 percent range. Simply put, you purchase an annuity for a certain amount, and in return you get monthly payments for life. An attractive advantage of annuities is that you can count on receiving payments throughout your retirement years. Some annuities will continue making payments to your surviving spouse or partner.

Most insurance companies offer annuities but under legally binding conditions and with a number of options. Two of them are Mass Mutual and Metropolitan Life. The insurance companies and the types of annuities are too numerous to state here. We advise conducting an online search for annuity-issuing insurance companies and the options that are available. Alternatively, contact your local life insurance agent for information.

Some financial advisers do not favor annuities, arguing that you can find a better retirement option for creating income. Other advisers argue that combining Social Security benefits, annuity income, and IRA income is the safest way to plan your total retirement income.

Certificates of Deposit (CDs)

CDs are savings accounts that guarantee a stated return for a certain period. They are issued by large and small banks across the country. You can purchase CDs from any bank no matter where you live. For example, while living in Virginia, you can buy a CD from a bank in Oregon. In addition, all CDs are insured by the Federal Deposit Insurance Corporation (FDIC), up to $250,000 per account.

The return on a CD will vary with economic conditions. For example, in 2024, twelve-month CDs from most banks were yielding about 5 percent. Go online now to find the current yield. For those who want to avoid all risk, a CD is a viable option.

DEBT-FREE RETIREMENT

One of the most serious mistakes workers can make is carrying debt into retirement—debt like home mortgages and car loan payments. Doing so will greatly impact your retirement income coming from assets like IRAs and Social Security payments, both of which will not increase more than a few dollars each year.

Reliable sources tell us 1) the average home mortgage amount across the US is approximately $150,000 and monthly payments are about $1,500; 2) the average monthly new car loan payment is $740 per month.[23] Going into retirement with a home mortgage payment of $1,500 per month and a new car loan payment of $740 per month when you have no salary is a fool's game. Why? Because in your declining years you will be faced with expenses you never imagined, particularly those related to health issues not covered by insurance. Common health issues that most retirees will face are hip replacements, knee replacements, cardiac malfunctions requiring bypass surgery, ALS, and Alzheimer's disease. All require postsurgical care, which in most situations will necessitate living in a rehabilitation center or hiring a home help aide, which may not be covered by insurance.

Planning for Debt-Free Retirement

Plan to pay off your home mortgage before retirement. Take money from your salary each month and place it in a separate account, or reduce the amount of loan time from thirty to just fifteen years. Talk with your mortgage company and car loan bank about adjusting the time factors and monthly payments to ensure that the mortgage and car loans will be paid off when you retire. This will require discipline, but it is well worth the effort. We can think of nothing more traumatic financially than taking a mortgage or car loan payment into retirement. Doing so almost guarantees that you will be needing another salaried job after formal retirement.

---

23 Maggie Davis, "Mortgage Statistics: 2025," Lending Tree, March 27, 2025, https://www.lendingtree.com/home/mortgage/u-s-mortgage-market-statistics/; Maggie Davis, "Average Car Payment and Auto Loan Statistics: 2025," March 18, 2025, https://www.lendingtree.com/auto/debt-statistics/.

PREPARING YOUR WILL OR TRUST

People live and people die, sometimes unexpectedly, but money matters keep living, not caring if you are ill prepared. Financial matters follow us to the grave, which is the main reason we prepare a will. For example, assume that you live in a home with your husband and suddenly he dies, leaving you with the house and all its attendant expenses for maintenance, taxes, and insurance. After the funeral, you look at his will and discover that the house, which had only his name on the deed, was left to his grown children. You had assumed that the house belonged to both of you, but now you discover it is not.

In some states the house that you cohabit with your lawful husband belongs to both of you, but in other states the owner is only the person named on the deed. Which is the law in your state? Look at your spouse's will. It may be an outdated copy you thought was still valid. However, at some point the will may have been changed, naming his children as the recipients of his house. What happens when you are served with a court order giving you a date to vacate the premises? Do you have enough money to buy or rent another place to live? If not, your next residence may be a tent on the street in Los Angeles, Chicago, Atlanta, or Philadelphia.

Review a copy of your spouse's will to determine whether you are the beneficiary of a life insurance policy or other possessions like an automobile or artwork. This financial information will help you assess your needs when you retire.

Preparing your will is something you should do right now. Consider the many factors in your personal life, like the health of your children, parents, or other significant family members. The importance of this cannot be overstated. For example, assume that you have a parent suffering a lifelong illness like Parkinson's disease. You may be supporting that parent now with income from your salary, but what will happen if you are the unfortunate victim of a fatal accident the day after you retire? Where is the money coming from to care for your sick parent? From your savings? Your monthly IRA check? Insurance? The best way to cover a future expense after you are gone is to buy a term life insurance policy right now. The younger you are, the less the policy will cost. The best way to find an insurance policy is to conduct an online search or consult your insurance broker for advice on selecting an insurance company to buy your policy. A reputable source for this information is AARP (AARP.org).

You must hire a lawyer to prepare a legally secure will or trust to dispose of your possessions and care for those you leave behind. Most lawyers in your neighborhood will do this for a modest fee, like $1,000. For easy-to-understand information on preparing your will, go online to "Will Preparation Checklist" on CurleyBusinessLaw.com.

The Revocable Living Trust

What is the difference between a revocable living trust and a will? A revocable living trust allows you to distribute property after you die and avoids the probate court process. A will is a final set of instructions for how to manage your affairs. While a living trust can distribute assets, it does not handle rights and debts.

The revocable living trust serves different purposes from a will, but they can overlap. A will goes into effect when you die. The trust goes into effect as soon as it is created and remains under your control until you die. The trust and will must work together to give you and your beneficiaries the best financial advantages. Seek advice from your lawyer and tax preparation consultant.

Review and update your will yearly or whenever there is a change in your financial life, which could be when dealing with a job termination, a substantial inheritance, or health matters in your family.

FINANCIAL ADVISERS

Establishing a retirement account and preparing a will and trust requires time, patience, financial acumen, passion, and energy. If you do not get it right, your retirement account could languish, resulting in an unpleasant retirement. If you are not quite sure about how to establish and manage a retirement account, there are several options:

- Go online to government sources for information and advice. These include the Internal Revenue Service, Bureau of Labor Statistics, and Social Security Administration.
- If you are employed, ask for advice from your HR director and the company legal department.
- If you are self-employed, consult with your tax preparation manager.
- If your employer does not offer a 401(k), seek advice from a financial planner at an asset management firm like Fidelity, where the advice might be free or for a small fee.
- If you are technology savvy, consult online sources like NerdWallet (NerdWallet.com). Click on "Investing" and then on "Explore Guides and Tips."
- Review "Twelve Retirement Planning Mistakes to Avoid," US News and World Report on USNews.com.
- Review "The Rule of 25" on RetireGuide.com. It offers advice for preretirement planning, including annuities.
- Review Annuity Resources (AnnuityResources.org).

KEY TAKEAWAYS

- Begin financial planning for retirement as early as possible in your career. Your first job is the ideal time

to begin planning. However, if you overlooked this opportunity, you can begin in mid-career or late career as well.
- Never take early withdrawals from your retirement account like a 401(k) except in dire emergencies.
- Check your retirement account at least once every month.
- Consult your HR director about company pension plans and their benefits for you.
- It's never too late to establish a retirement account.
- Seek advice from a financial planner if you need retirement investing information.
- Prepare your will now and review it each year.
- The right financial plan is there waiting for you. It's your job to find it. Use AI.
- Pay off mortgages and car loans before retirement.

PRINT AND DIGITAL RESOURCES
- FederalRetirement.net, run by Dennis Damp
- Go online to SuzeOrman.com for retirement planning advice written in the vernacular.
- "Top Ten Ways to Prepare for Retirement" by the US Department of Labor (DoL.gov) (Go online and enter "planning for retirement.")
- Consumer Financial Protection Bureau (CFPB.gov). This is a federal government agency offering excellent financial retirement planning advice.
- AARP (AARP.org)

CHAPTER 32

MAINTAINING INSURANCE COVERAGE

INSURANCE MATTERS

Insurance is one of the most disliked industries. Some consider it boring. Others think it is unnecessary. Still others believe it is just a way for greedy companies and their sales reps to take money out of your pocket. It is something most workers tolerate and act upon only when required or obliged to do so. How and why did the insurance industry ever come to the US?

Let's shed light on insurance by looking at it historically. In the US the first insurance company was established in Charleston, South Carolina, in 1735 and covered only loss from fires, which was a welcome and needed initiative for both homeowners and small businesses. Then in 1752 a smart guy in Philadelphia founded a homeowners insurance company to broaden the coverage. His name was Benjamin Franklin. He was trying to devise a way to reduce risk of losing possessions in a home or commercial property by accident or fire. He named the company the Philadelphia Contributionship. It is still in existence 275 years later, insuring homes and commercial properties, and is based in Philadelphia. It now offers expanded coverage that includes flood, wind, water, jewelry, earthquake, sinkhole, personal liability, and death itself.

The American insurance industry includes companies that are among the oldest in the country, with some founded in the mid-1800s. Some of them are the Hartford, founded in 1810; Southern Mutual, founded in 1847; Mutual of Omaha, founded in 1909; and MetLife, founded in 1868.

Insurance planning is not quick or pleasant. It takes time, patience, counseling, and gazing into an uncertain future. It will, however, make your retirement peaceful and happy and even leave time for pickleball, golf, tennis, and yoga.

Retirement planning advice for insurance matters is readily available from both state and county counselors, in person, at government offices. Begin the process by calling the main number for your county and asking to be transferred to the seniors counseling department.

What Does Insurance Really Do?

Life is filled with risk. Living is dangerous. People die, and we live in a litigious society. Nobody is immune to liability. This is why you need insurance. Your liability exposure does not stop when you retire. You must build the cost of insurance policy premiums into your retirement planning. If you need evidence of the necessity of carrying insurance, talk with a claim adjuster for a multiline company like State Farm or Allstate. And remember to consult AI.

How Much Insurance Will I Need in Retirement?

The short answer to this question is that you will need the same kind of insurance coverage in retirement that you needed when in mid-career. You will always need the following insurance policies:

- Medical and dental
- Long-term care
- Life

- Long-term disability
- Auto
- Homeowners
- Business liability insurance if you own your own business

Why We Need Medical Insurance

Let's construct a typical situation. You are doing yard chores or working in the kitchen and cut your thumb. The bleeding will not stop. You go to the emergency room at your nearest hospital or urgent care center for treatment. The doctor says it's nothing too serious and inserts three stitches to close the wound and stop the bleeding. Your bill is $450. In addition, the doctor gives you a prescription for an antibiotic, which costs $50. The total bill for your fun in the kitchen is $500, but your medical insurance covers only $200.

But there's more that can happen. You go to your general practitioner for your annual checkup. Piece of cake, you think. You are sixty-six, have no pain, your energy level is high, you can think clearly, you do not use drugs, and your alcohol intake is an occasional glass of wine. Life is good. The doctor says you are in good shape, but tests show a very slight abnormality, which the doctor contends could be the beginning of a kidney stone. As a precautionary measure, he recommends an abdominal CT scan.

"Nothing to mess with," he says, "so let's be on the safe side."

Two days after the scan, the doctor calls you in to review the results. He seems more serious than usual and asks you to sit in his office. He's behind the desk, report in hand, and says, "Well, the good news is that you do not have a kidney stone and most everything else looks good. However, there is one thing that is not so good. We discovered a growth on the tail end of your pancreas, which is likely malignant. We believe you have pancreatic cancer, and you must have this treated immediately."

Pancreatic cancer? You know this is a life-threatening

situation, having known two workers your age who died from this pernicious cancer only two months after surgery. Two weeks later you are in the hospital undergoing surgery for pancreatic cancer, something that happens only to the other guy, or so you used to believe. After five days in the hospital you are released to recover at home. The total bill for your experience with pancreatic cancer, that killer you never expected, is $65,000, plus loss of income from work, which was not covered because you did not have long-term disability insurance. After you receive all benefits from your company insurance, you still have bills to pay to the tune of $5,000. You are shocked because you were planning to cut your medical insurance to the bone when you retire. Now you're beginning to think about revising your retirement financial savings to include more medical insurance coverage, a wise decision.

Serious medical problems occur not only to workers still on the job but to retirees also. If you do not have adequate medical insurance, that cost will come directly from your own financial resources. Such occurrences do not stop when you retire. They continue until you die, and you must have the money to pay for your medical needs, to include not only doctor costs but also prescription costs, which could be astronomical if you develop something like atrial fibrillation (AFib) and need daily doses of costly blood thinners to prevent a stroke.

RETIREMENT MEDICAL INSURANCE: MEDICARE

This government plan starts at age sixty-five. Until then you can continue with your employee medical plan and benefits if you are still working. (Social Security benefits can start sooner. Medicare and Social Security are two separate programs.)

The enrollment period for Medicare is quite complicated and will require planning on your part to prepare your application at the appropriate time so you will not miss any benefits or incur penalties. Here is a summary of the Medicare plan:

- Medicare Part A covers hospital, skilled nursing care, nursing-home care, and hospice care.
- Medicare Part B covers diagnostic testing and preventive healthcare, such as the annual medical checkup and some eye care.
- Medicare Part C and Medicare Advantage are plans offered through other health insurance agencies and carriers that can be tailored to suit your personal situation. Both include Part A and Part B and may or may not include prescriptions, dental, and eye care.
- Medicare Part D covers prescription drugs offered through different agencies and insurance companies. Premiums and deductibles can be quite expensive and can be tailored to suit your health status and chronic health problems.
- Medigap plans are supplemental to Parts A and B. They cover out-of-pocket expenses not covered by Medicare.
- Dental insurance is separate from Medicare unless it is factored into a Medicare Advantage plan. Coverage can be tailored to suit your needs, including maintenance, and your premiums will be adjusted accordingly.

It's all quite complicated, but there are organizations to help, such as your local senior citizen organization; State Health Insurance Assistance Programs, known as SHIP; and AARP. Also, contact the Centers for Medicare and Medicaid Services (CMS.gov) to obtain the official US government Medicare handbook, which gives a complete review of the various Medicare options and requirements, of which there are many. It's not one size fits all. Costs and coverage options can change every year, so visit the Medicare site frequently (Medicare.gov).

LONG-TERM CARE (LTC)

LTC covers the cost for employing a home healthcare aide to assist retirees with everyday activities like taking a bath, taking prescription medicines, walking up and down stairs, and other medical and nonmedical activities. It also includes nursing-home care and assisted living in a separate facility. Consider purchasing LTC insurance while you are still healthy because you might not qualify for it when you need it in retirement. The cost of this insurance can be extremely high depending on your age, state of health, and location. For comprehensive information about LTC insurance, visit AARP.org and see the "Long-Term Care Insurance Explained" article at NerdWallet.com.

The bottom line, so to speak, is this: Plan to buy only the best medical and drug insurance policies during your retirement. Health issues will increase in your declining years. You will not regret buying the best.

LIFE INSURANCE

Life insurance is a benefit given by many employers to full-time employees, the value of which is usually one year's salary. If your base salary is $80,000, your life insurance will be the same. This is a term life insurance policy and will cease the day you leave your job.

The reality of life is that on some day, you are going to die. Date and time unknown. What we know without a doubt, however, is that your survivors will be left with reduced financial resources if you do not have life insurance. The solution? Purchase a life insurance policy independent of that provided by your employer.

There are different types of life insurance policies, the cost of which, again, will vary with your age and the state of your health. The best and least expensive policy to buy now is term life insurance. The policy pays a stipulated amount to your beneficiary in return for a premium you pay each month. The internet and your personal insurance agent will give you the names of reputable insurance companies and the approximate premium. How much should you purchase? Our recommendation is no less than $1 million. Yes, that's one million dollars. The approximate monthly premium for that term policy for a male in good health is approximately $200, less for a female. It may sound like a lot, but when you calculate the expenses your beneficiary will need in retirement, it is a very small amount to pay each month. For a quick look at the numbers, go to SelectQuote.com.

LONG-TERM DISABILITY (LTD) INSURANCE

As Guardian Insurance explains, "Disability insurance is sometimes referred to as income replacement because it pays you benefits to replace a portion of the income you lose if you're unable to work due to a prolonged illness or injury."

As with most insurance policies, LTD has many variables that include retirement status, age, type of injury, preexisting insurance, workers' compensation, and gender. Most companies will discontinue your LTD coverage when you reach a certain age, usually seventy-five. Some of the most popular companies writing this policy are Unum, Northwestern Mutual, and Guardian.

AUTO INSURANCE

There are two main parts to auto insurance: personal injury liability protection and property damage protection. Of course, there are add-ons like personal medical coverage, uninsured motorist coverage, storm damage, and more. Insurance companies offer a plethora of coverages, and you can explore these by speaking with a sales agent or going online. There are few differences in coverage from one company to another, and some coverages are mandatory. Every state except Florida now requires a minimum amount of personal liability and property damage insurance before they will issue a driver's license, no exceptions. In addition, almost half of all states require uninsured and underinsured personal injury coverage.

The temptation is great for retirees to purchase only the minimum required auto insurance. That is a big mistake. As you plan for retirement with all its attendant expenses, add in your auto insurance premiums. For personal injury protection, carry a minimum of $1 million, and for property damage a minimum of $500,000.

But why so much? Assume you are retired at age seventy-eight and driving your new Tesla to Costco to buy mouthwatering filets and sockeye salmon. You can almost taste it as you near the store, and your distraction causes you to take your eye off the road as you approach a stoplight. The light turns red, but you ignore it and run into the car stopped in front of you. This common rear-end collision causes a cervical spine fracture to the driver and a torn rotator cuff for the passenger. Two years later you are sued and you go to court. The jury awards the driver $1 million for permanent neck injury and $300,000 to the passenger with the rotator cuff injury, which required surgery and six months of physical therapy. *No problem*, you think. *I have insurance to cover this*. However, in an effort to save money for retirement when you were sixty-one, you reduced your auto coverage to the bare minimum of $50,000 for personal injury and $25,000 for property damage resulting from your negligence. Now where do you find the money to pay?

There are many auto insurance companies to select for coverage. Some have excellent reputations for rendering timely service and advice and reasonable premiums. Some give discounts to seniors. Some are noted for excellent claim service. Two of the best, based on personal experience, are State Farm, the world's largest auto insurer, and Nationwide Allstate. The five largest in rank order are State Farm, Geico, Progressive, Allstate, and USAA.

HOMEOWNERS INSURANCE

Homeowners insurance prevents you from risk of loss stemming from accident, injury, and liability for irresponsible actions in your residence, which could be a home or an apartment. But why do you even need this insurance when retired and living in a small two-bedroom 800-square-foot apartment? Think of the serious implications for just a minute. Let's say that someone trips over a frayed rug in your apartment, falls down, and suffers a skull fracture that results in loss of income from work and possibly permanent injury. You are sued and a jury finds you liable and directs you to pay the injured person $2 million. If you do not have homeowners insurance, where will you get the $2 million? And if you do have a homeowner's policy but with liability coverage up to $500,000, where will you get the additional $1.5 million? *But*, you think, *this only happens to other people, not me*. Think again. There is verifiable evidence proving that most serious injuries happen at home.

The five largest homeowners insurance companies are State Farm, Allstate, Liberty Mutual, USAA, and Farmers Insurance Group. Go online to compare coverages and cost of premiums. Better yet, visit the three companies closest to your home and speak with an agent. Learn if their policies cover water damage from an overflowing toilet, injury caused by one of your pets, and flood damage from a hurricane or tornado.

BUSINESS LIABILITY INSURANCE AND LLC COMPANIES

Some workers choose to run a small business in retirement and need insurance. Business insurance protects you from unexpected risks in running a small business, whether it be a restaurant or a business that you operate from home. Accidents, lawsuits, and natural disasters like a flood or tornado could put you out of work and make you personally responsible for loss to one of your customers. It is even necessary for gig workers who might be in a consulting business that gives advice to customers, like financial advice such as selecting equities.

There are many aspects to running a small business, and we suggest reviewing the Small Business Administration website (SBA.gov). Many companies provide small business insurance policies, and they provide advice and premium quotes online. Just google "small business insurance" for a comprehensive list of potential insurers for your business.

Forbes Advisor tells us that the main advantage to an LLC is that it provides limited liability protection. Owners' personal assets can be protected from business debts and lawsuits against the business. An LLC can have one owner (known as a "member") or many. Businesses as well as individuals can be members of an LLC. For information, google "LLC protection."

KEY TAKEAWAYS

- Living is dangerous, now and during retirement. Risk is with us twenty-four seven.
- The purpose of insurance is to limit risk of loss and liability.
- Without exception, you will need the following insurances when retired: medical, dental, life, auto, homeowners.
- You will need small business insurance if you own a business when retired, no exceptions.
- Always seek counseling if in doubt about insurance matters.
- Free retirement counseling is available from your local government offices.

PRINT AND DIGITAL RESOURCES

- The Small Business Administration (SBA.gov)
- Social Security Administration (SSA.gov)
- SelectQuote (SelectQuote.com)
- Centers for Medicare and Medicaid Services (CMS.gov)
- Medicare (Medicare.gov)
- Suze Orman (SuzeOrman.com)
- AARP (AARP.org)
- ACA enrollment information (ObamacarePlans.com)

CHAPTER 33

OVERCOMING LOSS OF IDENTITY

Identity for most workers is based on job title and company affiliation. Loss of identity causes much anxiety for retirees. Let's say you're Paul, a new kid on the retirement block. After forty years working in the private sector and landing an executive position and title, you are no longer Paul Brown, marketing director for Tech Solutions Inc. Now you are just plain Paul. How do you find a new identity, something to replace that fancy title? This is a big challenge, and the search for answers is a serious and necessary undertaking for retirees.

There are three types of identity: family identity, social identity, and work identity, which is the identity we covet most because it says to the world, "Look at me! I'm known throughout my industry and in my company as a success, someone to follow, someone to envy, someone to know and admire, someone with a six-figure income." When you attended company meetings and receptions at industry trade shows at major convention centers like the Javits in NYC, you proudly wore your name tag advertising your name, position, and company. Coworkers treated you with respect and sought your advice.

But the day after retirement, the Paul you saw in the mirror every day vanished. It's a lonely feeling. You feel invisible. Your profile on LinkedIn now says "retired." And in a timespan lasting less than six months, industry and company workers are referring to your replacement as Bob Smith, marketing director. This sudden change in identity to just plain Paul, or Joe, Kelsey, or Henry, is enough to send most workers into a state of grieving.

It's the same for hands-on workers like Walter, a painter who completed work on multimillion-dollar houses in affluent neighborhoods. When people drove past one of his masterpieces, they would say, "Walter worked on that house. Didn't he do great work? He was truly a master painter. He's retired now. Wonder what happened to him."

And so goes the loss of identity problem. It affects all workers when they retire. Some take it in stride and establish a new work identity with an encore career, but most don't. What's the solution? How do you live with a past identity and craft a new face in the mirror?

TRANSITIONING TO A NEW IDENTITY

All retirees face the identity problem upon retirement. It takes time and patience to create a new identity independent of your last job and employer. To ease the burden of transitioning to a new identity, begin the process while still in the workplace, not the retirement space. Think of retirement not as the end of your career but as the beginning of a new one. Also, remember your former on-the-job identity. Don't throw it away. It was part of your success story, and you can wear it proudly throughout your retirement.

The Transition Process

Nothing happens without a plan, which takes time and much thought to create. Here are several initiatives that will move you in the right direction as you search for purpose, meaning, and a new identity in your retirement years.

One year before you plan to retire, begin to redefine your identity. Concentrate on who you are independent of your company and your work title. Play down your work status by cutting back on appearances and speeches for your company and your industry. Attend fewer trade shows, and when possible, remove your job title from your name tag. Use only your name and company name.

Everyone has a family identity. Begin relating more to this identity while still in the workplace. If someone asks what you do, say that you are a mother or father or son or daughter. Respond, "I spend much of my time helping my recently graduated daughter find her spot in the workplace" or "In addition to my job, I'm really busy taking care of my father, who recently had a serious health problem."

Everyone has a social identity, maybe as a member of a political party, a faithful church member, or a food pantry volunteer. Begin spending more free time on these pursuits, and tell people how you function in these activities when asked, "What do you do?"

In the course of your work, you may have adopted a persona in conflict with your character. Redefine the persona and show your true character.

Decide how you will find meaning in your retirement years. It could be through volunteer work with needy individuals. It could be working in an encore career, full- or part-time, pursuing something you have always liked but could not pursue because the remuneration was less than you needed to cover expenses. And it could be pursuing an advanced degree either online or in person at your closest college.

KEY TAKEAWAYS

> - Every retiree faces identity challenges.
> - Begin transitioning to a new identity before retirement.

- Identity transition is a multistep process.
- Your former identity contributed to your success. Remember it fondly.
- Retirement is not an end to your career. It is a new beginning along with a new identity.

DIGITAL RESOURCES

- *Don't Retire, Rewire* by Jeri Sadler
- "Five Ways to Avoid Having a Retirement Identity Crisis" on RevolutionizeRetirement.com
- "Retirement can mean a loss of identity—how to bring happiness to your next act" on MarketWatch.com
- "Loss of Identity after Retirement—How to Adjust" on MutualofOmaha.com

CHAPTER 34

PURSUING AN ENCORE CAREER

"Encore career" refers to a career change when it comes in retirement years. Google "encore career" and you will be inundated with ideas and advice about how to tackle the challenge of transitioning to a new career. Pursuing an encore career could result in finding the most interesting job in your career cycle. Contrary to widespread opinion, an encore career does not have to be a nonpaying volunteer job. For example, substitute K–12 teaching is a delightful job that pays a daily wage in addition to providing meaning, purpose, and identity.

Second career paths are not usually motivated by money. Encore careers are typically motivated by social impact and a sense of personal fulfillment. Frequently, they are concentrated in education, environmental affairs, public service, and healthcare.

The pursuit of an encore career in retirement has become almost routine for most workers reaching the usual retirement age of sixty-five. Today, the majority of workers at age sixty-five are not physically burned out as were workers who did hard physical work in past generations. Encore careers need not be concentrated in full-time corporate jobs. There are other ways to use your retirement years to find purpose, meaning, and identity.

Many types of jobs are labeled as encore careers:

➤ Gig jobs that are hands-on or white-collar, focusing on a

specific market niche for a stated period
- Specific consulting in person or online
- Specialty photography
- Writing
- Executive recruiting in an industry you know well and in which you have multiple contacts with influential hiring managers
- Substitute teaching at the K–12 level
- Full- or part-time work with a political party
- Teaching English to students in a foreign country, like Poland, through the NYC-based Kosciuszko Foundation

An encore career does not have to be a job with a specific title for a specific company. There are many avenues one can take to find a suitable, interesting, and meaningful encore career.

SELECTING AN ENCORE CAREER PATH

Many workers find it taxing to decide how to explore encore careers. As they near retirement, they find this task as confusing as they did when selecting their first jobs in their mid-twenties. We addressed that concern in detail in chapter 4, "Matching the Real You with a Real Career." In that chapter, a creative and easy-to-navigate device called the NEXTERCISE is a fail-safe shortcut to link you with a meaningful career.

The main features of the NEXTERCISE:
- Determining your multiple interests
- Identifying your multiple skills
- Matching your interests and skills with a career demanding both your interests and skills
- Selecting an industry that identifies with your matched skills and interests
- Selecting companies within your chosen industry that offer compatible career opportunities

RETIREES WHO ESTABLISHED AN ENCORE CAREER

Here are several retirees who wish their story to be told as an example to others exploring encore careers:

David from Lancaster, Pennsylvania, retired from a great sales position with a nationwide printing company. Shortly thereafter, David accepted nonpaying jobs with his high school alma mater for many years. At his university alma mater, he maintained his former fraternity house and managed full house renovations. All these activities take a fair amount of David's time, but they have provided meaning in his retirement years. Now he plays pickleball almost daily, paints beautiful pictures, and enjoys summers with his grandchildren at the beach. To sum up his retirement, David says, "How sweet it is! Thank you, Social Security, Medicare, and my work pension!"

Jenny from Silver Spring, Maryland, has had a peripatetic work career. She began her working life as an aspiring actress. Her day job was as a waitress. She soon moved on to freelance film production after obtaining her master's degree in film from American University. When her two sons came along, film work's long and irregular hours made continuing in that field difficult. She took to writing and had a book published but soon found most writers need a day job to pay the bills! She then turned to her avocation and encore career: gardening. She began working for the Audubon Naturalist Society (now called Nature Forward) as an environmental educator bringing lessons to classrooms in the county and consulting on best practices for schoolyard gardens. She ended her career as a full-time consultant teaching adults about native plant gardening. Postretirement, she has continued with an encore career, offering her expertise as a native plant and food garden consultant for entities such as the City of Silver Spring and nonprofit organizations interested in supporting recent immigrants and food-insecure individuals.

Michael from Chesapeake, Virginia, retired from a national sales manager position with a company publishing K–12 instructional materials for special-needs and at-risk students. He selected a four-part encore career: 1) selling K–12 instructional materials as an independent sales representative in several nearby states; 2) leading religious and secular activities in his local Catholic church, for which he does not get paid; 3) conducting nonpaying volunteer services in his local Knights of Columbus chapter, where he was twice elected grand knight supervising 120 members; and 4) serving as a board member of the Black Fives, a foundation to research, preserve, teach, and honor the pre-NBA history of African Americans in basketball. Michael's multifaceted encore career gives him meaning, satisfaction, and purpose in addition to commission payments for his work as an independent sales representative.

John from Minneapolis, Minnesota, built his encore career as a K–12 substitute teacher after owning his own executive recruiting business, Meeker and Associates, for twenty five years. After earning his MA at the University of North Carolina and PhD at the University of Michigan, he held academic and research positions at Michigan. In addition, Dr. Meeker was the US national sales manager for the company that produced *The Oregon Trail* software for K–12 schools. His career path included executive-level positions in sales and marketing with companies producing services and products for the K–12 and college education markets. These work activities required him to live in Texas, New York, New Jersey, and Michigan. He is totally satisfied with his encore career as a substitute teacher, which not only pays but also provides satisfaction, meaning, and purpose during his retirement years.

Christine from San Francisco, California, received her MBA from St. Mary's College and worked as vice president of sales and marketing with an educational software firm. Later in her career she retired from a COO position with the Greaves Consulting Group. Then Christine pursued an encore career as a board member with nonprofit organizations catering to high school and college students with significant financial needs. She continues in her passion for education as a board member for Cristo De La Salle High School East and Catholic Charities of San Francisco. Her encore career gives her the ultimate job satisfaction and life meaning.

What can we learn from these encore career workers, all of whom are in their mid-sixties to late seventies? They are telling us that one can find meaning, value, purpose, and even a paycheck working in encore careers during retirement.

KEY TAKEAWAYS

- Your postretirement years will bring peace and happiness if you continue working in an encore career.
- Encore careers include both volunteer nonpaying jobs and paying jobs.
- Encore careers don't just happen. Plan for them during the mid-career of your full-time job.

DIGITAL RESOURCES

- Read "How to Start an Encore Career After 50" on MoneyGeek.com.
- *Encore: Finding Work that Matters in the Second Half of Life* by Marc Freedman
- Find information on retirement financial planning and guidance at FederalRetirement.net.

CHAPTER 35

PEACE, HAPPINESS, AND PICKLEBALL IN RETIREMENT

PEACE: WHAT IT IS AND HOW TO ACHIEVE IT

Retirement, the third part of the work cycle, can be the most peaceful time of your life. But peace will not be included in your corporate severance package. You must plan ahead for a peaceful retirement. So, what is peace?

Peace in retirement means living without stress. It is something you must achieve on your own by identifying and eliminating those things in life that generate stress. Items that cause stress include concern about long-term financial matters, unfavorable relationships with your spouse, partner, or other family members, health matters like type 2 diabetes, and problems generating a new identity independent of your career or company affiliation.

Achieving Peace

Financial, insurance, and health matters cause the most stress for retirees. The first two can be resolved with judicious planning and advice from experts in the field, like your employment lawyer and financial advisers at asset management firms like Vanguard and Fidelity.

Poor health in retirement causes stress, but it can be

minimized if you use common sense and maintain your health by having annual or semiannual checkups with your physician and consulting AARP or similar organizations.

HAPPINESS: WHAT IT IS AND HOW TO DISCOVER IT

Achieving happiness is a very personal event and comes from within. There are hundreds of definitions for happiness. Happiness is something that makes you smile, like seeing good fortune come to a friend or family member. It is an emotional state characterized by feelings of satisfaction, joy, and contentment.

Some dictionaries define happiness as "luck." Broadly defined, it might be called a state of satisfaction with one's accomplishments or with life in general. However, happiness usually is tied to particular events. For some it might be prompted by seeing a grandchild begin to walk and talk and grow physically and intellectually. For another person happiness might be seeing one's children graduate from college with honors and land an entry-level job six weeks later. Other retirees achieve an emotional high when they derive satisfaction, meaning, and identity from their encore careers.

Physical Activity

Retirees both in America and other countries have never been so physically fit and have never lived so long. Physical fitness has prompted retirees to break away from the TV and rocking chair and participate in activities never before imagined into their seventies or even mid-eighties. Today you find retirees on lawnmowers and ladders maintaining the interior and exterior of their houses and purchasing campers and traveling to remote places like the Outer Hebrides. As for sporting activities, the next time you pass a tennis court, a golf course, or a steep hiking trail, notice the many seniors participating.

The Most Fun for Retirees

We don't know how it came about, but we know it's here to stay. Seniors are addicted to the sport and find it invigorating, competitive, social, and just a lot of fun. Of course we're talking about *pickleball*! Enjoy!

KEY TAKEAWAYS

- Work does not stop when you reach retirement, the third part of the work cycle. Work is that which you do to make money to buy the three items for survival: food, shelter, clothing. Work continues as you manage your finances, insurance, and encore career.
- Remember the basic meaning of life, and the picture will be clear: You are born. You die. And in between, you work.

CHAPTER 36

TEN TIPS FOR MAKING RETIREMENT WORK

Making your retirement peaceful and happy is a process based on planning while you are still employed. Contentment does not appear automatically the day you say goodbye to your employer. The choices made are strictly personal, but there are some tips that apply to all workers in retirement planning mode.

Tip 1. Maintain good health. Establish a regular physical exercise routine. Avoid tobacco, alcohol, and harmful drugs. Initiate a healthy diet. Maintain a healthy weight by using the half-double method of weight control, which means eating half of what you usually eat and doubling your exercise time. Meet with your doctor, in person, for periodic physical exams.

Tip 2. Downsize your living quarters before your retirement day. Begin working with a realtor several years before retirement to see what your options are. Moving to new living quarters can be filled with stress. Why spend some of your retirement years living with house-hunting stress?

Tip 3. Begin financial initiatives for retirement when you enter the workforce. Financial planning the day after you retire is a bit too late.

Tip 4. Life is filled with risk. Accidents happen every day, most in our own homes. Over 40,000 people are killed in car accidents every year. We live in a litigious society. To reduce risk, which continues during retirement, insurance is necessary. Rather than discontinuing or reducing coverage, maintain and maybe expand policies for healthcare, auto, life, homeowners, and long-term care Your retirement will be filled with peace and happiness if you reduce risk.

Tip 5. Consult with your HR director, employment lawyer, insurance agent, and asset management company (companies like Vanguard, Fidelity, or Prudential) several years before retirement to determine your retirement rights and benefits. Knowing that you are receiving all that is owed to you in retirement will bring you peace.

Tip 6. Your work identity will disappear the day after you retire. Begin building your new identity based on your personal and social identities before retirement.

Tip 7. An encore career can consist of several part-time jobs aligned with your interests and abilities. Use AI to help with this task.

Tip 8. Going forward, interesting encore careers may include artificial intelligence. Prepare for using AI before retirement, and your choice of encore careers will expand exponentially. Also, use the NEXTERCISE in chapter 4 of this book.

Tip 9. Starting an entrepreneurial business in retirement can provide much life satisfaction and meaning. If this is on your list of retirement options, begin planning several years before your retirement day.

Tip 10. Retirement is the third and final stage in your career cycle. You will enjoy it to the max if you are kind, courageous, compassionate, and engaged in an encore career.

ACKNOWLEDGMENTS

I offer my heartfelt thanks to the many individuals who have contributed to the writing and publication of *Hired! Fired! Retired!* I am especially grateful to my Koehler editor, Hannah Woodlan, and executive, Danielle Koehler at Koehler Books for their time and expertise, which made this book possible.

Also, I thank the following:

Marilyn Baker Weiss, my wife and certified nurse midwife, who reviewed the manuscript and offered much advice for improvement. She has worked on three continents: Africa, Europe, and America.

Alice Miller, station manager and host for WWFM, 89.1, the Classical Network, located in New Jersey, who reviewed the manuscript and offered valuable insight into the state of being employed.

Christopher Weiss, video producer and cofounder of RaffertyWeiss Media. His editorial and marketing expertise played a key role in the organization and chapter titles of this book.

Dennis Damp, Air Force veteran, author of twenty-eight books, guest on hundreds of radio and TV shows, and nationally recognized expert in all matters pertaining to federal government jobs and retirement. My thanks to Dennis for permission to include quotations from his bestselling books and websites.

Nicholas Johnson, JD, law professor at Fordham University Law School, who reviewed current legal content in this book.

My appreciation to the following workers, who offered their retirement stories found in chapter 34, "Pursuing an Encore Career":

David Bair, whose account of his encore career sets an example for the path retirees can take to make their retirement peaceful, happy, and meaningful.

Jenny Brown, who reviewed material on retirement and contributed by disclosing her encore career activities.

Michael King, who contributed his truly inspiring encore career bio.

Dr. John Meeker, who gave insight into his encore career as a substitute teacher.

Christine Whelan, whose encore career continues unabated at the University of San Francisco.

A special thank-you to Nick Johnson, Vice President of Finance at AssemblyAI, a California-based company specializing in speech-to-text and speech-to-understanding. Nick is recognized by TOP CFOs as a leader of finance for AI companies throughout the world. Having worked in many countries outside of the US, Nick helped us understand how the worldwide workplace really works.

My thanks to Mark Simon, Assistant Treasurer for Merck, a multinational pharmaceutical company, for his updating us on the current use of AI.

APPENDIX

UNITED STATES CONVENTION CENTERS

Every state has convention centers that host trade shows and conferences, which are the best places to find hiring managers and job opportunities. Managers, directors, and vice presidents from sales, marketing, product development, technology, advertising, human resources, event planning, and finance work in the trade show exhibit booths. CEOs and presidents usually "work the booth" also.

What do you do at a trade show? Stop at a booth, introduce yourself, and ask for help securing employment. Does it get easier than that? Potential employers are not hiding under rocks; rather, they hang out at convention centers.

Go online and contact the convention centers listed by state below. Each center will provide the dates and names of the trade shows for the entire year, and many will provide links to the companies attending. In addition, you will find the price of admission and other pertinent information that will make your visit there more profitable.

ALABAMA

Birmingham-Jefferson Civic Center, BJCC.org
2100 Richard Arrington Jr. Boulevard North
Birmingham, AL 35203
(205) 458-8400

ALASKA

Anchorage Convention Centers
AnchorageConventionCenters.com
555 West Fifth Avenue
Anchorage, AK 99501
(907) 263-2800

Juneau Centennial Hall Convention Center
Juneau.org/centennial
101 Egan Drive
Juneau, AK 99801
(907) 586-5283

ARIZONA

Phoenix Convention Center
PhoenixConventionCenter.com
111 North Third Street
Phoenix, AZ 85004
(602) 262-6225

Tucson Convention Center
TucsonConventionCenter.com
260 South Church Street
Tucson, AZ 85701
(520) 791-4101

ARKANSAS

Statehouse Convention Center
LittleRockMeetings.com
101 East Markham Street
Little Rock, AR 72201
(501) 376-4781
(800) 844-4781

CALIFORNIA

Long Beach Convention and Entertainment Center
LongBeachCC.com
300 Ocean Boulevard
Long Beach, CA 90802
(562) 436-3636

Los Angeles Convention Center
LACCLink.com
685 South Figueroa Street
Los Angeles, CA 90015
(between Wilshire Blvd and Seventh Street)
(213) 741-1151

San Diego Convention Center
VisitSanDiego.com
111 West Harbor Drive
San Diego, CA 92101
(619) 525-5428

Moscone Center
Moscone.com
747 Howard Street
San Francisco, CA 94103
(415) 974-4000

COLORADO

Colorado Convention Center
DenverConvention.com
700 Fourteenth Street
Denver, CO 80202
(303) 228-8000

CONNECTICUT
XL Center (formerly the Hartford Civic Center)
XLCenter.com
1 Civic Center Plaza
Hartford, CT 06103
(860) 249-6333

DELAWARE
Chase Center on the Riverfront
CenterontheRiverfront.com
815 Justison Street
Wilmington, DE 19801
(302) 425-3929

DISTRICT OF COLUMBIA
Walter E. Washington Convention Center
EventsDC.com
801 Mount Vernon Place Northwest
Washington, DC 20001
(202) 249-3000

FLORIDA
Fort Lauderdale/Broward Co. Convention Center
FtLauderdaleCC.com
1950 Eisenhower Boulevard
Fort Lauderdale, FL 33316
(305) 765-5900

Miami Beach Convention Center
MiamiBeachConvention.com
1901 Convention Center Drive
Miami Beach, FL 33139
(786) 276-2600

Orange County Convention Center
OCCC.net
9800 International Drive
Orlando, FL 32819
(407) 345-9800

Tampa Convention Center
TampaConventionCenter.com
333 South Franklin Street
Tampa, Florida 33602
(813) 274-8511

GEORGIA
Georgia World Congress Center
GWCC.com
285 Andrew Young International Boulevard Northwest
Atlanta, GA 30313
(404) 223-4000

HAWAII
Hawaii Convention Center
HawaiiConvention.com
1801 Kalakaua Avenue
Honolulu, HI 96815
(808) 943-3500

IDAHO
Boise Center
BoiseCentre.com
850 West Front Street
Boise, Idaho 83702
(208) 336-8900

ILLINOIS
McCormick Place
MccormickPlace.com
2301 South Lake Shore Drive
Chicago, IL 60616
(312) 791-7000

Navy Pier
NavyPier.com
600 East Grand Avenue
Chicago, IL 60611
(312) 595-7437

INDIANA
Indiana Convention Center
ICCLOS.com
100 South Capitol Avenue
Indianapolis, Indiana 46225
(317) 262-3400

IOWA
Iowa Events Center
IowaEventsCenter.com
730 Third Street
Des Moines, IA 50309
(515) 564-8000

KENTUCKY
Kentucky International Convention Center
KYConvention.org
221 Fourth Street
Louisville, KY 40202
(502) 595-4381

LOUISIANA
Ernest N. Morial Convention Center
MCCNO.com
900 Convention Center Boulevard
New Orleans, LA 70130
(504) 582-3000

MAINE
Cross Insurance Arena
TheCivicCenter.com
1 Civic Center Square
Portland, ME 04101
(207) 791-2200

MARYLAND
Baltimore Convention Center
BCCenter.org
1 West Pratt Street
Baltimore, MD 21201
(410) 649-7000

MASSACHUSETTS
Boston Convention and Exhibition Center
BostonConventionCenter.com
415 Summer Street
Boston, MA
(617) 954-2000

John B. Hynes Convention Center
MassConvention.com
900 Boylston Street
Boston, MA 02115
(617) 954-2000

MICHIGAN
Huntington Place Conference/Exhibition Center
HuntingtonPlaceDetroit.com
1 Washington Boulevard
Detroit, MI 48226
(313) 877-8777

MINNESOTA
Mayo Civic Center
MayoCivicCenter.com
30 Civic Center Drive Southeast
Rochester, MN 55904
(507) 361-5040

Duluth Entertainment Convention Center
DECC.org
350 Harbor Drive
Duluth, MN 55802
(218) 722-5573

Minneapolis Convention Center
MinneapolisConventionCenter.com
1301 Second Avenue South
Minneapolis, MN 55403
(612) 335-6000

MISSISSIPPI
Mississippi Coast Convention Center
MSCoastConventionCenter.com
2350 Beach Boulevard
Biloxi, Mississippi 39531
(228) 594-3700

MISSOURI

Kansas City Convention Center
KCConvention.com
301 West Thirteenth Street
Kansas City, Missouri 64105
(816) 513-5000

America's Center Convention Complex
ExploreStLouis.com
701 Convention Plaza
St. Louis, Missouri 63105
800-916-8938

MONTANA

Butte Silver Bow Civic Center
ButteCivicCenter.com
1340 Harrison Avenue
Butte, MT 59701
(406) 497-6400

Helena Civic Center
HelenaCivicCenter.com
340 Neill Avenue
Helena, MT 59601
(406) 447-8000

NEBRASKA

CenturyLink Center
CenturyLinkCenterOmaha.com
455 North Tenth Street
Omaha, NE 68102
(402) 341-1500

NEVADA
Las Vegas Convention and Visitors Authority
LVCVA.com
3150 Paradise Road
Las Vegas, NV 89109
(702) 892-0711

NEW HAMPSHIRE
Check out the convention centers in Maine and Massachusetts.

NEW JERSEY
Atlantic City Convention Center
ACCenter.com
1 Convention Boulevard
Atlantic City, NJ 08401
(609) 449-2000

Meadowlands Exposition Center,
MECExpo.com
355 Plaza Drive
Secaucus, NJ 07094
(201) 330-1172

New Jersey Convention and Exposition Center
NJExpoCenter.com
97 Sunfield Avenue
Edison, New Jersey 08837
(732) 417-1400

Wildwoods Convention Center
WildwoodsNJ.com/cc
4501 Boardwalk
Wildwood, NJ
(609) 729-9000

NEW MEXICO
Albuquerque Convention Center
AlbuquerqueCC.com
401 Second Street Northwest
Albuquerque, NM 87102
(505) 768-4575

NEW YORK
Buffalo Convention Center
BuffaloConvention.com
153 Franklin Street
Buffalo, NY 14202
(716) 855-5555

Jacob K. Javits Convention Center
JavitsCenter.com
429 Eleventh Avenue
New York, NY 10001
(212) 216-2000

NORTH CAROLINA
Charlotte Convention Center
CharlotteConventionCtr.com
100 Paul Buck Boulevard
Charlotte, NC 28217
(704) 339-6117

NORTH DAKOTA
Bismarck Event Center
BismarckEventCenter.com
315 South Fifth St.
Bismarck, ND 58504
(701) 355-1370

OHIO

Duke Energy Convention Center
Duke-EnergyCenter.com
525 Elm Street
Cincinnati, OH 45202
(513) 419-7300

Cleveland Convention Center
ClevCC.com
500 Lakeside Avenue East
Cleveland, OH 044113
(216) 928-1600

I X Center
IXCenter.com
1 1-X Center Drive
Cleveland, OH 44135
(216) 676-6000

Dayton Convention Center
DaytonConventionCenter.com
22 East Fifth Street
Dayton, OH 45402
(937) 535-5300

Glass City Center
GlassCityCenter.com
401 Jefferson Avenue
Toledo, OH 43604
(419) 355-3300

OKLAHOMA

Cox Business Center
CoxCenterTulsa.com
100 Civic Center
Tulsa, OK 74103
918-894-4350

OREGON

Oregon Convention Center
OregonCC.org
777 North Martin Luther King Boulevard
Portland, OR 97232
(503) 235-7575

PENNSYLVANIA

Pennsylvania Convention Center
PAConvention.com
1101 Arch Street
Philadelphia, PA 19107
(215) 418-4700

David L. Lawrence Convention Center
PittsburghCC.com
1000 Fort Duquesne Boulevard
Pittsburgh, PA 15222
(412) 565-6000

RHODE ISLAND

Rhode Island Convention Center
RIConvention.com
1 Sabin Street
Providence, RI 02903-1814
(401) 458-6000

SOUTH CAROLINA
Charleston Area Convention Center
MeetCharleston.com/convention-center/
5001 Coliseum Drive North
North Charleston, SC 29418
818-264-6812

SOUTH DAKOTA
Sioux Empire Fairgrounds
SiouxEmpireFair.org
100 North Lyon Boulevard
Sioux Falls, SD 57107
(605) 367-7178

TENNESSEE
Music City Center
NashvilleMusicCityCenter.com
201 Rep. John Lewis Way South
Nashville, TN 37203
(615) 401-1400

TEXAS
Austin Convention Center
AustinConventionCenter.com
500 East Cesar Chavez Street
Austin, TX 78701
(512) 404-4000

Kay Bailey Hutchison Convention Center
DallasConventionCenter.com
650 South Griffin Street
Dallas, TX 75202
(214) 939-2700

George R. Brown Convention Center
GRBHouston.com
1001 Avenida de las Americas
Houston, TX 77010
(713) 853-8000

Henry B. González Convention Center
SAHBGCC.com
800 East Market Street
San Antonio, TX 78296
(210) 207-8500

Waco Convention Center
WacoCC.com
100 Washington Avenue
Waco, TX 76702
(254) 750-5810

UTAH
Calvin L. Rampton Salt Palace Convention Center
VisitSaltLake.com/salt-palace-convention-center
90 Southwest Temple Street
Salt Lake City, UT 84101
(801) 534-4900

Dixie Convention Center
DixieCenter.com
1835 South Convention Center Drive
St. George, UT 84790
(435) 301-7770

VERMONT

Stoweflake Convention Center
Stoweflake.com
1746 Mountain Road
Stowe, VT 05672
(800) 253-2232

VIRGINIA

The Greater Richmond Convention Center
Richmondcenter.com.
403 North Third Street
Richmond, VA 23219
(804) 783-7300

The Virginia Beach Convention Center
VBCVB.com
1000 Nineteenth Street
Virginia Beach, VA 23451
(757) 385-2000

WASHINGTON

Meydenbauer Center
Meydenbauer.com
11100 Northeast Sixth Street
Bellevue, WA 98004
(425) 637-1020

Seattle Convention Center
SeattleConventionCenter.com
705 Pike St.
Seattle, WA 98101-2350
(206) 694-5000

Spokane Convention Center
Spokanecenter.com
334 West Spokane Falls Boulevard
Spokane, WA 99201
(509) 279-7007

WEST VIRGINIA
Charleston Civic Center
CharlestonCivicCenter.com
200 Civic Center Drive
Charleston, WV 25301
(304) 345-1500

WISCONSIN
Wisconsin Center
WisconsinCenter.org
400 West Wisconsin Avenue
Milwaukee, WI 53203
(414) 908-6000

WYOMING
Ford Wyoming Center
FordWyomingCenter.com
1 Events Drive
Caspar, WY 82601
(307) 235-84

THE AUTHOR

John Henry Weiss is the author of four books focusing on careers and the workplace. Additional writing experience includes articles published in the *Costco Connection* magazine; articles published by Ms. Career Girl; blogs for Talentmarks; and articles for FederalGovernmentJobs.net. Weiss has been quoted in the *New York Post* and other national publications. Previous full-time employment includes teaching in Chicago and working in editorial, and in domestic and international sales and marketing with publishers concentrating on the K–16 education market, companies such as Houghton/Harcourt and Apple. In addition, Weiss has twenty years of experience working as an executive recruiter placing CEOs, presidents, editors, sales managers, marketing managers, and a variety of director-level workers.

Contact Information
Email: Weiss4Jobs@aol.com
Website: JohnHenryWeiss.com

INDEX

AARP
    career resources of, 214, 219
    health resources of, 276–277
    insurance resources of, 253, 260, 261
    retirement resources of, 237, 253, 255, 260, 261, 266, 276–277
AARP (magazine), 219
AASA. *See* American Association of School Administrators
ACA. *See* Affordable Care Act
accounting/finance department, 26
administrative assistants, power of, 106–107
Adobe, 24
Advanced Micro Devices (AMD), 115
Aetna, 160
Affordable Care Act (ACA), 146, 149, 160, 167, 266
age
    and IRA withdrawals, 248
    and retirement, 232–233, 238–240
    and salary expectations, 181–182
Age Discrimination in Employment Act (ADEA) of 1967, 238
agenda, written, for interview, 59–61, 71
aging parent care, 168, 170–171
Agra, India, 15
AI. *See* artificial intelligence
The AI Lead (Lambert), 117
ALA. *See* American Library Association
alcohol, avoiding, 68, 191
Allstate, 44, 257, 263–264
American Airlines, 25
American Association of School Administrators (AASA), 199
American College of Nurse Midwives, 202
American Library Association (ALA), 199
American Physical Therapy Association, 202
American Society of Clinical Oncology, 202
angel funding, 98
annuities, 234, 249–250
Annuity Resources (AnnuityResources.com), 254
Apparel Sourcing show, 197
Apple, 24, 114, 120, 207, 208

aptitude
- discovering, 118–119
- NEXTERCISE for, 37–40, 118

Ardipithecus ramidus (Ardi), 17

artificial intelligence (AI), 114–116
- assistants in, 17
- education, for unemployed people, 173–174
- encore careers and, 280
- everyday transactions using, 8–9
- federal government and, 116
- jobs lost to, 8, 114
- media focus on, 1
- potential impact of, 1
- preparing for future of, 114–115, 126
- products and companies, 115
- resources on, 8
- résumé written by, as bad approach, 47, 50
- skills and proficiency with, 18, 50
- trade shows and, 202
- workplace transformed by, 4, 8–9, 126

AssemblyAI, 24, 115, 117

Assurity, 84

Atlanta Convention Center, 194

AT&T, 44

attorney. *See* employment attorney

at-will provision, 6, 30, 31, 32

automobile industry, 24–25, 124

automobile insurance
- largest providers of, 263–264
- maintaining in retirement, 258, 262–264
- maintaining after termination, 160, 162
- personal injury liability protection in, 262–263
- proof of, 162
- property damage protection in, 262–263
- state requirements for, 262–263

automobile loans, retirement and, 250–251

automobile shows, 202

awards and special recognition, on résumé, 49

Baby boomers, 27

banking and finance industry, 24

bank loans, 97

Bank of America, 24, 44, 132

banks, certificates of deposits in, 250

Barra, Mary, 42
Barron's (magazine), 128
BBC, 24
Beautiful.AI, 115, 117
beginning of interview, 61–63
benefits
    COBRA, 145–146, 160
    company-paid, 83–84
    FMLA provisions for, 33, 82–83
    government job, 25
    legally required, 82–83
    negotiating, 81, 85–86
    reduced, COVID-19 pandemic and, 3
    retirement, legally required, 243–244
    severance agreements and, 147–149
    Social Security, 82, 232–237
    termination and, 145–149, 160–162
    unemployment, 146–147
Bernstein, Brenda, 19, 52, 136
Best Buy, 132–133
"big three" (food, shelter, clothing)
    AI-assisted acquisition of, 17
    cost, during retirement, 234
    cost, during unemployment, 154–156
    evolution of search for, 16–17
    industries focused on, 21–22
    primary purpose of work and, 13, 18, 125
    survival of species and, 28
bipedalism (walking), and human self-sufficiency, 16–17
Black Data Processing Associates, 44
Black Professionals in Tech Network, 44
Bloom, Nicholas, 168–169
Bloomberg channel/*Bloomberg Businessweek,* 47, 128, 151, 158
BLS. *See* Bureau of Labor Statistics
Blue Cross, 160
board of directors, 26
body language, 58–59, 71, 179
body of interview, 61
Bolles, Richard, 218
Bologna Children's Book Fair (Italy), 200
The Book of US Government Jobs (Damp), 109, 113, 174
boss, as reason for quitting, 90
Branson, Richard, 96, 207
Brazil, population of, 124

break, taking after termination, 141–142, 226
breakfast interviews, 68–69
"breakout sessions," at trade shows, 186
Breeze, 84
Brewer, Rosalind, 43
Bright Hub, 104
Brooks, David, 123
budget
 retirement, 7, 233–234, 245–246
 unemployment, 153–157
Building a Better Vocabulary (Flanigan), 74
Bureau of Labor Statistics (BLS)
 benefit costs explained by, 81
 Employment Situation Summary of, 8
 government job data of, 105, 107
 JOLTS report of, 8, 158
 The Occupational Outlook Handbook of, 8, 19, 28, 103, 113–114, 117, 174, 184
 retirement resources of, 254
 termination resources of, 143, 144, 166, 174, 184
 termination statistics of, 6–7, 126, 131
Burger King, 101
business (calling) cards, 101, 185–186, 187, 189–190, 204
business liability insurance, 258, 264 265
Business Management Daily (online source), 86
BusinessNewsDaily.com, 93
business parks
 online/AI resources on, 205
 personal visits to, 185, 204–205

California
 convention centers and trade shows in, 193, 201, 286
 government jobs in, 106
 retirement benefits in, 243
 salary comparisons for, 184
calling (business) cards, 101, 185–186, 187, 189–190, 204
Campbell Soup Company, 22
Caprino, Kathy, 215
career. *See also specific topics*
 definition of, 2
 encore, 7, 234, 271–275
 NEXTERCISE on, 37–40
Career Builder (CareerBuilder.com), 203
career-centered questions, 4–5

career coaches, 210–219
    career counselors *versus,* 211
    credentials of, 212–214
    fees of, 212
    outplacement services *versus,* 216–217
    personal characteristics of, 211
    selecting, 214–215
    solution orientation of, 211
    training organizations for, 213–214
The Career Coaching Handbook (Yeates), 218
CareerContessa.com, 86
career counselors, 138, 210–219
    career coaches *versus,* 211
    credentials of, 212–214
    fees of, 212
    outplacement services *versus,* 216–217
    selecting, 214–215
    training organizations for, 213–214
Career Forward (Puma and Shi), 45, 74
career objectives, 111–117
    artificial intelligence and, 114–116
    mid-career changes in, 111–112
    outcomes of trying to fulfill, 116
    redefining process for, 112
    searching for, 112–114
caring, 122
CASA trade show, 194
cash savings
    certificates of deposit (CDs), 250
    protecting, after termination, 150–153
    retirement need for, 234
    six-month emergency fund of, 151–152
CDs (certificates of deposit), 250
Census Bureau, US, 8, 42, 184, 232–233
Centers for Medicare and Medicaid Services (CMS), 260, 266
CEO. *See* chief executive officer
CertaPro Painters, 102
certificates of deposit (CDs), 250
certifications
    of career coaches and counselors, 212–214
    on résumé, 49
    unemployment and need for, 173–174
CES. *See* Consumer Electronics Show
CFO (chief financial officer), 26

CFPB. *See* Consumer Financial Protection Bureau
character
    conflict with persona, 127, 269
    definition of, 121, 127
    discovering and rebuilding, 118, 121–122
    showing true, in retirement, 269
    six pillars of, 122
Character Counts!, 122, 123
Character.org, 123
Charleston, South Carolina, origins of insurance industry in, 23, 256
ChatGPT, 115
Chelle Law, 36
Chicago, convention centers and trade shows in, 128, 192, 194–195, 197, 198, 289
ChicagoHomeShow.net, 198
chief executive officer (CEO), 26
    minority firsts as, 43
    women as, 42, 43
chief financial officer (CFO), 26
childcare, 168, 169–170
China, population of, 124
Chipotle, 101
churches, counseling services of, 138, 217
Cigna, 160
Cisco, 44
Citigroup, 42
Citizens Bank, 234
citizenship, 122
civil service jobs, 108
Civil Service Retirement System (CSRS), 239–240
clergy, counseling from, 138, 217
C-level departments, 26
clothing
    AI-assisted acquisition of, 17
    cost, during retirement, 234
    cost, during unemployment, 155–156
    evolution of search for, 16–17
    working to provide, 13, 18, 125
clothing companies, 22
clothing industry trade shows, 197
CMS. *See* Centers for Medicare and Medicaid Services
CNBC, 47, 128, 133, 151, 158
COBRA benefits, 145–146, 160, 166
college costs, options for unemployed parent, 156–157

colleges, counseling services provided by, 217–218
college savings accounts (529), 153
Colorado, retirement benefits in, 243
community service, on résumé, 49
company culture, as reason for quitting, 91
company-paid benefits, 83–84
compensation objection, to job candidacy, 177, 181–184
compensation package, 80, 81. *See also* benefits; salary
competition, noncompete provision restricting, 6, 30
Conagra, 22
conferences. *See* trade shows
Connecticut, retirement benefits in, 243
Consolidated Omnibus Budget Reconciliation Act (COBRA), 145–146, 160, 166
consulting
- encore career in, 272
- self-employment in, 100–101

Consumer Electronics Show (CES), 187, 202
Consumer Financial Protection Bureau (CFPB), 255
contact information, on résumé, 48
continuing education, on résumé, 49
contract. *See* employment contract
convention centers, 186, 284–300
- finding jobs with, 192
- top, for trade shows, 192–196

conventions. *See* trade shows
corporate websites, 204
courtesy, and interview, 55–56, 68–69, 72–73, 78
Covey, Stephen, 55, 74
COVID-19 pandemic
- economic rebound from, 3, 9
- "essential" workers during, 3
- financial investments during, 150–151
- remote work during, 3, 84
- return to "normal" after, 3
- stress during, 3–4
- termination/layoffs during, 3, 132–133, 134
- work transformed by, 2–5

COVID-19 vaccine, 3
coworkers, relationship with, as reason for quitting, 90
Cramer, Jim, 128, 158
credentials, for career coaches and counselors, 212–214
Crosby, Olivia, 108
cryptocurrencies, 17

CSRS. *See* Civil Service Retirement System
currency, history of, 17
CVS, 23
CWM Environmental, 113

Dairy Queen, 101
Damp, Dennis, 28, 108–109, 113, 174, 239–240, 244, 255
data sources, 7–8
death, preparing for
    funeral insurance for, 166–167
    life insurance for, 83, 160, 163–164, 167, 252–253, 257, 261–262
    will for, 252–253
debt-free retirement, 250–251
Delhi, India, 15–16
Delta, 44
Delta Dental, 162
denial, as response to termination, 138–139
dental insurance
    as company-paid benefit, 83
    maintaining in retirement, 257, 260
    maintaining after termination, 160, 161–162
DentalPlans.com, 167
departmental organization, of companies, 26
depression
    marital problems and, 172
    termination and, 140, 172, 210
Deutsche Bahn, 25
developed countries, available jobs in, 126
digital employment sites, 203–204. *See also specific sites*
digital profile, 47, 51
dinner interviews, 68–69
director of department, 26
disability insurance
    long-term, 83–84, 164–167, 227, 258, 262
    short-term, 83
discretion, in job search while still employed, 53
discrimination
    DEI efforts *versus*, 41–42
    EEOC enforcement of laws against, 34–35
    goals of worldwide workplace *versus*, 125
diversity, equity, and inclusion (DEI), 41–42, 125
divorce, 168, 171–172
Don't Retire, Rewire (Sadler), 270
door-to-door job search, 204–205

Dow Jones, 24
downsizing, and job loss, 7, 134
downsizing, home, for retirement, 279
dress, appropriate
    for interview, 57, 71
    for job fairs, 185–186
    for trade show, 188
due diligence, in research on employer, 75

eBay, AI use by, 8–9
EducatetoAdvance.com, 74
education
    cost, 529 savings account for, 153
    cost, for unemployed parent, 156–157
    encore careers in, 271, 272
    industry trade shows of, 199–200
    lacking cited requirements for, 177, 180–181
    professional development, 83, 168, 172–174
    on résumé, 49
    unemployment and challenge of, 168, 172–174
education book fairs, international, 200
education objection, to job candidacy, 177, 180–181
ego, and salary expectations, 182
"8 Steps to Bouncing Back After Getting Fired" (TheMuse.com), 144
Ellison, Larry, 209
emergency fund, 151–152
Employee Retirement Income Security Act of 1974 (ERISA), 243–244
employment attorney
    for contract review, 30, 32, 36, 127
    for retirement review, 242
    for severance agreements, 148, 227
    for termination issues, 134–135, 138–139
employment contract, 6, 30–32, 127
    at-will provision in, 6, 31, 32
    consultation with attorney about, 30, 32, 36, 127
    noncompete agreement in, 6, 31–32
    retirement package and, 241–242, 244
    serious issues in, 31–32
Employment Crossing (EmploymentCrossing.com), 206
employment history, gaps in, 51
Employment Law (newsletter), 134
employment laws and regulations, federal, 33–36
Employment Situation Summary, 8
Encore (Freedman), 275

encore career, 7, 234, 271–275, 280–281
    artificial intelligence and, 280
    definition of, 271
    NEXTERCISE for, 272
    resources on, 275
    selecting, 272
    stories of retirees in, 273–275
    types of jobs in, 271–272
end of interview, 61, 66–67
English, teaching, in encore career, 272
Entrepreneur.com, 104
entrepreneurship, 25–26, 94–104
    attention and time required in, 94
    Branson's advice on, 96
    consulting business, 100–101
    encore career in, 281
    famous entrepreneurs in, 207, 208–209
    franchise opportunities for, 25–26, 101–102
    funding sources for, 95, 97–98
    human evolution and, 16–17
    interests *versus* profit potential in, 95
    jobs provided through, 126–127
    partnership, 100
    physical business site *versus* home office in, 95–96
    planning and research for, 94
    profile of people engaged in, 95
    rebuilding career through, 207–209, 227
    selecting business for, 103
    skills needed for, 94
    sole proprietor, 98–100
    written plan for, 208
environmental affairs, encore careers in, 271
environmental conservation, searching for jobs in, 113
Equal Employment Opportunity Commission (EEOC), 34–35
"equivalent" qualifications, 181
ERISA. *See* Employee Retirement Income Security Act of 1974
errors, on résumé, 50–51
"essential" workers, 3
ethics, character and, 121
Ethiopia, human evolution in, 16–17
etiquette
    for follow-up to interview, 73, 78
    for meal interviews, 68–69
    for quitting, 87–89
    for virtual interviews, 72

Events in America (website), 203, 206
executive branch, of companies, 26
exercise, in retirement, 277–278, 279

Facebook, 209. *See also* Meta
Fair Labor Standards Act (FLSA), 33–34
fairness, 122
false sense of security, 19, 46, 153–154
Family and Medical Leave Act (FMLA), 33, 82–83, 134
family identity, 119, 220, 224, 267, 269
family issues, termination and, 168–174
family money, businesses started with, 95, 97
Farmers Insurance Group, 264
fast food, spending on, 154–155
FDIC (Federal Deposit Insurance Corporation), 250
fear, as obstacle, 122
Federal Deposit Insurance Corporation (FDIC), 250
Federal Employees Retirement System (FERS), 239–240
federal government jobs, 107–109
    complex process of finding, 108
    environmental, 113
    locations outside Washington, D.C., 107–108
    number and diversity of, 105, 107
    political *versus* civil services, 108
    resources for exploring, 108–109, 113
    retirement from, 239–240
federal government retirement systems, 239–240
FederalJobs.net, 25, 28, 108, 109, 110, 244
federal laws and regulations, 33–36
federal minimum salary, 34
federal minimum wage, 33–34
FederalRetirement.net, 244, 255, 275
FedEx, 25
FERS. *See* Federal Employees Retirement System
Fidelity, 24, 153, 233, 247, 249, 254
finance industry, 24
financial advisers, 254
financial planning, 245–255
financial security
    during retirement, 233–234, 245–255, 276
    during unemployment, 150–158, 227
fired (firing), 7, 133. *See also* termination
    as blessing in disguise, 111–112
    COBRA eligibility after, 145
    daily statistics on, 126

for-cause nature of, 133
  résumé and interview after, 175–176
  12 tips for rebuilding career after, 226–227
529 College Savings Account, 153
"5 Questions Great Job Candidates Ask" (Haden), 65–66
Flanagan, Tammy, 244
Flanigan, Kevin, 74
Fleischauer, E. Alan, 123
flexible hours, family responsibilities and, 168
Florida
  automobile insurance in, 262–263
  convention centers and trade shows in, 193–194, 287–288
  state jobs in (Florida.gov), 107
Florida Educational Technology Conference, 193
FLSA. *See* Fair Labor Standards Act
FMLA. *See* Family and Medical Leave Act
follow-up, interview, 73, 78
fonts, for résumé, 51
food
  AI-assisted acquisition of, 17
  availability of and assistance for, 21
  cost, during retirement, 234
  cost, during unemployment, 154–155
  evolution of search for, 16–17
  survival of species and, 28
  working to provide, 13, 18, 125
food companies, 21–22
food industry trade shows, 197
food-stamp program, 21
Forbes.com/Forbes Advisor, 115, 117
Ford, 124
Fortune (magazine), 174
forward-looking approach, 54–55, 57–58
401(k) account, 247–248
  annual and change fees on, 153
  company provision for, 83
  evaluating, after termination, 152–153
  individual and employer contributions to, 247
  investment options in, 247–248
  IRS restrictions on, 248
  moving, 153
Fox TV Business News, 43, 151, 158
FRA (full retirement age), 233
France, retirement age in, 232

franchise(s), 25–26, 101–102, 227
    main names in, 101
    operation of, 102
    purchasing and fees, 102
Franchise Business Review, 104
FranchiseDirect.com, 102, 104
franchisee, 102
FranchiseProspector.com, 104
franchisor, 102
Frankfurt Book Fair (Germany), 200
Franklin, Benjamin, 23, 256
Fraser, Jane, 42
Freedman, Marc, 275
frequently asked questions, in interviews, 63–64
friendly approach to negotiation, 86
friendship, forging, in interview, 56, 68, 73, 77, 79, 180
full retirement age (FRA), 233
fun, in retirement, 278
funeral costs, 163, 166
funeral insurance, 166–167
FuneralWise.com, 166–167

Gallup poll, 90
gap years, 156–157
Gate One Travel, 142, 144
Gates, Bill, 94, 208
Gaylord National Resort and Conference Center (National Harbour, Maryland), 201
GCDF (global career development facilitator), 213
Geico, 263–264
gender
    DEI efforts and, 41–42
    employment laws/regulation and, 34–35
    organizations promoting women in workforce, 42–43
    termination and, 168
General Electric, 153–154
General Mills, 22
General Motors, 42
generations in workplace, 27
Generation X, 27
Generation Y (millennials), 27
Generation Z, 27
Georgia, convention centers and trade shows in, 194, 288
Geronimo, Aldus, 212

gig jobs, in encore career, 271–272
Girls Who Code, 43
Glassdoor.com, 78, 79, 217, 219
global career development facilitator (GCDF), 213
God, seeking help from, 218
"going postal," 139
Goldman Sachs, 24
GoodHire.com, 79
Goodloe, Paul, 43
Google searches, 113
government, as industry, 25
government jobs, 25, 105–110
    federal, 105, 107–109
    local, 105–107
    mistake of overlooking, 105
    number and diversity of, 105
    online listings of, 106, 107, 108–109
    political *versus* civil services, 108
    referrals and networking for, 107
    resources for exploring, 108
    retirement from, 239–240
    state, 107
    veterans hired for, 109, 110
government loans, 98
government-mandated benefits, 82–83
government retirement systems, federal, 239–240
grammar mistakes, on résumé, 51
Great Recession of 2008, 150–151
Great Resignation period (2022–2023), 111
grieving process, 137–144
    acceptance in, 140
    anger in, 139
    denial in, 138–139
    depression in, 140
    five solutions for working through, 141–143
    humiliation in, 139
    professional counseling for, 138, 139, 140
    prolonged *versus* abbreviated, 138
    stages of, 137
Guardian Insurance, 262
Guardian Life, 84

Haden, Jeff, 65–66, 74

happiness
　　definitions of, 277
　　in retirement, 277–278
The Hartford (insurance company), 257
Harvard Business Review, 225
Hawaii Convention Center, 194, 288
hazardous working conditions, OSHA and, 34
health, and retirement, 276–277
Healthcare.gov, 160, 167
healthcare industry, 23
　　encore careers in, 271
　　trade shows of, 201–202
　　women in, 42
Healthcare Information and Management Systems Society, 201
health insurance
　　as company-paid benefit, 83
　　maintaining in retirement, 257, 258–260
　　maintaining after termination, 145–146, 159–161, 227
　　need for, 258–259
Hewlett Packard, 132
Hilton, 192, 196
hiring process
　　digital profile in, 47, 51
　　employment attorney for, 30, 32, 36, 127
　　employment contract in, 6, 30–32, 127
　　interview in, 53–79 (*see also* interview)
　　negotiation in, 80–86
　　offer letters in, 29–32
　　overcoming opposition to job candidacy in, 177–184
　　résumé in, 46–52
Holiday Inn, 196
holidays, 83
Hollub, Vicki, 42
home mortgages, retirement and, 250–251
homeowners insurance
　　maintaining in retirement, 258, 264
　　maintaining after termination, 159, 160, 162
honesty, in interview, 55–56, 175–176
Hormel Meats, 22
hotels, trade shows in, 192
housing costs
　　during retirement, 234
　　during unemployment, 155

housing industry, 22
housing industry trade shows, 198–199
"How Entrepreneurs Measure Up" *(The Wall Street Journal)*, 95
"How to Get a Job in the Federal Government" (Crosby), 108
How to Write a Killer LinkedIn Profile (Bernstein), 52
How to Write a Stellar Executive Résumé (Bernstein), 52
HR Specialist (organization), 35, 36, 134, 135
human resource professionals, career counseling by, 211–212
human resources department, 26
human resources (HR) specialists, 35
humiliation, termination and, 139
Hyatt, 192
hybrid model, for remote work, 85

IBM, 44
ICF. *See* International Coaching Federation
identity
    COVID-19 pandemic and, 4
    discovering, 118, 119, 227
    family, 119, 220, 224, 267, 269
    maintaining and rebuilding, 224–225
    personal, 119, 220, 224, 267, 269
    redefining processing and, 112
    retirement and, 7, 235, 267–270, 280
    searching for career objectives and, 112–114
    social, 119, 220, 225, 267, 269
    termination and loss of, 17, 118, 119, 132, 223–225, 227
    work, 17, 119, 132, 220–225, 267
    work cycle and, 17–18
Illinois
    convention centers and trade shows in, 128, 192, 194–195, 197, 198, 289
    retirement benefits in, 243
immigration, 13–16, 126
Inc. Magazine, 74
income
    class status by, 81
    retirement and loss of, 235
INC. online magazine, 65–66
Indeed.com, 149, 203
independent sales representative, 103
index funds, 247–248, 249
India
    gap between rich and poor in, 15

immigration to US from, 16
population of, 124
technology industry in, 15–16
Indiana Bankers Association Annual Convention, 195
Indianapolis Convention Center, 195
individual retirement account (IRA), 232–234, 248–249
    age and withdrawals from, 248
    average amount in, at age 65, 233
    budgeting and, 245–246
    combined with other income, 250
    company provision for, 83
    IRS restrictions on, 249
    planning for adequate retirement and, 246–247
    protecting, during unemployment, 150, 152–153
    required minimum distribution from, 246, 248
    Roth, 248
Indonesia, population of, 124
industrial parks
    online/AI resources on, 205
    personal visits to, 185, 204–205
industries. *See also specific industries*
    best trade shows for job hunting by, 196–202
    corporate websites, 204
    job titles specific to, 20
    large and important, 21–22
    matching NEXTERCISE results with, 39–40
inheritance, 252–253
Inspiring Character (Character.org), 123
insurance
    automobile, 160–161, 258, 262–264
    dental, 83, 160, 161–162, 257, 260
    funeral, 166–167
    homeowners, 159, 160, 162
    life, 83, 160, 163–164, 167, 252–253, 257, 261–262
    long-term care, 257, 261
    long-term disability, 83–84, 160, 164–167, 227, 258, 262
    maintaining in retirement, 234, 256–266, 280
    maintaining after termination, 159–167
    medical, 83, 145–146, 159–161, 257, 258–260
    necessity of, 159
    planning for, 257
    purpose of, 257
    resources on, 166–167, 266
    short-term disability, 83

insurance industry, 23–24
    annuities offered by, 249–250
    history of, 23, 256–257
    largest automobile insurers in, 263–264
    largest homeowner insurers in, 264
    trade shows of, 201
Insure.com, 167
integrity, 122
interests
    aptitude and, 118–119
    NEXTERCISE on, 37–40, 118
Internal Revenue Service (IRS), 248, 249, 254
International Coaching Federation (ICF), 213, 214
international education book fairs, 200
International Home and Housewares Show, 195
International Restaurant and Food Service Show, 197
International Society for Pharmaceutical Engineering, 202
International Society for Technology in Education (ISTE), 199
interview, 53–79
    appropriate dress for, 57, 71
    basic rules of, 55–56
    beginning of, 61–63
    body language in, 58–59, 71
    body of, 61, 63–64
    content in, 57–58
    courtesy and etiquette for, 55–56, 68–69, 72, 78
    describing self in, 62–63
    end of, 61, 66–67
    five topics to incorporate in, 61–62
    follow-up after, 73, 78
    forging friendship in, 56, 68, 73, 77, 79, 180
    forward-looking approach in, 54–55, 57–58
    frequently asked questions in, 63–64
    handling overqualified objection in, 179–180
    honesty in, 55–56, 175–176
    inquiring about next steps in, 66–67, 73
    interviewer's judgment and checklist in, 56–59
    interviewing interviewer in, 61, 65–66
    learning during, 54–55, 77–78
    listening in, 54–55
    meal (breakfast, lunch, or dinner), 68–69
    panel, 67–68
    praying for help with, 218
    process of, 61–67

purpose of, 54
red or yellow flags about company in, 78
rehearsal for, 64
research about employer before, 75–76
resources on, 53
roles, responsibilities, and respect in, 54
setting tone and direction of, 62
smiling in, 58–59, 71
terminated employee and, 175–176, 226
verbal communication in, 57
virtual, 69–73
written agenda for, 59–61, 71

introspection
 career-centered questions for, 4–5
 maintaining and rebuilding identity through, 225
 redefining process in, 112

investments
 definition of, 150
 monitoring, 150–151
 protecting, during unemployment, 150–153
 reliance on, during retirement, 232–234

Investopedia.com, 9, 28, 167
Iowa Events Center, 195
iPhones, AI-manufactured, 114
IRA. *See* individual retirement account
ISTE. *See* International Society for Technology in Education

Jaipur, India, 15
Javits Center (New York City), 128, 192, 195–197, 202, 294
Jewelers International Showcase, 193–194
job(s). *See also specific topics*
 clothing company, 22
 definition of, 2
 expectations for fulfillment in, 111
 government, 25, 105–110
 healthcare, 23
 shelter company, 22
 small businesses and, 126–127

job candidacy, opposition to
 compensation objection and, 177, 181–184
 education objection and, 177, 180–181
 overcoming, 177–184
 overqualification objection and, 177–180

job fairs, 185–186, 226

job interview. *See* interview
job loss, AI and, 8
Job Loss, Identity, and Mental Health (Norris), 225
Job Openings and Labor Turnover Survey (JOLTS), 8, 158
Jobs, Steve, 94, 120, 207, 208
job-specific résumé, 47–48
job titles, 20
Johns Hopkins Hospital, 23
Johnson, Nick, 15
Johnson & Johnson, 23
Johnson O'Connor Research Foundation, 119, 123
JOLTS. *See* Job Openings and Labor Turnover Survey
JP Morgan Chase & Co., 24, 44
juggernaut, work as, 1, 4, 9

Kentucky Fried Chicken (KFC), 101
Kiyosaki, Robert, 158
Korn Ferry (KornFerry.com), 204
Kosciuszko Foundation, 272
Kraft Heinz, 22
Kroger, 21–22
Kübler-Ross, Elisabeth, 137

Lambert, Brian, 117
Langhorne, Pennsylvania, industrial park, 204
language skills
    hiring chances improved by, 18
    immigration and, 16
Las Vegas Convention Center, 187, 202
laws, federal employment, 33–36
lawsuits, over terminations, 134, 138–139
lawyer. *See* employment attorney
layoffs, 7, 133. *See also* termination
    as blessing in disguise, 111–112
    COVID-19 pandemic and, 3
    daily statistics on, 126
    mass, 132–133, 147
    notification requirement for, 147
    12 tips for rebuilding career after, 226–227
learning, lifelong, 240
learning about employer
    after interview, 78
    before interview, 75–76
    during interview, 54–55, 77–78

Lee Hecht Harrison, 217, 219
legal contract. *See* employment contract
legal department, 26
legally required benefits, 82–83
legal rights
    employment contract and, 6, 30–32
    federal laws and regulations on, 33–36
    migrants', 35
    minority, organizations promoting, 43–44
    retirement and, 280
    termination and, 134–135, 138–139, 145–149
    veterans', 35
    women's, organizations promoting, 42–43
Lennar Corporation, 22
"let go," 133–134. *See also* termination
liability insurance
    automobile, 262–263
    business, 258, 264–265
    homeowners, 264
Liberty Mutual, 264
life insurance
    beneficiaries of, 252
    as company-paid benefit, 83
    maintaining in retirement, 252–253, 257, 261–262
    maintaining after termination, 160, 163–164, 167
    recommended amount of, 262
    resources on, 253
lifelong learning, 240
LinkedIn, 51, 52, 76, 96, 98, 128, 203, 267
Lipman, Joanne, 123
listening, in interview, 54–55
living trust, revocable, 253
L.L. Bean, 22
LLC companies, 264–265
loans
    bank, 97
    government, 98
    retirement and, 250–251
local government, as largest employer in US, 105
local government jobs, 105–107
    application instructions for, 106
    number and diversity of, 105
    online listings of, 106
    personal visit in search for, 106–107

    referrral and networking for, 107
London Book Fair (United Kingdom), 200
long-term care (LTC), 257, 261
long-term disability insurance (LTD)
    employer and payment for, 83–84
    maintaining in retirement, 258, 262
    maintaining after termination, 160, 164–167, 227
lower class, income of, 81
Lowe's, 44
LTC. *See* long-term care
LTD. *See* long-term disability insurance
lunch interviews, 68–69
Lydians, 17

Mad Money (TV program), 158
Maine
    retirement benefits in, 243
    salary comparisons for, 184
manager of department, 26
mandatory retirement, 238–239
marital problems and divorce, 168, 171–172
marketing department, 26
MarketWatch.com, 270
Marriott, 192, 196
Maryland
    convention centers and trade shows in, 201, 290
    retirement benefits in, 243
MassMutual, 23, 249–250
mass terminations, 132–133, 147
McCormick Place (Chicago), 128, 192, 194–195, 197, 289
McDonald's, 8–9, 101–102, 114
meal interviews, 68–69
meaning in work, 125
    COVID-19 pandemic and, 4
    NEXTERCISE on, 37–40
"meaning of life," 18, 278
Medicaid, 161
medical insurance
    as company-paid benefit, 83
    maintaining in retirement, 257, 258–260
    maintaining after termination, 145–146, 159–161, 227
    need for, 258–259
Medicare, 82, 160–161, 243–244, 259–260
    annual changes in, 260

       enrollment period for, 259–260
       resources on, 260, 266
Medicare Advantage, 260
Medicare Part A, 260
Medicare Part B, 260
Medicare Part C, 260
Medicare Part D, 260
Medigap plans, 260
Medtronic, 23
mental health counseling, 138, 139, 211
Meta, 114–115, 209
MetLife, 23, 257
Metropolitan Life, 249–250
MGX, 116
Miami Beach Convention Center, 193–194, 287
Microsoft, 24, 207, 208
middle class, income of, 81
migrants' rights, 35
military career
       FMLA coverage during, 82
       meaning and purpose in, 125
Military.com, 95
military veterans. *See* veterans
millennials (Generation Y), 27
minimum distribution from IRA, required, 246, 248, 249
Minimum Retirement Age, for federal employees, 240
minimum salary, federal, 34
minimum wage, federal, 33–34
minority employment
       DEI efforts and, 41–42
       organizations promoting, 43–44
mobility, 13–16
Molecular Medicine Convention, 193
Mondelez International, 22
money
       employer's goal of making, 126
       history of, 17
       as motivation, 78–79
       required, for comfortable retirement, 233–234
       retirement and, 233–234, 245–255, 276
       sources, for starting own business, 95, 97–98
       unemployment and, 150–158
MoneyGeek.com, 275
Monster (Monster.com), 203, 219

Moody's, AI use by, 8–9
More in Common (organization), 44
mortgages, retirement and, 250–251
Moscone Center (San Francisco), 192, 193, 286
Ms. Career Girl, 42
Musk, Elon, 14–15, 25, 94, 207, 209
Mutual of Omaha, 84, 257, 270

NAACP. *See* National Association for the Advancement of Colored People
NAHB. *See* National Association of Home Builders
NAMIC. *See* National Association of Mutual Insurance Companies
National Association for the Advancement of Colored People (NAACP), 43–44
National Association of Biology Teachers, 200
National Association of Home Builders (NAHB), 198
National Association of Mutual Insurance Companies (NAMIC), 201
National Auto Dealers Association, 193
National Board of Certified Counselors, 211
National Career Development Association (NCDA), 213
National Council for Teachers of English, 200
National Council for the Social Studies, 200
National Council of Teachers of Mathematics, 200
National Organization for Women (NOW), 42–43
National Restaurant Association, 197
National Science Teachers Association, 200
National Urban League, 44
Nationwide Allstate, 263–264
NCDA. *See* National Career Development Association
negotiation, 80–86
    basic rules for, 85–86
    benefits, 81, 85–86
    hesitancy or fear in, 80, 81
    insidious connotation of, 85
    remote work, 84–86
    salary, 80–81, 85–86
    severance agreement, 148–149, 227
NerdWallet, 254, 261
Nestlé, 22
New Jersey
    retirement benefits in, 243
    unemployment compensation in, 147
New York Boat Show, 192
New York City, convention center and trade shows in, 128, 192, 195–196, 197, 202, 294

New York International Auto Show, 202
New York State
    convention center and trade shows in, 128, 192, 195–196, 197, 202, 294
    retirement benefits in, 243
New York Travel Show, 192
NEXTERCISE, 37–40, 48, 113, 118, 143, 208, 226, 272
Next! The Power of Reinvention in Life and Work (Lipman), 123
noncompete provision, 6, 30, 31–32
nonverbal communication, 58–59, 179
Noomii: The Professional Coach Directory (Noomii.com), 214–215
Norris, Dawn R., 225
North Carolina, state government jobs in, 113
North Cascades Institute, 113
Northwestern Mutual Insurance Co., 84, 165–166
notice, resignation, 88–89
notice, retirement, 241–242
notification, for plant closings and mass layoffs, 147
NOW. *See* National Organization for Women
Nurse Practitioners in Women's Healthcare, 201
NY NOW, 196

Obamacare (Affordable Care Act), 146, 149, 160, 167, 266
Occidental Petroleum, 42
occupation, definition of, 2
Occupational Health and Safety Act (OSHA), 34
The Occupational Outlook Handbook (BLS), 8, 19, 28, 103, 113–114, 117, 174, 184
offer letters, 29–32
    at-will provision in, 30, 31, 32
    noncompete provision in, 30, 31–32
    serious issues in, 31–32
Office of Personnel Management (OPM), 107, 109, 244
office parks
    online/AI resources on, 205
    personal visits to, 185, 204–205
O'Neill, Eugene "Tip," 106
OneTen (organization), 44
online college studies, 157
online job sites, 203–204. *See also specific sites*
online outplacement services, 216
OpenAI, 8, 115–116, 117
OpenSourceAI (AI.Meta.com), 117
Operation Warp Speed, 3

OPM. *See* Office of Personnel Management
opposition, to job candidacy
    compensation objection and, 177, 181–184
    education objection and, 177, 180–181
    overcoming, 177–184
    overqualification objection and, 177–180
Oracle, 116, 209
Orange County Convention Center (Florida), 193, 288
Oregon, retirement benefits in, 243
organizational structure, of companies, 26
Orlando Home Show, 193
Orman, Suze, 237, 255, 266
OSHA. *See* Occupational Health and Safety Act
outplacement services, 210–211, 215–217
    cost per terminated employee, 215
    cost per terminated executive, 215–216
    mixed reviews for, 216
    offerings of, 216
    resources on, 216–217
    severance package including, 216
    traditional model of, 216
    virtual, 216
overqualified objection, 177–180
overtime pay, federal law on, 33–34

Packaging Corporation of America, 113
paid sick leave, 83
paid vacations, 83
panel interviews, 67–68
paper money, invention of, 17
parental leave, 33, 82–83
Parting.com, 166
partner, starting business with, 100
part-time jobs
    family responsibilities and, 168, 171
    retired workers holding, 245
PARWCC. *See* Professional Association of Résumé Writers and Career Coaches
Paycheck, Johnny, 89, 141
Payne, Charles, 43
PayPal, 14
peace, in retirement, 276–277
pension plans, 83, 232, 234, 249
PepsiCo, 22, 44

persona
- as apparent or public "you," 120, 127
- conflict with character, 127, 269
- discovering, 118, 119–121
- Jobs's, 120
- redefining, in retirement, 269
- Shakespeare on, 121
- theatrical origin of term, 119–120

personal identity, 119
- family and, 119, 220, 224, 267, 269
- individual characteristics and, 119
- retirement and, 267, 269
- termination and, 220, 227, 244

personal injury liability
- automobile insurance for, 262–263
- homeowners insurance for, 264

personal inventory, after termination, 142
personal visits, in job search, 106–107, 185, 204–205
Pew Research Center, 5, 8, 143, 144, 232
PGA Golf Industry Show, 193
Pharma Expo, 202
Philadelphia, trade shows in, 192, 198–199
Philadelphia Contributorship, 23, 256
Philly Home and Garden Show, 198–199
photos, avoiding on résumé, 51
physical activity, in retirement, 277–278, 279
pickleball, 278
"Plan for the Retirement You Want" (AARP), 237
PMI. *See* Project Management Institute
PMP. *See* project management professional (PMP) training
political jobs, 108
Portland, Maine, industrial park, 204
power, as motivation, 78–79
practice
- for interview, 64
- for quitting, 87

prayer, 218
Pregnant Workers Fairness Act, 35
prescription drug coverage, Medicare, 260
president, of company, 26
pride in work, 125, 132
Principal Financial Group, 84
private sector, 105
Procter and Gamble, 204

product development, 26
production department, 26
profession, definition of, 2
Professional Association of Résumé Writers and Career Coaches (PARWCC), 213
professional development education, 83, 168, 172–174
profit sharing, 83
Progressive, 263–264
Progressive Insurance Boat Show, 195
Project Management Institute (PMI), 174, 184
project management professional (PMP) training, 174
promotion policy, as reason for quitting, 91
property damage protection
    automobile, 262–263
    homeowners, 159, 160, 162
Prudential, 247, 249
psychologists, career counseling by, 211–212
Psychology Today, 119, 123, 219, 225
public sector, 105. *See also* government jobs
public service, encore careers in, 271
Puma, Grace, 45, 74

"qualifying life event," 146
questions
    career-centered, 4–5
    frequently asked, in interviews, 63–64
    for interviewing interviewer, 65–66
    for learning about employer, 75–79
    NEXTERCISE, 37–40
    written agenda, for interviewee, 59–61, 71
Quest Outplacement, 217
quitting, 87–94
    company culture and, 91
    compensation issues and, 92
    crude manner of, 87, 89
    financial reserves for, 92
    giving ample notice in, 88–89
    graceful (proper) manner of, 87–89
    Great Resignation period (2022–2023), 111
    lifestyle-working condition disconnect and, 91
    motivation/reasons for, 5, 89–92
    preparation for, 46–47
    promotion policy and, 91
    relationship with boss and, 90

relationship with coworkers and, 90
  securing another job before, 92
  verbal resignation for, 87–88, 92–93
  written resignation for, 87, 88, 93

race and ethnicity
  DEI efforts and, 41–42
  employment laws/regulations and, 34–35
  organizations promoting minority employment and, 43–44
  population statistics on, 42
Radiological Society of North America, 201
receptionists, power of, 106–107
recession, 150–151
Reconfigurement (Fleischauer), 123
recruiters
  encore career as, 272
  at trade shows, 190
redefining process, 112
red flags, about company, 78
regret, as obstacle, 122
regulations, federal employment, 33–36
rehearsal
  for interview, 64
  for quitting, 87
relocation, after retirement, 234
remote work
  benefits of, 85, 168
  COVID-19 pandemic and, 3, 84
  family responsibilities and, 168–169
  global workplace and, 15
  hybrid model of, 85
  negotiating for, 84–86
  willingness to sacrifice wages for, 168–169
required minimum distribution (RMD), 246, 248, 249
research about employer, 75–79
  after interview, 78
  before interview, 75–76
  during interview, 54–55, 77–78
research and development department, 26
research after termination, 142–143
resignation. *See also* quitting
  giving ample notice in, 88–89
  Great Resignation period (2022–2023), 111
  proper process of, 87–89

verbal, 87–88, 92–93
written, 88, 93
respect, 122
responsibility, 122
restaurant spending, 154–155
résumé, 46–52
    additions to and deletions from, 48
    AI experience articulated on, 50
    AI-written, as bad approach, 47, 50
    common mistakes on, 50–51
    formatting and style of, 51
    gaps in employment history on, 51
    general *versus* job-specific, 47–48
    main parts of, 48–50
    metrics missing from, 51
    multiple, for door-to-door job search, 204
    multiple, for job fairs, 185–186
    multiple, for trade shows, 187
    new, for terminated employee, 175, 226
    preparing to write, 47–48
    purpose of, 47
    research before submitting, 75–76
    up-to-date, importance of, 46
RetireFederal.com, 244
RetireGuide.com, 254
retirement, 7, 231–281
    artificial intelligence and, 280
    budget for, 7, 233–234, 245–246
    comfortable, money required for, 233–234
    data on, 232–233
    debt-free, 250–251
    dynamic/changing concept of, 7, 232
    encore career after, 7, 234, 271–275, 280
    exact date of, 241
    financial security/planning in, 233–234, 245–255, 276
    four major issues of, 7
    fun in, 278
    happiness in, 277–278
    health during, 276–277, 279
    in higher *versus* lower cost locations, 234
    insurance after, 234, 252–253, 256–266, 280
    learning and activity after, 240
    loss of identity in, 7, 235, 267–270, 280
    loss of income in, 235

    mandatory, 238–239
    number of workers entering, per day, 233
    peace in, 276–277
    physical activity in, 277–278, 279
    private-sector, 239
    process of, 241–244
    public-sector, 239–240
    reasons for and circumstances of, 241
    required benefits in, 243–244
    resources on, 235–237, 242, 244, 254, 255
    "shoulda," "woulda," and "coulda" in, 231
    10 tips for, 279–281
    timing of, 7
    transitioning to new identity in, 268–269, 280
    two big challenges in, 235
    verifying and reviewing documents/details in, 241–242
    winding down toward, 243, 268–269
    written statement of, 241
retirement accounts, 232–234, 246–250. *See also specific types*
    company provision for, 83
    protecting, during unemployment, 150, 152–153
retirement age, 232, 238–240
retirement counseling, 244
retirement planning, 231–237
    debt management/elimination in, 250–251
    financial, 233–234, 245–255
    financial advisers for, 254
    resources for, 235–237
    timing of, 235, 246–247, 280
    wills and trusts in, 252–253
revenue goals, company's missing of, 90
revocable living trust, 253
RevolutionizeRetirement.com, 270
RG Group, 24
Rich Dad Poor Dad (Kiyosaki), 158
rights, legal
    employment contract and, 6, 30–32
    federal laws and regulations on, 33–36
    migrants', 35
    minority, organizations promoting, 43–44
    retirement and, 280
    termination and, 134–135, 138–139, 145–149
    veterans', 35
    women's, organizations promoting, 42–43

RMD. *See* required minimum distribution
The Road to Character (Brooks), 123
Robert Half (RobertHalf.com), 203
Roman currency, salt as, 17
Roosevelt, Franklin D., 238
Roth retirement plan, 248
RSA Cybersecurity show, 193
"The Rule of 25" (RetireGuide.com), 254

Sadler, Jeri, 270
safety margin, in cash savings, 151–152
salary
    compromise on, 183
    dissatisfaction with, as reason for quitting, 92
    ego and, 182
    federal minimum, 34
    negotiating, 80–81, 85–86
    objection to job candidacy over, 177, 181–184
    Roman origin of word, 17
    rubrics for unemployed workers, 183–184
    severance, 147–149
    worker's age and, 181–182
salary-comparison research, 80, 184
sales department, 26
sales representative, independent, 103
salt, as currency, 17
Sam's Club, 43
San Diego Convention Center, 201, 286
San Francisco, convention center and trade shows in, 192, 193, 286
savings
    certificates of deposit (CDs), 250
    protecting, during unemployment, 150–153
    retirement need for, 234
    six-month emergency fund of, 151–152
    using, to start business, 95, 97
SBA. *See* Small Business Administration
Schwab, 247
security, false sense of, 19, 46, 153–154
security, financial
    during retirement, 233–234, 245–255, 276
    during unemployment, 150–158
SelectQuote.com, 262, 266
self-employment, 25–26, 94–104
    attention and time required in, 94

Branson's advice on, 96
   consulting, 100–101
   encore career in, 281
   famous entrepreneurs and, 207, 208–209
   franchise opportunities for, 25–26, 101–102
   funding sources for, 95, 97–98
   interests *versus* profit potential in, 95
   partnership, 100
   physical business site *versus* home office for, 95–96
   planning and research for, 94
   profile of people starting own businesses, 95
   rebuilding career through, 207–209, 227
   selecting business for, 103
   skills needed for, 94
   sole proprietor, 98–100
   written plan for, 208
self-sufficiency
   bipedalism (walking) and, 16–17
   work and, 13, 17
separation or divorce, 168, 171–172
SEP (Simplified Employee Pension) plan, 249
Servpro Cleaning Services, 101, 102
The Seven Habits of Highly Effective People (Covey), 55, 74
severance agreements, 147–149
   content of, 148
   negotiating, 148–149, 216, 227
   outplacement in, 216
   time to review and consult attorney on, 147–148, 227
sex discrimination
   DEI efforts *versus,* 41–42
   EEOC enforcement of laws against, 34–35
Shakespeare, William, 121
shelter
   AI-assisted acquisition of, 17
   cost, during retirement, 234
   cost, during unemployment, 155
   downsizing, in retirement, 279
   evolution of search for, 16–17
   working to provide, 13, 18, 125
shelter companies, 22
shelter industry trade shows, 198–199
Sheraton, 192
Shi, Christiana Smith, 45, 74
SHIP. *See* State Health Insurance Assistance Programs

short-term disability insurance, 83
sick leave, paid, 83
Silent Generation, 27
Simplified Employee Pension (SEP) plan, 249
Simply Hired, 203
six-month emergency fund, 151–152
"Six Pillars of Character," 122
skills
    aptitude and, 118–119
    cited education requirements *versus*, 180–181
    NEXTERCISE on, 37–40
Small Business Administration (SBA), 98, 104, 207, 265, 266
small businesses, 126–127
smiling, in interview, 58–59, 71
SNAP (Supplemental Nutrition Assistance Program), 21
social identity, 119, 220, 225, 227, 267, 269
socially conscious businesses, 114
social media
    business start-up and, 101
    career resources on, 128
    digital profile on, 51
    finding funding sources through, 98
    Generation Z and, 27
    interview questions about, 64
    screening applicants through, 69
Social Security, 82, 232–237
    age and, 232–233, 238–239
    budgeting and, 245–246
    calculation of benefits, 232
    combined with other income, 250
    legal requirement for, 243–244
    maximum benefits of, 233
Social Security Act of 1935, 238
Social Security Administration (SSA), 242, 254, 266
Society for HR Management (SHRM), 35, 36
SoftBank, 116
sole proprietor, 98–100
solicitation, prayers of, 218
Southern Mutual, 257
SpaceX, 14, 25, 207
spelling errors, on résumé, 50–51
Spotify, 24
SSA. *See* Social Security Administration
Starbucks, 36, 43, 101

Stargate, 116
State Farm, 23, 257, 263–264
state government jobs, 107
State Health Insurance Assistance Programs (SHIP), 260
Statista.com, 110
status, as motivation, 78–79
stock options, 83
StocktonCA.gov, 106
stress
        COVID-19 pandemic and, 3–4
        freedom from, in retirement, 276–277
structure, workplace. *See* workplace structure
Su, Lisa, 115
substitute teaching, as encore career, 271, 272
summary, on résumé, 48
supplemental insurance, with Medicare, 260
Supplemental Nutrition Assistance Program (SNAP), 21
survival, financial, 150–158
survival of species, 28
SuzeOrman.com, 237, 255, 266

table manners, 68–69
"Take This Job and Shove It" (song), 89, 92, 141
Tampa Convention Center, 193, 288
Target, 44
technology department, 26
technology industry, 24
        AI use, manufacturing, and development in, 114–116
        Black/minority employees in, 44
        demands of working in, 114
        gender gap in, 43
        in India, 15–16
technology skills
        importance of acquiring, 18
        on résumé, 49
        unemployment and education for, 173–174
technology trade show, 187, 202
telephone interviews, 69–73
telephones calls, during interviews, 68
termination, 6–7, 131–227
        acceptance of, 140
        anger over, 139
        at-will provision for, 6, 30, 31, 32
        benefits of time off after, 118

as blessing in disguise, 111–112
career counseling after, 210–219
COVID-19 pandemic and, 3, 132–133, 134
daily statistics on, 6–7, 126, 131, 153
denial as response to, 138–139
depression over, 140
discovering aptitude after, 118–119
discovering identity after, 118, 119, 227
discovering persona after, 118, 119–121
discovering and rebuilding character after, 118, 121–122
education challenge after, 168, 172–174
evaluating work–life balance after, 143
family issues after, 168–174
financial security after, 150–158, 227
Great Resignation period (2022–2023), 111
grieving process after, 137–144
humiliation over, 139
insurance after, 145–146, 159–167, 227
lawsuits over, 134, 138–139
loss of identity in, 17, 132, 223–225, 227
maintaining and rebuilding identity after, 224–225
marital problems with, 168, 171–172
mass, 132–133, 147
mental health counseling after, 138, 139, 140, 211
monitoring cost of necessities after, 153–157
moving forward after, 141–143
noncompete restrictions after, 6, 30, 31–32
outcry after, 131–132
outplacement services in, 210–211, 215–217
overcoming opposition to job candidacy after, 177–184
personal inventory after, 142
redefining process after, 112
research after, 142–143
résumé and interview after, 175–176, 226–227
searching for career objectives after, 112–114
severance agreements in, 147–149, 216, 227
starting own business after, 207–209
taking break/travel after, 141–142, 226
terminology for and types of, 7, 133–134 (*see also specific types*)
12 tips for rebuilding career after, 226–227
unemployment compensation after, 146–147
unexpected, 131
up-to-date résumé as preparation for, 46
workplace/legal rights and, 134–135, 138–139

term life insurance, 163, 253, 261–262
Tesla, 14, 24–25, 207
thanksgiving, prayers of, 218
thank-you note, for interview, 73, 78
TheGreatCourses.com, 74
Tomé, Carol, 42
"Top 10 Franchises" (FranchiseDirect.com), 102
"Top 10 Ways to Prepare for Retirement" (US Department of Labor), 235–236, 255
"The Top Five Regrets of Mid-Career Professionals" (Caprino), 215
trade shows, 128, 172, 185, 186–203, 226
    appropriate dress for, 188
    avoiding alcohol at, 191
    best for job hunting, by industry, 196–202
    establishing relationships at, 189
    fee for attending, 187–188
    hiring managers at, 190–191
    interest-specific, finding, 203
    lunch as networking opportunity at, 191
    names for, 186
    online listing of, 192, 203
    preparation checklist for attending, 187–188
    purpose of, 186
    recruiters at, 190
    script for talking to company representative at, 189–190
    sites of (convention centers), 186, 284–300
    sponsorship and costs of, 186
    top, 192–196
    travel and accommodations for, 188
    what you do at, 188–189
transition process, in retirement, 268–269, 280
transportation costs, 156, 234
transportation industry, 24–25, 124
transportation industry trade shows, 202
travel, after termination, 142–143
trust (financial), revocable living, 253
trustworthiness
    in character, 122
    in negotiation, 86
tuition assistance, 83
"Twelve Retirement Planning Mistakes to Avoid" (US News and World Report), 254
Twenge, Jean, 27
typefaces, for résumé, 51

typos, on résumé, 50–51
Tyson Foods, 22

unemployment compensation, 35, 146–147, 243–244
unemployment insurance, 82
unemployment rate
    COVID-19 pandemic and, 3, 132
    focusing on employment rate *versus*, 143
Union Pacific Railroad, 25
unions, 35–36
United Healthcare, 23
United Kingdom, retirement age in, 232
United Parcel Service (UPS), 25, 42
United States
    employment laws and regulations of, 33–36
    federal AI initiative in, 116
    government jobs in, 25
    healthcare as percentage of GDP of, 23
    immigration to, 13–16, 126
    as job basket of world, 126
    net worth and wages in, 81
    population and workforce of, 124–125
    retirement age in, 232
US Census Bureau, 8, 42, 184, 232–233
US Department of Commerce, 143, 144
US Department of Defense, 125
US Department of Health and Human Services, 108
US Department of Justice, 113
US Department of Labor. *See also* Bureau of Labor Statistics
    COBRA resources of, 146
    Fair Labor Standards Act and, 33–34
    Family Medical Leave Act and, 33
    The Occupational Outlook Handbook of, 8, 19, 28, 103, 113–114, 117, 174, 184
    retirement data/resources of, 232, 235–237, 242
US Office of Personnel Management (OPM), 107, 109, 244
universities, counseling services provided by, 217–218
Unum, 84, 166
upper class, income of, 81
UPS (United Parcel Service), 25, 42
USAA, 263–264
USA Jobs (USAJobs.gov), 108–109, 110
US News and World Report, 254

vacation, after termination, 142–143
vacation pay, 83
values, character and, 121
Vanguard, 24, 153, 237, 242, 247–249
venture capital, 98
verbal communication, in interview, 57
verbal resignation, 87–88, 92–93
veterans
    as entrepreneurs, 95
    government jobs for, 109, 110
    job fairs for, 185
    trade show discounts for, 188
veterans' rights, 35
VetFran.com, 104
vice presidents, of companies, 26
Villanova University, 174
Virgin Atlantic, 96, 207
Virginia, retirement benefits in, 243
virtual interviews, 69–73
    etiquette for, 72
    in-person preferred over, 69–70
    preparation checklist for, 70–72
    as screening tool, 69
    smiling during, 71
    time allotted for, 72
virtual outplacement services, 216
vocation, definition of, 2
volunteering, encore career *versus*, 271

wages. *See also* salary
    federal minimum, 33–34
    lower, COVID-19 pandemic and, 3
    lower-, middle-, and upper-class, 81
Walgreen, 43
walking (bipedalism), and human self-sufficiency, 16–17
The Wall Street Journal, 24, 46, 47, 76, 95, 128, 133
Walmart, 44, 105
Walter E. Washington Convention Center (Washington, D. C.), 196, 287
WARN. *See* Worker Adjustment and Retraining Notification Act
Warsaw, Poland, 16
Washington, D. C., convention centers and trade shows in, 196, 287
Watts Architectural and Engineering, 113
Weather Channel, 43
Wells Fargo, 24, 97

What Color is Your Parachute (Bolles), 218
wills, 252–253
window cleaning, entrepreneurship and, 98–100
women
 best companies for working mothers, 174
 CEO and executive-level, 42
 DEI efforts and, 41–42
 employment laws/regulations and, 34–35
 in workforce, organizations promoting, 42–43
Women's Media Center, 43
Women Who Code, 43
work
 as juggernaut, 1, 4, 9
 origin and evolution of, 16–18
 primary purpose of, 13, 18, 125
 survival of species and, 28
 terms used to describe, 1–2
"work cities," in India, 15
work cycle, 7, 19
 individual experiences of, 9, 17–18
 retirement as part of, 7, 231, 240, 281
Worker Adjustment and Retraining Notification Act (WARN), 147
worker's compensation insurance, 82, 243–244
work experience, on résumé, 48–49
work history, evaluating, 143
work identity, 119, 220–225
 building, on the job, 220–224
 personal identity *versus*, 224
 retirement and loss of, 267–270, 280
 termination and loss of, 17, 132, 223–225, 227
working classes, net worth and wages of, 81
WorkingMothers.com, 174
work–life balance, 91, 114, 143
workplace
 AI and changes in, 4, 8–9
 COVID-19 pandemic and, 2–5
 diversity, equity, and inclusion in, 41–42
 generations in, 27
 transformation of, 2–5
 worldwide, 13–19, 124–128, 232
workplace rights
 employment contract and, 6, 30–32
 federal laws and regulations on, 33–36
 minority, organizations promoting, 43–44

       termination and, 134–135, 138–139, 145–149
       women's, organizations promoting, 42–43
workplace structure, 20–28, 124
       departmental, 26
       importance of understanding, 20
       large and important industries in, 21–22
worldwide workplace, 13–19
       mobility/immigration and, 13–16, 126
       population and geography of, 124–125
       remote work and, 15
       retirement as changing concept in, 232
       12 tips for understanding, 124–128
Wozniak, Steve, 207, 208
written agenda, for interview, 59–61, 71
written resignation, 88, 93
written retirement statement, 241
wrongful discharge, 134

XPO Logistics, 25

Yahoo! Finance, 81
Yeates, Julia, 218
yellow flags, about company, 78

ZipRecruiter, 203
Zoom
       COVID-19 pandemic and, 3
       interviews via, 69–73
       outplacement services via, 216
Zucker, Rebecca, 225
Zuckerberg, Mark, 94, 115, 209

www.ingramcontent.com/pod-product-compliance
Ingram Content Group UK Ltd.
Pitfield, Milton Keynes, MK11 3LW, UK
UKHW041903230426
12049UKWH00002B/25